Philosophy and Methodology in the Social Sciences

Philosophy and Methodology in the Social Sciences

BARRY HINDESS

Department of Sociology
University of Liverpool

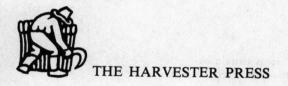

THE HARVESTER PRESS

First published in 1977 by
THE HARVESTER PRESS LIMITED
Publisher: John Spiers
2 Stanford Terrace, Hassocks, Sussex.

© B. Hindess 1977

British Library Cataloging in Publication Data

Hindess, Barry
  Philosophy and methodology in the social
  sciences.
  1. Social sciences – Methodology
  I. Title
  300′.1′8   H61
ISBN 0–85527–344–5

Printed and bound in Great Britain by
Redwood Burn Limited, Trowbridge & Esher

Acknowledgements

I should like to thank all those who have read and commented on my drafts of chapters for this book or on the articles and papers from which the chapters have been derived. I am particularly grateful to Paul Hirst, Bryn Jones and Stephen Savage, who have each read some chapters, and to Elizabeth Kingdom, who has read the entire manuscript, for their extremely helpful comments and suggestions.

Earlier versions of chapters 2 and 3 and of parts of chapter 5 have appeared in *Economy and Society* (in vol. 1, no. 1, vol. 2, no. 3, and vol. 2, no. 2 respectively). I am grateful to the Editors of *Economy and Society* and to the publishers, Messrs. Routledge & Kegan Paul Ltd., for permission to reproduce this material.

Contents

Introduction

The first six chapters of this book provide a systematic critique of epistemological and philosophical interventions in the social sciences and of prescriptive methodology in general. The first chapter examines the methodological doctrines of Max Weber and his definition of sociology as a science of social action. I argue that Weber's definition of sociology is based on an essentially religious, metaphysical conception of man, that his methodology is relativistic and irrationalist, and that his concept of scientific objectivity is a façade for an underlying notion of verisimilitude, of plausibility and subjective conviction. The next two chapters deal directly with phenomenology and phenomenological sociology. The first is an extended critique of the work of Alfred Schutz, showing that it reduces the social sciences literally to story-telling and, further, that far from being an application of Husserl's philosophy it represents a vulgar psychologistic distortion of it. The second examines Husserl's conception of the nature of the sciences and of philosophy in *The Crisis of European Sciences and Transcendental Phenomenology* and argues that, despite its rigour, Husserl's epistemology is structured around a number of crucial contradictions which render it ultimately incoherent. It follows that there can be no rational or coherent phenomenological 'foundation' of the social sciences. In the next three chapters I have developed an extended critique of empiricist methodologies and of their epistemological bases in the positivist and neo-positivist philosophies of Carnap, Mill, Popper and others.

Two of these chapters have been published elsewhere and, save for minor revisions and corrections, they are reprinted here without change. The rest have their origin in lectures or seminars prepared for various audiences during the last few years. These have been heavily revised and expanded for publication in their present form. In all cases my approach has been abstract and theoretical. I have been concerned to examine the concepts and relations between concepts entailed in the methodological and epistemological doctrines in question and to investigate what might be called the logical character of the systems of concepts involved, in particular their relative coherence and consistency. I propose no methodology or epistemology as an alternative to the positions criticized here. On the contrary I argue that the problems which these disciplines pose are false problems and that they arise only as a function of a conception of knowledge which can be shown to be fundamentally and inescapably incoherent. Epistemology and such derivative doctrines as methodology and philosophy of science have no rational or coherent foundation. In particular, then, there can be no rational or coherent prescriptive methodology. These arguments are outlined below.

If these chapters merely bring together the substance of arguments that I have put forward in one form or another over recent years, then my concluding chapter must be seen as a development of some of my earlier positions and a correction of others. The precise character of these corrections will be discussed in later sections of this Introduction. For the present it is enough to say that while some of the positions taken up in the earlier chapters must now be regarded as untenable my main conclusions concerning the coherence of epistemology and the possibility of prescriptive methodology remain untouched by these changes.

Philosophy and Methodology

In sociology and more generally in the social sciences methodology is taken to be a discipline, bordering on philosophy, whose function is to examine the methods which are used or which should be used to produce valid knowledge. It is in this sense that Talcott Parsons refers to:

'the questions of the grounds of empirical validity of scientific propositions, the kinds of procedures which may on general grounds be expected to yield valid knowledge.' (*The Structure of Social Action* p.23)

Methodology lays down procedures to be used either in the generation or in the testing of propositions by those who wish to obtain valid knowledge. These procedures, as Parsons also notes, are justified by means of philosophical arguments. It is clear that methodology's claim to prescribe correct procedures to the sciences must presuppose a form of knowledge which is in some sense superior to that produced in the sciences. Scientific knowledge is thought to be valid only if its production conforms to the prescribed procedures; it follows that the prescriptions of methodology cannot be validated by scientific knowledge. Access to this special kind of knowledge is thought to be provided by philosophy. Methodology, then, presupposes a particular kind of relationship between philosophy and the sciences in which the one is able to judge and to validate the claims to knowledge advanced by the other. Different philosophies may conceive of that relationship in somewhat different terms but it is well represented in Winch's assertion that:

'The difference between the respective aims of the scientist and the philosopher might be expressed as follows. Whereas the scientist investigates. the nature, causes and effects of *particular* real things and processes, the philosopher is concerned with the nature of reality as such and in general.' (*The Idea of a Social Science,* p.8)

The 'nature of reality as such and in general' can be known quite independently of the particular little investigations of the sciences. If, then, some 'science' were to pretend to knowledge of an object falling outside the realm of 'reality as such', then that 'science' would be an illusion: it could not give knowledge of particular real things at all. In principle and in practice Winch's philosophy claims to judge the sciences. Indeed Winch proceeds to castigate much of sociology for failing to conform to the findings of his own (or rather Wittgenstein's) philosophical investigations. Whilst nothing could be further from my intention than to attribute a scientific status to the products of sociology, this example may serve to illustrate the general character of the relationship between philosophy and the sciences as it is conceived by philosophy itself and as it is presupposed by any methodological discourse. Methodology lays down procedural rules for scientific practice which it derives by means of a 'knowledge' provided by philosophy. Methodology is the product of philosophy and the sciences are the realization of their methodology.

In this book I intend to expose and to destroy the myths of methodology and, in particular, philosophy's claims to an esoteric 'knowledge' from which these myths derive. If the claims of philosophy to a special kind of knowledge can be shown to be without foundation, if they are at best dogmatic or else incoherent, then methodology is an empty and futile pursuit and its prescriptions are vacuous.

Methodological prescriptions may be derived from epistemology, a conception of the forms of knowledge that are possible and of the conditions in which valid knowledge may be achieved, or from ontology, a conception of what exists. In the one case prescriptions relate to what is thought to be the character of knowledge as such, and in the other they relate to what are thought to be the essential properties of the object of investigation. Where ontological doctrines are invoked with respect to the social sciences they generally concern an alleged distinction between the essential properties of things social and those of (all other) things natural which, far from being established by scientific investigation, is supposed to call for a corresponding distinction in scientific methods of investigation. I shall comment first on epistemology and secondly on the doctrine of the distinctive character of the objects of the social sciences.

An epistemology is a theory in which knowledge is conceived in terms of both a *distinction* and a *correspondence* between two realms. It is concerned with a distinction and a correspondence between a realm of knowledge, of propositions, concepts, beliefs, etc., and a realm of objects, variously conceived in terms of 'real objects', 'phenomena', 'experience', 'sense-data', 'the given', and so on. By virtue of the distinction between, say, the *concept* 'dog' which does not bark and the *real* dog which does, the precise character both of the correspondence involved in a genuine knowledge and of the conditions in which a genuine knowledge may be said to exist becomes problematic. Epistemology attempts to pose and to answer the problems that arise in this area. For example, early logical positivism as represented in Carnap's *The Logical Structure of the World* conceived of knowledge in terms of propositions on the one hand and the given, namely, 'cross-sections of consciousness' and 'remembrance of similarity' on the other. The elementary propositions of knowledge represent the relational structure of the given and they 'point to' its content. Thus the distinction between knowledge and its object is acknowledged and, at least in intention, a bridging correspondence is established.

A conclusive critique of epistemology in all its forms has been outlined by Althusser in his analysis of the structure of 'the empiricist conception of knowledge'. I discuss that analysis and critique in chapter 7. For the purposes of this Introduction it is enough to say that Althusser's concept of 'the empiricist conception of knowledge' designates a conception which counterposes subject to object, knowledge to being, theory to fact, and so on, and which represents genuine knowledge as a function of a process which bridges the distinction between knowledge and its object. Althusser describes that process as an operation of abstraction which is thought to be carried out by a 'subject', whether an individual − an empirical or transcendental individual − or a community of scientists, or whatever. There can be various conceptions of the 'subject' and the 'object' from which it abstracts knowledge but in all cases the structure of the empiricist conception of knowledge establishes some form of fundamental opposition between, say, 'theory' and 'fact', 'men' and 'world', 'transcendental subjectivity' and 'transcendent objectivity', and so on. All epistemology takes some such opposition as constitutive of its theory of knowledge, the aim of which is to lay down the conditions in which valid knowledge is possible. Its conception of 'knowledge' is therefore a function of the particular form in which this opposition is conceived. Epistemology involves a definite conception of the 'subject', the 'object' and the relation between them and it derives its protocols for the evaluation of knowledge from its own 'knowledge' of that relation. 'Empiricism' in this general sense is by no means restricted to the British empirical tradition and its associates since it subsumes the classical rationalist epistemologies which, while they do not conceive the subject as a merely passive recipient of knowledge, nevertheless retain the fundamental structure of distinction and correlation between knowledge and the world. Weber's conception of knowledge, for example, is clearly empiricist in this sense. It presents a knowing subject as confronted by an infinity of given facts so that the subject is capable of knowledge of the world only through the intervention of values which act as a principle of selection in determining what he may or may not choose to investigate.

The inescapable circularity of epistemology is evident for, however, it may conceive the distinction between knowledge and the world, its theory of knowledge logically presupposes a knowledge of the conditions in which knowledge takes place, that is, of the terms of the opposition, 'subject' and 'object', and of the nature of the relation between them. Thus the epistemological specification of the criteria of the validity of all knowledge must presuppose the validity of the prior 'knowledge' from which that specification is derived. Many instances of the general structure of empiricism and of the inescapable problems to which it gives rise are examined in the following chapters.

Two consequences of this critique of epistemology may be noted. The first is that there can be no epistemological protocols of scientific practice and no extra-scientific guarantees that what the sciences or other epistemologically approved disciplines produce is real knowledge. To the extent that methodological doctrines are derived from epistemology their rules and protocols have no rational or coherent foundation and methodology's claims to prescribe for scientific practice are vacuous. Secondly, knowledge can no longer be conceived as involving a relation of 'abstraction' between knowledge on the one hand and the world on the other. There can be no question of maintaining both a *distinction* and a *correlation* between a real object located outside knowledge and an object of knowledge constituted within knowledge. It follows that the classical epistemological problems of knowledge, concerning criteria for the validity of knowledge, can no longer arise. In particular, then, there can be no question of the evaluation of particular substantive discourses, say, Political Economy or Sociology, in terms of epistemologically defined criteria. This last point raises a general problem of the terms in which a coherent critique of determinate theoretical discourses may be conducted. I return to this problem in Chapter 7.

So much for epistemology and epistemologically derived methodologies. But, in the social sciences in particular, methodological doctrines pertaining to the general character of knowledge as such are frequently combined with implicit or explicit ontological conceptions of the distinctive character of the object of investigation. These conceptions are ontological, and therefore philosophical, to the extent that the recognition of that distinctive character is thought to be not the *product* of scientific investigation but rather its *precondition*. Winch maintains, for example, that:

'the central problem of sociology, that of giving an account of the nature of social phenomena in general, itself belongs to philosophy. In fact, not to put too fine a point on it, this part of sociology is really misbegotten epistemology. I say "Misbegotten" because *its problems have been largely misconstrued, and therefore mishandled, as a species of scientific problem.' (op. cit.* p.43 emphasis added)

Not only does philosophy tell us 'the nature of reality as such and in general' but it also tells us the distinctive character of one particular kind of reality, that is, 'the nature of social phenomena in general'. In the absence of such knowledge sociology cannot proceed without fundamental error.

Winch's thesis is only one, and by no means the most rigorous, of the many positions which pretend to a special knowledge of 'the nature of social phenomena in general'. Nevertheless, and in spite of considerable variation, these positions can be shown to be a function of what I shall call the rationalist conception of action.[1] In its most general form this conception presents a realm of ideas, a realm of nature, and a mechanism of the realization of ideas in the realm of nature, namely, human action. This mechanism may be thought to operate at the level of the individual human subject, that is, as a function of its consciousness and will, or at some supra-individual level of determination which subsumes the actions of individuals to its functioning. But however the mechanism may be conceived, its effect is to constitute some portion of the realm of nature as a product of extra-natural determinations. In this sense social phenomena may be conceived as both natural and extra-natural. The rationalist conception of action condemns all positions which fail to acknowledge the extra-natural determination of social phenomena as 'naturalistic' or 'positivistic'. In its view 'naturalism' or 'positivism' commits the fundamental error of treating social phenomena as things. The things of nature are to be the object of natural scientific investigations but where the things of nature are the products of rationalist mechanism they must also be *understood*.

I have defined the rationalist conception of action in its most general form, because, as the debates in the social sciences and history have made abundantly clear, it is not confined to any particular philosophical or epistemological position and it may even be combined with a positivist methodology. It is well known, for example, that in *The Rules of Sociological Method* Durkheim adopts as his first and most fundamental rule that we 'consider social facts as things' (*Rules* p. 14) and he insists that, in the observation of social facts, 'all preconceptions must be eradicated'. (*ibid.* p.31) However, he also conceives of social facts as 'representations', as 'states of the collective consciousness' which are different in kind from those of the individual but are nevertheless of the order of 'ideas', 'concepts' and 'images'. [2] In Durkheim's sociology suicide rates and many other manifest phenomena are conceived as manifestations or expressions of the state of the social consciousness.

Now in referring to the *rationalist* conception of action I do not intend to suggest that this conception must involve a rationalist epistemology. Rationalist epistemology conceives of the world as a rational order in the sense that its parts and the relations between them conform to concepts and the relations between them, the concept giving the essence of the real. Where rationalist epistemology presupposes an *a priori* correspondence, a pre-given harmony, between ideas and the world, the rationalist conception of action postulates a mechanism of the realization of ideas. For example, in Weber's conception of action as 'oriented in its course' by meanings the relation between action and its meaning is one of coherence and logical consistency: the action realizes logical consequences of its meaning. Is it necessary to point out the theological affinities of this conception of action? Whilst theology postulates God as the mechanism *par excellence* of the realization of the word, the rationalist conception of action conceives of a lesser but not essentially dissimilar mechanism.

Two sets of problems may be noted which arise within any form of the rationalist conception of action. The first is that what actually appears in nature is not the idea as such but only what is thought to be its expression. Thus, in the investigation of what it regards as social phenomena, the rationalist conception must not only postulate that some set of given phenomena are indeed the expression of some ideal totality, a system of ideas, but it must also speculate as to the ideas that are expressed in those phenomena. The inescapably speculative character of rationalist conceptions should be abundantly clear from my discussions of Weber, Schutz and Husserl. [3]

The other set of problems may be indicated as follows. The rationalist conception of action postulates *first* a system of ideas (ultimate values, rules, presuppositions, or whatever), an ideal totality, and *secondly* processes of realization of the ideas in that totality. The ideas govern action in the sense that the relation between all actions and the ideas of the totality is one of coherence and consistency. For example it may be said that action is governed by a system of ultimate values if all actions conform to those values, that is, if actions which conflict with them are precluded. Thus, whatever processes of realization may be invoked, they are somehow constrained (it is never clear quite how) to conform to the prior determination of the ideal totality. Problems arise if it is possible for an ideal totality to contain contradictory ideas, for example, conflicting ultimate values. If two contradictory ideas are involved in a given totality then rationalist mechanisms of realization must be indeterminate. Expressions of one idea should be precluded by the other idea.. Thus, if contradiction is possible the action cannot be represented simply as the realization of one idea, since in the event of an action which realizes one of two conflicting ideas there is nothing in the ideas by themselves to account for the realization of one rather than the other in the action. For example, if, as in the case of Winch, conduct is held to be a matter of following rules, then, .in the event of logical contradiction, the rules themselves cannot determine conduct. Short of adopting the relativist position which denies the existence of logical contradiction, the rationalist conception of action can only conceive of the situation as indeterminate. [4] The alternative is to conceive of rationalist mechanisms as functioning by courtesy of quite different extra-rational determinations. Hence the alternatives for the rationalist conception of action are either theoretical indeterminacy or the achievement of theoretical determination at the price of incoherence. This critique is developed in greater detail in Chapter 7.

The consequences of these problems for any methodological doctrine based on a rationalist conception of action must be clear. But there is another consequence of some importance for the argument of this book. If the rationalist conception of action is untenable, then, in particular, no substantive theoretical discourse in Sociology, History, Political Economy, and so on, can be conceived as the product of rationalist mechanisms, as the realization of a methodology, of an author's presuppositions, or what have you. It follows that no critique of methodology can be carried over to a critique of those theoretical discourses which represent themselves as the product of a methodology. Similarly, the Althusserian critique of the empiricist conception of knowledge cannot be carried over into a critique of what might seem to be a substantive empiricist discourse. If the rationalist conception of action is untenable then there can be no process in which the empiricist conception of knowledge is realized. I will return to the significance of this point.

'Understanding' the Social World

Perhaps the most sustained body of work concerned to establish the distinctive character of the subject matter of social scientific and historical investigation is that of German neo-Kantian philosophy of history. Few of the major works of this tradition have been translated into English and it is probably best known in the English-speaking world, if only indirectly, through the writings of Max Weber. Neo-Kantian philosophy includes several quite distinct and often opposing tendencies but, rather than attempt to cover their differences in this Introduction, I shall confine myself to giving a general characterization of the main features of the neo-Kantian conception of history.[5] The methodological writings of Max Weber are examined in Chapter 1.

Neo-Kantian philosophy elaborates a distinction between the natural and the social or cultural sciences on the basis of certain features of Kant's conception of theoretical and practical reason. For the purposes of a schematic exposition it is probably best to begin by considering two sets of problems. First there are the problems posed by Humean empiricism with respect to the status of certain concepts often held to be essential for science. If all knowledge is to be based on experience, and on experience alone, then it is easy to show, for example, that there can be no warrant for the assertion that one event is the *cause* of another. Experience may tell us that the events occur together or in close proximity but we cannot experience any causal connection between them. Thus the concept of causality and, by the same token, all other concepts pertaining to the notion of scientific determination appear to have no foundation in experience. A second set of problems arises out of the notion of scientific determination itself; if every phenomenon has a cause, as science seems to suggest, then what remains of the notion of human freedom? How can human action be free and at the same time determined? Kant's reply to Humean empiricism provides a solution to the second set of problems so that Kant can, in his view, maintain without contradiction both that man is free and that human action, as an event in nature, must be governed by natural determinations. This conception of man as both free and determined is the foundation for the neo-Kantian conception of history.

Kant disputes Humean empiricism on the one hand by admitting that all knowledge *begins with* experience and on the other hand by denying that all knowledge *arises out of* experience:

> 'For it may well be that even our empirical knowledge is made up of what we receive through impressions and of what our own faculty of knowledge (sensible impressions serving merely as the occasion) supplies from itself. If our faculty of knowledge makes any such addition, it may be that we are not in a position to distinguish it from the raw material, until with long practice of attention we have become skilled in separating it.' (*Critique of Pure Reason, B,* pp.1-2)

By postulating a faculty of knowledge which 'supplies from itself' certain features of empirical knowledge Kant is able to save the field of nature for scientific determinism and also to save human freedom from the determinism of nature. Man is possessed of the faculties of sensibility, understanding and reason by virtue of which he is receptive to sensory givens, capable of organizing these givens into knowledge, and of synthesizing his knowledge into systems. These faculties cannot be the *object* of empirical knowledge since they provide the conditions of the *possibility* of empirical knowledge.

Kantian empiricism imposes a distinction between sensible and supersensible objects. Sensible objects are objects of sensory experience, that is, they are the product of impressions *and* of what our cognitive faculties supply from themselves; they must therefore be distinguished from supersensible objects, from things as they are in themselves. Thus whilst sensible objects are immanent to experience there is a realm of supersensible objects, or *noumena,* that is transcendent. The totality of sensible objects constitutes the realm of nature. Its contents are distributed in space and time as a function of our faculty of sensibility and they are governed by natural causality as a function of our faculty of understanding. Nature is therefore a realm of scientific determination whilst man as a transcendental object, i.e. as the possessor of cognitive faculties, is external to the realm of nature.

> 'Man, however, who knows all the rest of nature solely through the senses, knows himself also through pure apperception; and this, indeed, in acts and inner determinations which he cannot regard as impressions of the senses. He is thus to himself, on the one hand

phenomenon, and on the other hand, in respect of certain faculties the action of which cannot be ascribed to the receptivity of sensibility, a purely intelligible object.' (*ibid.* pp. 574–5)

Now, since there are forms of experience and forms of the understanding it follows that certain types of knowledge exist which are totally independent of experience, for example, mathematics, geometry, and certain conceptions of the natural sciences: the concept of 'law of nature', the conception that every phenomenon has a cause in previous phenomena, etc. That knowledge, which is provided by pure reason, is not a knowledge of objects, since these are constituted as a function of experience, and it is not a knowledge of *noumena*. In Kant's view any claim to a knowledge of *noumena* is entirely speculative and any attempt at argument or demonstration with regard to such claims is dialectical, that is, worthless rubbish. In particular, concepts such as 'God', 'freedom', 'immortality', which refer to transcendent objects belong to the sphere of faith but not of knowledge. As far as such objects are concerned Kant finds it 'necessary to deny *knowledge,* in order to make room for *faith*' (*ibid.* p.xxx). Faith and the objects of faith are introduced by Kant specifically with reference to morality. They may be necessary for morality but they are no part of knowledge.

'The doctrine of morality and the doctrine of nature may each, therefore, make good its position. This, however, is only possible in so far as criticism has previously established our unavoidable ignorance of things in themselves, and has limited all that we can theoretically *know* to mere appearances.' (*ibid.* p.xxix)

Hence Kant's distinction between theoretical and practical reason. Theoretical reason is concerned with the knowledge of appearances, with the realm of nature. Practical reason is concerned with morality and its conditions, in particular with 'freedom (in the strictest sense) as a property of our will.' (*loc. cit.*) Practical reason is a sphere of thought concerning practical and moral considerations and it includes a sphere of pure practical reason which subsumes these considerations under general principles, but it cannot be a sphere of *knowledge*.

Now human action is pertinent both to theoretical and to practical reason: it is part of nature and therefore governed by law and it is the action of a rational being, which can act according to a *conception* of law. Every human subject has an empirical character and an intelligible character. With regard to the former, this subject 'would have to conform to all the laws of causal determination. To this extent it could be nothing more than a part of the world of sense, and its effects, like all other appearances, must be the inevitable outcome of nature.' (*ibid.* p. 568) In its intelligible character, on the other hand, 'this same subject must be considered to be free from all influence of sensibility and from all determination through appearances.' (*loc. cit.*) Human action is both free and determined. In so far as it is an object of *knowledge* action is of the order of nature and is subject to causal determination. But as an object of *thought* in the sphere of practical reason it is free and undetermined — it is the expression of a will.

For Kant, then, the sphere of history is a sphere of natural determinations. While, for purposes of practical reason we must conceive of man as free and undetermined, if we are concerned with *knowledge* we must restrict ourselves to the order of appearances. We may *believe,* as a matter of *faith,* that action is the expression of the will of a free actor but we cannot hope to *know* the *noumena;* we can know only the order of appearances within nature. Kant insists on this point in the opening lines of his "Idea for a Universal History":

> 'Whatever concept one may hold, from a metaphysical point of view, concerning the freedom of the will, certainly *its appearances, which are human actions, like every other natural event are determined by universal laws.*' (Kant 1963, p.11 emphasis added)

Human history is a part of nature.[6] For Kant the distinction between practical and theoretical reason implies no corresponding distinction between the social or cultural sciences and the natural sciences.

The neo-Kantians do not agree. The neo-Kantian treatment of the cultural or historical[7] sciences is completely opposed to Kant on this point. As far as these disciplines are concerned the most striking feature of the nineteenth century 'return to Kant' in German philosophy and historiography, from Dilthey to Windelband and Rickert, lies in its invoking what Kant could only regard as a speculative claim to knowledge. To take just one example, consider the following passage from Rickert's Preface to the Sixth and Seventh German edition of his *Science and History:*

> ' "spirit" means something essentially different from, and even in great measure independent of, all merely physical existence. It is akin to what Hegel, using a terminology now taken up once again,

called "objective spirit" in contrast to "subjective spirit". What remains as mere "unspiritual" inner life can thus be subsumed under "nature" . . . on this hypothesis, what distinguishes culture from the whole of nature is not, then, its psychical, but its objectively "spiritual" content, i.e., the sum total of that which is not perceptible by the senses but which can be grasped only in a nonsensorial manner and which gives life its importance and meaning . . .' (p.xv)

Here Rickert retains a form of the distinction between sensible and supersensible, 'that which is not perceptible by the senses', and lays claim to a form of knowledge of the latter. It is the objectively spiritual content of cultural phenomena which delimits that particular portion of nature as precisely the expression of extra-natural meanings and it is the task of the sciences of culture and of history to grasp 'in a nonsensorial manner' the content that is expressed in these phenomena. Cultural phenomena must be treated not only as events in nature but also as the expression of meanings — they must be *understood*.

Now, whatever 'common humanity'[8] may be invoked to account for the miraculous faculty of *understanding,* it is clear that the neo-Kantian sciences cannot be other than essentially speculative in character. In retaining the distinction between sensible and supersensible and in laying claim to a *knowledge,* and not merely *faith,* with regard to the latter, the neo-Kantian theories are condemned by their own concepts to recognize a necessary indeterminacy in the relation between sensible phenomena and the 'meanings' that may be read into them. The very delimitation of a certain sphere of phenomena as cultural, rather than merely natural, requires that they be known to be the expression of some, as yet unknown, objective meaning, and the 'understanding' of any given cultural phenomenon requires an indeterminate process of speculative interpretation. This process of interpretation, in the nature of the case, is always open to challenge by alternative, equally speculative interpretations. The dependence of these positions on a rationalist conception of action is evident: cultural phenomena are the product of acts of expression. We shall see in Chapter 1 that Weber's neo-Kantian positivism and his insistence on 'causally adequate' explanation in no way escapes the rationalism and the necessary element of speculation of neo-Kantian historiography.

In Chapters 2 and 3 we shall see that while Schutz and Husserl depart from neo-Kantianism in several respects they do not depart either from the rationalist conception of action of from its speculative consequences. The doctrines of Schutz have been taken over to a greater or lesser extent in the so-called phenomenological sociology and in parts of ethnomethodology, two of the more fashionable anti-positivist tendencies in contemporary sociology. The far more rigorous and serious work of Husserl has had little direct impact on the social sciences; it is known, if at all, largely through the vulgarizations of Schutz, Merleau-Ponty, and others. In Chapter 2 I argue that far from being based on the work of Husserl, Schutz's 'phenomenology' perpetrates a vulgar humanist and psychologistic distortion of Husserl's philosophy. The critique of Schutz's conception of history and the social sciences in that chapter is therefore directed not against the phenomenology of Husserl but only against some of its grosser misrepresentations. The argument of that chapter, then, leaves open the possibility that the rigorous transcendental phenomenology of Husserl might form the basis of a coherent phenomenological social science and science of history. In Chapter 3 I examine Husserl's own theory of the history of the sciences and of philosophy, and I argue that no such possibility exists. Husserl's position is shown to be structured around a central contradiction between his objective of a rational, non-subjectivist history of the sciences and the transcendental empiricist epistemology in terms of which that objective is to be realized. The effect of this contradiction between one set of Husserl's concepts and another is a theoretical discourse structured by a series of logical discrepancies and a denegatory play on words which glosses over the discrepancies. Husserl's epistemology is shown to be impossible without these necessary discrepancies and to be ultimately incoherent as an epistemology because of them. Thus there can be no Husserlian theory of knowledge unless these contradictions are also present and no corresponding realization of that theory in 'positive' knowledges.

There are, of course, forms of the rationalist conception of action which do not involve the neo-Kantian distinction between sensible and supersensible objects or the phenomenological demarcation between transcendental subjectivity and objects in the world. For example, the dominant tendency in recent British philosophy has been to reject any distinction between 'consciousness' on the one hand and 'body' on the other: there are not two kinds of object here but only one. Persons are distinguished from other types of object not in that they combine two kinds of entity in one but rather in that certain types of description are pertinent to persons and not pertinent to other things. We attribute an intention to a person who hits me over the head but not to an apple which falls on me from a tree.[9] In these cases the basic rationalist conception of action is retained – men realize ideas, apples falling off trees do not. While the rejection of the doctrine of two kinds of entity in one person has definite theoretical effects, it cannot avoid the fundamental problems of the rationalist conception of action and the speculative effects which it imposes. I have not discussed this position at any length in this book but it may readily be subsumed under the general critique of the rationalist conception of action developed in Chapter 7.

Positivism and Positivist Methodology

The term 'positivism' is used in a number of different senses in the social sciences and in philosophy. I use it here to refer to a distinctive type of epistemology characterized by its insistence that we can know reality only on the basis of experience. There is no pure *a priori* knowledge of the kind that Kant suggests and there are no objects which lie beyond the realm of sensible phenomena. Positivism asserts the claims of experience as the ultimate foundation of human knowledge and denies the possibility of meaningful discourse concerning supersensible objects. Further, since all knowledge is based on experience there can be no foundation for the ontological doctrines which underlie the rationalist demarcation between the sciences of nature and those of history and culture. If positivist philosophy presents a definite conception of the forms and conditions of knowledge then positivist methodology proceeds to derive and to elaborate a definite system of rules and protocols both for knowledge in general and for scientific knowledge in particular. In the social sciences the dominant positivist methodologies are the varieties of systematic empiricism, the methodology of deductive testing proposed by Popper and his associates, and the vulgar positivist epistemology of model-building. The first have been subjected to a devastating critique by David and Judith Willer in *Systematic Empiricism: critique of a pseudo-science*. In spite of the weakness of their own conception of science and empiricism their thorough and systematic demolition of many of the dominant positivist methodological doctrines cannot be too highly recommended. Rather than attempt to repeat their arguments I shall be concerned in Chapter 4 to outline the basic features of positivist epistemology and to demonstrate the inescapable circularity and ultimate dogmatism of even the most sophisticated positivist epistemology. Popper's position, which deviates from positivism in certain limited respects is examined in Chapter 6. The epistemology of model-building, in which knowledge is said to be obtained through the construction of models on the basis of given facts, is discussed in Chapter 5.

As an epistemology positivism falls under the general critique of the empiricist conception of knowledge outlined above. Its conceptions of the forms of knowledge that are possible and of the criteria for the validity of claims to knowledge logically presuppose a 'knowledge' of the conditions in which knowledge takes place, that is, of the terms of the opposition: 'subject'/'object', and of the character of the relation between them. Thus, the specification of the criteria for the validity of knowledge must presuppose the validity of the knowledge from which that specification is derived. Positivism faces the additional problem that the attributes of the knowing subject which are required for its theory of knowledge cannot, even on its own terms, be established on the basis of experience alone. In this respect positivist epistemology presupposes what it must regard as a metaphysics, that is, a form of knowledge not reducible to experience. It presupposes what its own criteria must dismiss as meaningless. Thus, quite apart from the general problems of the empiricist conception of knowledge, positivist epistemology and its secondary discourses on methodology and philosophy of science are logically incoherent and rationally indefensible.

But there is a further set of problems for any positivist epistemology which concerns its conception of the relations between the propositions of science on the one hand and the phenomena of experience on the other. Concepts such as 'electromagnetic field', 'electron', 'proton', 'the geometrical structure of relativistic space-time continua', can hardly be considered to refer to objects of direct experience. How, then, can we be sure that to speak of such entities is not to introduce surreptitious metaphysical elements into scientific discourse? In the later work of Carnap such problems are resolved in terms of his distinction between the languages of theory and of observation. There is a language of observation whose elementary propositions express the relational structure of the given and point to its content. These propositions are strictly irreducible and they refer only to what is given in experience. They contain no theoretical admixture. The theoretical language, on the other hand, refers to objects and properties of objects that are not given in experience. Carnap proposes a number of rigorously defined conditions which can ensure that a theoretical term or proposition is meaningful, that is, empirically significant. The details of these proposals need not concern us here. What must be noted at this point is that the concept of an a-theoretical observation language makes possible a very precise conception of the testing of theory against observation. The testing of theory against irreducible statements of observation is equivalent to a direct comparison between theory and the real. If they fail to correspond then the theory is false and it may therefore be rejected.

So far so good. Now, many positivist philosophers have disputed the possibility of drawing any hard and fast distinction between the languages of theory and of observation. In fact, as I argue in Chapter 5, that distinction involves a definite conception of logic and pure mathematics as being independent of any empirically given conditions. In effect their propositions must be true in all possible states of affairs. Logic and pure mathematics give a knowledge of the structure of the given that is arrived at independently of the given itself. It is clear that this conception of logic and pure mathematics is incompatible with the fundamental positivist doctrine of the reducibility of all knowledge to experience. Thus the distinction between theoretical and observational languages cannot be sustained within any strict positivist epistemology.

What are the implications of the rejection of the notion of an a-theoretical observation language for the positivist doctrine of the testing of theory against experience? The answer to this question is given in Chapter 6 where I examine Popper's methodology of deductive testing. It is true that Popper has always rejected certain features of positivist epistemology, notably the thesis of an a-theoretical observation language and the doctrine of the meaninglessness of metaphysics. Nevertheless he insists that the sciences advance by the testing of theory against the 'facts', that is, against descriptions of observations. If all observation is to some extent theoretical then how is it possible to maintain that all knowledge is reducible to observation and that theory is to be tested against the 'facts' of observation? For Carnap there is no problem: theory is to be tested against the observation statements because the latter really do designate the given and they really do express its relational structure. But, if there is no a-theoretical observation language then observation statements do not strictly designate the given nor do they strictly express its relational structure. Why then test theory against observation statements? If observation statements do not express the structure of the real, if they are always to some extent theoretical, then there is no reason why we should accept a theory if it conforms to them and reject it as false if it fails to conform. The doctrine of reduction and of the testing of theory against the 'facts' of observation can be defended only within a strict positivist epistemology by reference to its strict observation language. If the existence of an a-theoretical observation language is denied then these doctrines have no possible rational foundation. I argue this case at length in relation to Popper's epistemology in Chapter 6 but the argument applies equally to all those, for example Quine and Hempel who dispute the possibility of a rigorous distinction between theoretical and observation languages while retaining a residual positivist commitment to the doctrine that knowledge is reducible to the phenomena of experience.

The argument of Chapters 4 to 6, then, is that positivist epistemology in all its forms and the related doctrines of deductive testing and of model-building are logically incoherent and rationally indefensible. Positivist methodology, philosophy of science, and other derivative discourses are therefore untenable. It follows that the sciences cannot be conceived as either testing or measuring theory against the standard of the real. The protocols of positivist epistemology or of Popper's 'critical rationalism' therefore have no pertinence to any 'empirical' investigations.

The Critique of Empiricism and the Production of Theoretical Discourse

Finally, it is necessary to consider the implications for the critique of empiricist positions of my analysis of the rationalist conception of action elaborated in Chapter 7 and outlined above. Chapter 7 opens with a distinction between two levels or forms of critique of empiricism: one directed at epistemology and related doctrines, the other directed at what are thought to be products of an empiricist process. For example, the authors of *Systematic Empiricism* elaborate a critique of particular epistemologies and methodological positions but they also insist that empiricism is a real process of the production of knowledge. Thus their concept of empiricism provides the basis for a critique of substantive positions which are held to be the products of an empiricist process. Similarly the far more rigorous and sophisticated work of Althusser contains both an analysis and critique of the empiricist conception of knowledge and a distinction between science and theoretical ideology as the products of distinct types of process of production of knowledge. The production of theoretical ideology is a process dominated by empiricism. Thus Althusser's concept of the empiricist conception of knowledge on the one hand and his concepts of science and theoretical ideology on the other provide the foundation for an 'Althusserian' critique of work in Sociology, Political Economy, History — in short, of all substantive theoretical discourses that can be represented as empiricist and therefore ideological. Much of the argument of this book is based on Althusser's critique of the empiricist conception of knowledge but, in other publications, I have sometimes adopted the second 'Althusserian' mode of critique. For example, in our Introduction to *Pre-Capitalist Modes of Production* Paul Hirst and I have suggested:

> 'The empiricism of the academic social sciences and of much Marxist scholarship has serious theoretical effects. In so far as certain facts are represented as 'given' in the real or as 'given' by history they must fall below the level of theoretical determination: they cannot be the product of an explicit theoretical practice. The empiricism of these disciplines therefore ensures that these 'facts' are ideological constructs and that their 'theories' are, at best, sophisticated theoretical ideology.' (p. 3)

This critique is of no great importance for the major arguments of *Pre-Capitalist Modes of Production* but its general character is clear. There is a real empiricist process of knowledge and it results in ideological knowledge not in scientific knowledge.

Chapter 7 examines the Willers' concept of systematic empiricism and the 'Althusserian' critique of empiricism. In both cases I argue that, however effective their respective critiques of methodology and epistemology may be, their conceptions of empiricism as a real process of production of knowledge and of science as a distinct type of real process generate insurmountable problems and result in a logically impossible theory of the process of production of knowledge. Consequently the anti-empiricist critique of theoretical discourses other than those of epistemology and methodology is an invalid and logically ineffective form of critique.

Now, these arguments raise a more general problem which I consider in the third part of Chapter 7. It concerns not the demarcation of science from non-science but rather the manner in which the process of production of theoretical discourse, scientific or otherwise, is conceived in terms of the realization of extra-discursive conceptual relations. What is at stake here, whether what is thought to be realized in theoretical discourse is conceived as a methodology, an author's presuppositions, or even a theoretical (scientific or ideological) problematic which governs the order of appearance of concepts in the production of discourse, is what I shall call the rationalist conception of the production of discourse. This is a special case of the more general rationalist conception of action outlined above in that the relation between what appears in the discourse and the extra-discursive conditions implicated in its production is conceived as one of coherence and logical consistency — the order of concepts in the discourse realizes ideas and relations between ideas that are held to govern the production of that discourse. I argue that the rationalist conception of action is untenable and that it can be maintained only at the price of theoretical incoherence. The rationalist conception of the production of discourse is therefore untenable. Theoretical discourse cannot be conceived as the outcome of a rationalist process of production. It follows that a rigorous distinction must be maintained between problems concerning the logical properties of the order of concepts of a discourse and problems concerned with the process of production of discourse. I conclude the chapter by considering the implications of that distinction for the analysis of discourse and for the question of the terms in which a rational and coherent critique of particular discourses may be conducted.

What are the consequences of these arguments for the critique of epistemological and methodological positions developed in the preceding chapters? One consequence has already been noted, namely, that the critique of methodology cannot be extended to a critique of those substantive discourses which are represented as if they were the product of the application of methodological protocols. If there is no rationalist process of production of discourse then it is impossible to maintain that methodological or other protocols may be effectively realized in particular theoretical discourses. Similarly Althusser's critique of the empiricist conception of knowledge cannot be extended into a critique of what might seem to be a substantive empiricist discourse. But there is a second consequence which should be noted before I conclude this Introduction. Although, my examination of methodological and epistemological positions in the first six chapters is primarily concerned with their concepts and the relations between their concepts there are also a number of passages in which I counterpose these positions to a quite different conception of science. For example, in the chapter on Popper I assert, in contradiction to Popper's position, that:

> 'the sciences work upon constructs which are produced through the operation of its theory and instruments (and these latter in their turn depend upon theory). It follows that the relations between theory, instrument and observation must be conceived as internal to the practice of the science concerned.'

At work in this and other passages is a particular rationalist conception of the process of production of scientific knowledge developed in the work of Bachelard and Althusser. It follows from my critique of the rationalist conception of action that this conception of the process of production of scientific knowledge cannot be sustained. However, this conception plays no significant part in my examination of the coherence of epistemological and methodological doctrines. Thus, while some of the positions taken up in these chapters must now be regarded as untenable, my conclusions concerning the coherence of epistemology must stand.

1. The Methodology of Max Weber

In a series of essays published together in English under the title of *The Methodology of the Social Sciences* (hereafter: *Methodology*) and again in the first part of *Economy and Society*, 'The Fundamental Concepts of Sociology', Weber attempts to define the general character of the social and cultural sciences and to establish general canons of proof and demonstration for use in their investigations. These texts are by no means equivalent. *Economy and Society* is presented as a systematic elaboration and classification of general concepts while the essays in the *Methodology* are more polemical in tone and more discursive in style. *Economy and Society* concerns itself with sociology (as Weber conceives it) while the *Methodology* essays are more concerned with problems of the definition of history as a cultural science and with problems of historical proof and explanation, sociology being relegated to the status of an ancillary discipline, a useful tool which no historian should be without. Nevertheless there are few significant epistemological differences between these texts and they involve identical conceptions of the nature of the social and cultural sciences as the sciences of *action* in general and of social action in particular.[1]

In this chapter I examine Weber's definitions of action and of sociology as a science of social action as given in the opening paragraphs of *Economy and Society* and the forms of proof which he outlines there and in *Methodology* in relation to the concepts of ideal type, causal explanation and causal significance, objective possibility and probability. While *Economy and Society* refers mainly to sociology its most general concepts – action, meaning and behaviour – serve to define the social and cultural sciences as a whole specifically as sciences of action in contrast to the natural sciences. The definition of action in terms of extra-phenomenal, transcendent meanings is crucial to Weber's conceptions of the social and cultural sciences and of the particular theoretical and methodological problems that may arise within them. Action is not the product of psychological causes, it is the phenomenal expression of transcendent meanings. I consider first the general concepts of action, meaning and behaviour, secondly Weber's epistemology and the role of values within it, and finally, his more 'technical' conceptions of scientific objectivity. Weber's definition of sociology is based on an essentially religious metaphysical conception of man, his methodology is relativistic and irrationalist, and his concept of scientific objectivity is a façade for an underlying notion of verisimilitude, of plausibility and subjective conviction.

1.1 Meaning, Action and Behaviour

'The fruit of the tree of knowledge, which is distasteful to the complacent but which is, nonetheless, inescapable, consists in the insight that every single important activity and ultimately life as a whole, if it is not to be permitted to run on as an event in nature but is instead to be consciously guided, is a series of ultimate decisions through which the soul – as in Plato – chooses its own fate, i.e. the meaning of its activity and existence.' (*Methodology*, p.18)

Apart from its overt religious and mystical overtones the conception of human action outlined in this passage reappears in Weber's definition of action in the first paragraph of *Economy and Society*:

'In "action" is included all human behaviour when and in so far as the acting individual attaches a subjective meaning to it' (*The Theory of Social and Economic Organisation* – hereafter: *Theory* – p.88)

Here the distinction between 'action' and 'behaviour' reproduces the earlier distinction between 'an event in nature' and action guided by 'meanings', 'values' and other such human attributes and the peculiar character of the relation that obtains between these two realms is fundamental to Weber's conception of *Man* and therefore of the human or cultural sciences.

It should be noted that while Weber refers us to 'the fruit of the tree of knowledge' for a constitutive element of his sociology he makes no attempt to establish this alleged 'knowledge'. In the absence of the slightest attempt at proof or demonstration we appear to be confronted by an arbitrary and dogmatic assertion that plays a crucial role in Weber's definition of sociology as 'a science which attempts the interpretative understanding of social action'. Elsewhere Weber makes it clear that we owe the fundamental definition of the object of the social or cultural sciences to philosophy. For example, he refers to 'the transcendental presupposition of every cultural science', namely:

> 'that we are *cultural beings,* endowed with the capacity and the will to take a definite attitude toward the world and to lend it *significance*'. (*Methodology,* p.81)

The fundamental concepts of the social sciences are to be based on a 'knowledge' provided by philosophy, in particular by the neo-Kantian philosophy of Rickert and Windelband mixed with more than a pinch of Dilthey. This 'knowledge', such as it is, is constitutive of the social sciences; it cannot be established within them. Weber's social sciences are constituted by what he imagines to be established in philosophy.

Whatever the status of that alleged 'knowledge' the precise character of the relation that is supposed to hold between meanings and actions remains obscure. It is obscure not only in the work of Weber but in all those texts which peddle non-natural 'meanings' as the constitutive elements of the social sciences. 'Action' is distinguished from 'behaviour' by means of the subjective meaning which is attached to it. Or again:

> 'Action is social in so far as, by virtue of the subjective meaning attached to it by the acting individual (or individuals), it takes account of the behaviour of others and is thereby oriented in its course' (*Theory,* p.88)

What are the mechanisms which enable meanings to produce their effects? How, in the case of social action, does meaning 'take account of the behaviour of others' in such a way as to orient action 'in its course'? If Weber does not and indeed cannot answer these questions, it is, as we shall see, because the relation of meaning to behaviour is not a relation 'in nature' between one phenomenon and another but a relation between phenomena and extra-phenomenal, non-natural entities, an expressive and teleological relation which vitiates any attempt at a rigorous Weberian theory of action.

Nevertheless the concept of 'subjective meaning', however obscure and ill-defined it may be, plays a crucial role in Weber's sociology. Social relationships, social collectivities (e.g. the state),[2] the different types of action, and so on, are all defined by reference to meanings. For example, in the case of economic action:

> ' "economic" processes and objects are characterized as such entirely by the meaning they have for human action in such roles as ends, means, obstacles, and by-products . . . these phenomena have a peculiar type of subjective meaning. This alone defines the unity of the corresponding processes, and this alone makes them accessible to subjective interpretation.' (*Theory,* p.158–9)

Subjective meanings cannot be conceived as epiphenomenal, as something which merely accompanies action; on the contrary they enter in to the definition of the distinct types of action and it is primarily with respect to their meanings that actions are to be classified. Thus the substantive concepts of Weber's social theory involve an essential reference to meanings. In effect the general notion of the human subject – making decisions, interpreting situations, acting 'in terms of' meanings and intentions and in relation to similarly constituted actors – appears as an unquestioned and essential basis of Weber's theory of action. What is distinctive, however, is not so much the conception of the human subject as agent, which in one form or another characterizes the academic social sciences, but the manner in which Weber's human subject is alleged to function, in particular the peculiar relation of meaning and action which is constitutive of Weber's sociology. In the following chapter we shall see that it is largely with respect to how this peculiar relation is to be conceived that Weber has been criticized by social phenomenology.

Now, if Weber explains anything about 'meaning' it is not how it relates to overt behaviour. Instead he offers a distinction between two kinds of meanings: 'the actually existing meaning' which refers to a given actor or actors and 'the theoretically conceived *pure type* of subjective meaning attributed to the hypothetical actor or actors in a given type of action' (*Theory,* p.89). The term 'actually existing' is confusing. The distinction made here is not between a 'real' meaning and one that is postulated by the social scientist, it is between two postulated meanings, one referring to a particular given actor or actors, the other referring to actors engaged in particular types of action. The crucial point for Weber's conception of meaning and its relation to overt behaviour is made in the sentence which follows. 'In no case does it refer to an objectively "correct" meaning or one which is "true" in some metaphysical sense'. (*ibid.*) In the social sciences or in history 'meaning' is always something attributed by an observer.[3] 'Meanings' are not sensible phenomena; they are not events 'in nature'. Rather they belong to the supersensible essence of Man, an essence that in Weber's neo-Kantian epistemology must be conceived as radically exterior to the realm of nature. Meanings may be *expressed* in the realm of nature but they do not reside there.[4]

We can now approach the fundamental theoretical problems deriving from a 'transcendental presupposition' such as Weber's and the peculiar character of the relation it effects between 'meaning', 'action' and 'behaviour'. Weber's definition of action implies a reference to human behaviour that is not action, i.e., that has no subjective meaning attached to it. There are psychophysical processes that cannot be considered meaningful action at all and the line between action and behaviour is always difficult to determine. Indeed:

'A very considerable part of sociologically relevant behaviour, especially purely traditional behaviour, is marginal between the two' (*Theory*, p.90).

The category of action that is marginal between action and behaviour occupies a central position in Weber's sociological theory and in his investigations of the differences between the development of rationality in the West and its non-development elsewhere. Section 2 of 'The Fundamental Concepts of Sociology' distinguishes four basic types of social action according to their mode of orientation. Two are defined as rational: *zweckrational,* defined in relation to a system of discrete individual ends and the rational estimation of means available for their attainment;[5] *wertrational,* involving a conscious belief in an absolute value and its implementation independently of any prospects of successful realization. The others, traditional and affectual orientations, are explicitly conceived as on the borderline of meaningful orientation. In so far as they cease to be marginal they 'shade over' into one or other of the rational action types. We may therefore conclude that action is *essentially* rational and that it deviates from rationality only to the extent that it is polluted by an admixture of behaviour, i.e., to the extent that it becomes 'an event in nature'. [6]

Now the existence of a mass of human behaviour that is not action at all and, presumably, of a great deal more that is on the borderline raises the question of the relative proportions of the rational or meaningful and of the merely natural in any given society. More generally, given that there is always a great deal of mere behaviour, why is it necessary to define sociology as a science of social *action* in particular rather than of a more general range of behaviours?

Consider first the question of the relative proportions of action and mere behaviour in any given society. It is clear that Weber's concepts preclude any empirical determination of those proportions since meanings are supersensible entities. They may be *postulated* by the observer but they cannot be empirically discovered. Weber is undeterred. In a very revealing discussion of the potentialities of the subjective understanding of animal behaviour Weber tells us that biological analogies:

> 'may throw light on the question of the relative role in the early stages of human social differentiation of mechanical and instinctive factors, as compared with that of the factors which are accessible to subjective interpretation generally, and more particularly to the role of consciously rational action. It is necessary for the sociologist to be thoroughly aware of the fact that *in the early stages even of human development, the first set of factors is completely predominant.* Even in the later stages he must take account of their continual interaction with the others in a role which is often of decisive importance. This is particularly true of all 'traditional' action and of many aspects of charisma.' (*Theory,* p.106, emphasis added)

There are two levels in man: the mechanical and biological, *viz.,* the animal; and the level of subjective meanings, of the rational essence of man. The former is predominant in the early stages of human development. [7] It is easy to recognize here the traditional religious and metaphysical dichotomy of body and soul, material and spiritual, etc. Weber, following much of German philosophy of history, represents this metaphysical dichotomy as achieving a certain realization in history. [8]

In defining sociology as a science of action, that is, of the realization of human purposes, Weber in no way denies that there is always a great deal of mere behaviour. But *purpose,* subjective meaning and rationality, is nevertheless represented as what is specifically and essentially human. History is, *inter alia,* a process of realization of that essence.[9] It is in this sense that, in the Introduction to his studies of the World Religions, Weber can refer to the rationalizing development of Western civilization (in contrast to the ossification and stagnation of the East), as lying 'in a line of development having *universal* significance and value' (*Protestant Ethic,* p. 13). [10]

It is this conception of the rational essence of man which necessitates the definition of the social and cultural sciences as sciences of action, of human purposes and their realizations. More precisely, it is the valuation of this alleged rational essence that is decisive here. The mere fact that some behaviour is meaningful and other behaviour is not does not suffice, in Weber's epistemology, to define the field of action as a distinctive area of scientific investigation. 'Value-relevance' is decisive for the constitution of the theoretical objective of *Economy and Society.* [11] For all its generalizing and systematizing tendencies *Economy and Society* does not escape the theoretical relativism and irrationalism consequent upon the attempted definition of objects of investigation on the basis of their relevance for values. The inescapable relativism and irrationalism of Weber's doctrine of value-relevance is examined below.

Similarly, it is the essential rationality of action that entails Weber's insistence that psychological and irrational elements in behaviour are to be interpreted as leading to deviations from the pure type of rational action. It is only by comparison with an ideal type, with the theoretical construct of a rational course of action, that:

> 'it is possible to understand the ways in which actual action is influenced by irrational factors of all sorts, . . . in that they account for the deviations from the line of conduct which would be expected on the hypothesis that action were purely rational (*Theory,* p.92)

At this point Weber adds that 'rational types' are only a methodological device.. Nevertheless, for reasons of 'methodological convenience', sociologists are enjoined to work with rational action types and to interpret the causal significance of all other behavioural elements merely 'as accounting for the deviations from this type' (*ibid.*). Here it is clear that rationality is presupposed as essential and that only that presupposition can justify Weber's insistence on the use of rational idea types. [12]

Finally, in this section, it should be noted that Weber's conception of action as the realization of meanings or purposes involves a necessary reference to values as the ultimate source of purposes. The precise theoretical status of these 'ultimate values' is brought out most clearly in the passage from the *Methodology* cited at the beginning of this section and again in the following:

> '[We] must recognize that general views of life and the universe can never be products of increasing empiricial knowledge, and that the highest ideals, which move us most forcefully, are always formed only in the struggle with other ideals which are just as sacred to others as ours are to us.' (*Methodology*, p.57)

The essence of human action, as opposed to mere behaviour, must therefore be conceived as involving rationality and ultimate values. It is the choice of ultimate values, and therefore of the meaning of life, and the attempt to realize those values which distinguishes action from 'an event in nature'. Values are conceived as radically exterior to the world of nature since it is precisely their intervention which distinguishes essentially human *action* from merely natural *behaviour*. Values intervene in the natural, or material, world through the medium of their attempted realization in action but they are not part of that world and they cannot be formed within it.

Thus the fundamental concepts of Weber's social science are defined by reference to an extra-natural, if not super-natural, realm of values, meanings, purposes. Weber's 'man' is a sensible-supersensible unity, a combination of natural elements pertaining to behaviour and non-natural elements pertaining to action. Sociology, the 'science' of social *action*, is defined as a science of the expressions of those extra-natural elements in the realm of nature. [13] Given the essentially religious character of its fundamental concepts Weber's sociology must be unremittingly hostile to all forms of materialism. The claim that Weber's work may be interpreted as a footnote to Marx or that it is a correction of Marx's 'one-sided' emphasis on the role of economic factors in history is completely without foundation. [14]

1.2 Knowledge, Values and Meanings

We have seen that the Weberian concept of action is predicated on a dichotomy between the phenomenal or empirical realm of events in nature and an extra-phenomenal realm containing, *inter alia,* meanings, values and the like. Whilst entities of the former realm are thought to be subject to empirical observation and therefore to empirical canons of proof those of the latter are not strictly empirical at all – they may be *expressed* in the phenomenal realm but they do not reside in it. The presence of meanings, values and other attributes of rational beings in the transcendent is disclosed by philosophy which also supplies us with the invaluable information that some, if not all, behaviours of human animals are expressions of those particular transcendent entities. To each phenomenal human animal there corresponds a transcendent rational being which expresses itself in and through the behaviours of that animal. The task of the student of action, the social scientist or historian, is to investigate the phenomenal expressions of transcendent meanings and thereby to account for the appearance of those phenomena and for the relations which obtain between them.

1.2.1 Value-relevance and concept formation

Weber's methodological protocols are a function of his epistemological conception of the relation between the knowing subject (the scientist) and the realm of nature which confronts him together with certain complications deriving from the fact (alleged by neo-Kantian philosophy) that certain natural phenomena are also expressions of transcendent meanings. While nature itself is conceived of as a realm of mechanical regularity and mechanical causation the expressions of meanings in nature cannot be conceived in the same way. Following the neo-Kantian epistemology of Rickert, Weber argues that the differences in the objects of the natural and the cultural sciences in no way preclude the development of objective knowledge in the latter. The fact that the student of action must investigate values does not entail that his knowledge must be purely subjective and evaluative.

In addition Rickert's neo-Kantianism involves a conception of nature and of everything within it as infinite in all significant respects. While some sciences investigate general regularities and produce nomological knowledge others (the cultural sciences) investigate individual cases and produce ideographic knowledge. Yet no complete description of any event or situation is possible. All description of particular events or situations therefore requires some principle of selection. For Rickert and for Weber that principle is provided by values: it is their relevance to values that determines which particular phenomena are pertinent to investigation in the cultural sciences and which are not. Once again, however, the intervention of values is thought not to preclude objectivity. The selective principle of value-relevance does not depend on the investigator's own subjective valuation of phenomena but only on the relevance of phenomena to particular values. The values in question may or may not be shared by the investigator himself but in principle his own subjective valuation should play no part in scientific investigation. However, unlike Rickert, Weber denies that there are universal objective values in terms of which the relevance of cultural phenomena may be assessed. On the contrary:

> 'the highest ideals, which move us most forcefully, are always form-
> ed only in the struggle with other ideals which are just as sacred to
> others as ours are to us.' (*Methodology*, p.57)

What are the consequences of this conception of the role of values in scientific investigation?[15]

First, there is an inevitable discrepancy between concepts and the reality to which they relate. Whatever event or situation we may investigate its infinity ensures that we must always ignore certain of its features as not pertinent to the values in question. Hence Weber's comments on what he calls 'the economic interpretation of history', i.e., Marxism. The economic interpretation:

> 'is antiquated at best. The explanation of everything by economic
> causes *alone* is never exhaustive in any sense whatsoever in *any*
> sphere of cultural phenomena, not even in the 'economic' sphere
> itself ... [The] 'one-sidedness' and the unreality of the purely
> economic interpretation of history is in general only a special case
> of a principle which is generally valid for the scientific knowledge of
> cultural reality' (*Methodology*, p.71)

That 'generally valid' principle is that there can be no objective study of ' "social phenomena" independent of special and one-sided viewpoints' (*ibid.*, p.72).

Secondly, all concepts are a product of values. Thus, in the essay 'Objectivity in Social Science and Social Policy' Weber insists that the very definition of a phenomenon as 'economic' is a product of values.

> 'The quality of an event as a "social economic" event is not

something which it possesses "objectively". It is rather conditioned by the orientation of our cognitive interest, as it arises from the specific cultural significance which we attribute to the particular event in a given case' (*ibid.,* p.64)

The implications of this position are devastating. Different values will have the result that different events or configurations will be judged to be historically significant and consequently that different concepts are to be used in their investigation. Furthermore the imputation of causes is also supposed to be a function of value-relevance. For example:

'an exhaustive causal investigation of any concrete phenomena in its full reality is not only practically impossible – it is simply nonsense. *We select only those causes which are to be imputed in the individual case, the "essential" feature of an event*' (*ibid.,* p.78, emphasis added)

Thus, with regard to the same historical event, say, the development of modern capitalism, different investigators may quite legitimately attribute entirely different causes without departing in any way from the highest Weberian standards of 'objectivity' and 'value-freedom'.

Finally, a third consequence is that any idea of a universally valid classification or theory is entirely meaningless because our interests, and therefore our concepts, are subject to change – so long as 'a chinese ossification of intellectual life' (*ibid.,* p.84)[16] does not set in and spoil everything.

'The light of the great cultural problems moves on. Then science too prepares to change its standpoint and its analytical apparatus and to view the streams of events from the heights of thought. It follows those stars which alone are able to give meaning and direction to its labours' (*ibid.,* p.112)

Weber's metaphysical and fundamentally religious conception of the relation of man to the world of nature therefore entails a systematic epistemological relativism, a relativism defined at the level of cultural values rather than individual subjectivities[17] but a relativism nonetheless. In this respect the cultural sciences, as Weber defines them, might seem to be a not unpleasant pastime but they could hardly be considered a serious intellectual pursuit for grown men. However, utter relativism notwithstanding, Weber proceeds to elaborate canons of *causal* explanation, *objective* possibility, *causal* adequacy, and the like. Is it possible to attach any coherent intellectual content to these notions? Before proceeding to examine this question it is necessary to consider the implications resulting from the introduction of transcendent elements into Weber's concept of action.

1.2.2 Knowledge of actor's meanings

The social scientist or historian is concerned with the study of action and with its causal explanation by means of 'subjective interpretation', that is, by reference to its meaning for the actor or actors concerned. Unfortunately the meaning of an action is a transcendent entity; it is not a phenomenon and cannot be subjected to empirical observation. While its behavioural expression may appear in the realm of empirical phenomena the meaning itself cannot. The social scientist is therefore constrained to work with meanings which he postulates in order to account for the behaviour with which he is concerned. Action is distinguished from mere behaviour, from the effects of 'mechanical and instinctive factors' (*Theory,* p.106), by the fact that it has meaning for the actor, and actions are distinguished from one another by their different meanings, all of which are equally unobservable.

On the one hand, therefore, the Weberian sociologist must attempt to classify and to differentiate actions by reference to the meanings which they express. To that end he may, should he feel so inclined, make use of the categories elaborated by Weber in *Economy and Society* for such a purpose. On the other hand, while behaviours may be subjected to empirical observation, their meanings, if indeed they do have meanings, are specifically excluded from the realm of observation. Nevertheless, if he is to investigate *action* and to provide causal explanation by reference to its meanings he must be able to distinguish action from mere behaviour and to establish the meanings of the actions thus distinguished. How is the poor man to proceed?

It should be noted that neo-Kantian philosophy has nothing to offer at this point. That philosophy tells us, if we care to listen, that some human behaviour expresses a transcendent meaning and that there is a sense in which that meaning accounts for the corresponding behaviour. However, if meanings could be established by empirical observation they would cease to be transcendent. Thus while meaning expresses itself in behaviour it is not a phenomenal attribute of behaviour; its presence or absence cannot be established by any procedure appropriate to the investigation of natural phenomena. Meaning may be postulated by the student of action but in no case is it 'an objectively "correct" meaning or one which is "true" in some metaphysical sense' (*Theory*, p.89).

This radical disjunction between meanings postulated by the investigator and those intended by actors is central to Weber's conception of the social and cultural sciences. The possibility of subjective interpretation requires that both actor and investigator be similarly constituted as rational transcendent beings. But that condition of the possibility of subjective interpretation in general establishes no necessary relation between the meanings of the investigator and those of the actor. 'Meanings' are essentially unknowable, they are a product of the actor's free and undetermined choice of ultimate values.[18]

The Weberian student of action must therefore be constrained to analyse and to classify behaviours by reference to the meanings which he has to postulate in order to account for them.[19] His classification and analysis of human behaviour is thus a function of the meanings which he himself proposes. There can be no question of proof or demonstration of the adequacy of the postulated meanings, i.e., of their identity with such real meanings as the behaviour in question may actually express. Indeed Weber's injunctions concerning the use of rational ideal types might seem to allow free reign to the investigator in his postulation of meanings; if behaviour appears not to conform to its proposed meaning he can always toss in a few irrational factors to account for the deviation. In this respect the sociologist's postulation of meanings appears to be limited only by the power of his imagination – and if he has access to a good library even that limit may be readily overcome.

The absurdity of this situation is evident, yet it is an inescapable consequence of the Weberian definition of action and of the peculiar character of the concepts which the student of action is required by that definition to use. Weber describes the distinctive concepts of the social and cultural sciences as 'pure' or 'ideal' types. If, for Weber, there is always a necessary discrepancy between concepts and the reality to which they refer then ideal types are doubly discrepant with respect to the reality of action to which they refer. On the one hand they are constituted by the intervention of value-relevance as a selective criterion; on the other they involve the speculative postulation of meanings. These concepts involve a necessary reference to non-empirical meanings and they may also refer to observable phenomena, overt behaviour, means and objects in a situation of action, and so on.

In the formation of these concepts the requirement of the causal explanation of action by means of the subjective interpretation of meanings implies that meanings should occupy the central and primary place. Meanings and relations between meanings must therefore provide the fundamental principles of organization and construction of ideal type concepts. The social scientist or historian will tend to work with concepts formed by a double abstraction in relation to the historical situations with which he is concerned: abstraction by value-relevance and a further quite distinct abstraction in the interests of forming concepts organized according to the principle of subjective interpretation. In the first section of *Economy and Society,* for example, Weber tells us that:

> 'In *all* cases, rational or irrational, sociological analysis both abstracts from reality and at the same time helps us to understand it, in that it shows with what degree of approximation a concrete historical phenomenon can be subsumed under one or more of these concepts' (*Theory,* p.110)

It is the second abstraction and the requirements of 'understanding' that are at issue here. These account for the problematic character of the 'approximation' between 'concrete historical phenomena' and ideal type concepts. Weber proceeds:

> 'For example, the same historical phenomenon may be in one aspect "feudal", in another "patrimonial", in another "bureaucratic", and in still another "charismatic". In order to give a precise meaning to these terms it is necessary for the sociologist to formulate pure ideal types of the corresponding forms of action which in each case involve *the highest degree of logical integration by virtue of their complete adequacy at the level of meaning.* But precisely because this is true, it is probably seldom if ever that a real phenomenon can be found which corresponds exactly to one of these ideally constructed pure types' (*ibid.,* emphasis added)

As a general rule 'complete adequacy on the level of meaning' precludes empirical adequacy in the sense of a correspondence between concept and phenomena. Here the doctrine of the primacy of meaning which leads Weber to concentrate on meanings and (logical) relations between them in the construction of ideal types requires that those types must tend to be 'one-sided accentuations' of reality.

There is therefore an inevitable discrepancy, not only between reality and the sociologist's ideal type concept, but also between ideal types and the 'historical individuals'[20] (abstracted from the real thorough considerations of value-relevance) to which the ideal types are to be applied. This second discrepancy is crucial. It follows that the utility of ideal types cannot be evaluated in terms of the extent to which they correspond or fail to correspond to the real. Instead their utility consists in showing 'with what degree of approximation' concrete historical phenomena can be subsumed under these concepts. We have seen an example of this position in Weber's comments on the use of rational types to determine the causal effectivity of irrational factors: 'they account for the deviation which would be expected on the hypothesis that action were purely rational.' (*Theory,* p.92)

Thus apart from its rational coherence at the level of meaning – a consideration whose pertinence is clearly restricted to the case of rational types only – there can be no question of the validity of any ideal type concept. Ideal types do not correspond to the real; they define and measure the extent to which phenomena do not correspond to them. They may be more or less *useful* but they cannot be more or less valid. In this respect the theory of knowledge through ideal types reproduces the basic features of the epistemology of models. I examine that epistemology in Chapter 5. For the present it is enough to note that in defining the relations between *concepts* and the *real* as an extra-theoretical relation of similarity or difference the epistemology of models or ideal types precludes rigorous conceptual investigation of any real event or situation. When is the *difference* between ideal type and the real significant? Under what conditions does that difference require that the ideal type be abandoned in favour of another, more useful type? Since concepts *are* types there can be no *theoretical* evaluation of these differences.

In terms of the epistemology of ideal types the judgement of the usefulness of a type concept must be considered to be theoretically arbitrary. At this point the Weberian apologist might be tempted to suggest that the problem of *theoretical* arbitrariness may be overcome by invoking considerations of 'value-relevance': the difference between type and reality is significant if it is relevant to the values governing the investigation. But that 'solution' is no solution at all. First, Weber's concepts of objectivity and value-relevance require that considerations of value-relevance should intervene only in the initial, 'pre-theoretical', selection of the object of investigation. Thereafter value-relevance has no further part to play: theories and concepts must confront the tribunal of the facts. Now, the theoretical arbitrariness implicit in the epistemology of ideal types ensures that the evaluation of the usefulness of type concepts cannot be objective in this sense. Once values are called in to perform a theoretical task then 'objectivity', 'value-freedom' and the like must go by the board. Weber's conception of scientific objectivity is a logical impossibility; it contradicts the fundamental concepts of his epistemology. I return to this point in the following section.

Secondly, however relevant to values the difference between type and reality might be, that relevance has no determinate theoretical implications: are we to 'account for' that difference by invoking some irrational mechanical or biological factors or are we to discard our ideal type and try another? The arbitrariness entailed in the epistemology of ideal types is essentially theoretical and the invocation of value-relevance at this point leaves that theoretical arbitrariness untouched. Finally we should recall that ideal types involve a necessary reference to non-empirical meanings as well as to observable phenomena. Any *comparison* between type and reality must therefore be restricted to the latter. For the rest, as we have seen, there is no reason why the social scientist should not let his imagination run wild. He has nothing to lose but the chains of reason.

1.3 Weberian Conceptions of Proof and Demonstration

We have seen that Weber's epistemology requires that cultural values play an essential part in the definition of the object of scientific investigation. Values themselves are located in the extra-phenomenal transcendent sphere. They cannot be proved or established in or by the sciences and there is no sense in which values can be considered universally valid or objective. The individual's choice of values is essentially free and undetermined, that is, it does not take place within the realm of nature and it cannot be subject to any natural determination. The formation of values cannot be subsumed under scientific laws. But if the choice of values is not dependent on the sciences, the sciences are nevertheless essentially dependent on the intervention of values. The constitution of the distinct sciences and of their particular objects of investigation takes place on the basis of considerations of value-relevance. Different values determine different objects of investigation by their differential partitioning of the infinite phenomenal world into value-relevant and non-relevant phenomena. The result, as we have seen, is that the formation of scientific concepts and the attribution of causes are inescapably coloured by the initial choice of cultural values. Concepts, explanations, laws, all are dependent on values and, since there are no objective or universal values, Weber's position involves an essential epistemological relativism.

Relativism is the logically inescapable consequence of Weber's epistemology. Yet it is well known that Weber insists on 'value-freedom' and 'scientific objectivity', that he elaborates standards of adequacy for sociological explanation and for the determination of causal significance and objective possibility. Indeed, as Lukacs has noted:

'On several occasions, Weber defends himself against the reproach of relativism. However, he holds up his formalist and agnostic method as the only truly 'scientific' method, as he argues that it permits nothing to be introduced into sociology that cannot be proven precisely.' (Lukacs, 1972, p.394)

Lukacs, in many respects one of the most perceptive critics of Weber's irrationalism,[21] continues:

'For him, only *technical* criteria can be expected from sociology; in other words, only "which means for the achievement of a proposed end are appropriate or inappropriate" can be investigated. On the other hand it can "determine the consequences which the application of the means to be used will produce in addition to the eventual attainment of the proposed end." *Everything* else will be outside the domain of science, an 'irrational' article of faith. Thus, Weber demands the "neutrality of sociology, the total absence of value judgements, he desires it purged of all apparently irrational elements".' (*ibid.*, pp.394–95)

What is the status of Weber's technical criteria of 'scientific objectivity' and 'value-freedom'? Is it possible that, at least at this technical level, Weber escapes the irrationalism and relativism of his more general epistemology? I have shown above that Weber's conception of the use of ideal types in sociological explanation involves an inescapable theoretical arbitrariness. To the extent that it depends on the use of such ideal types, then, Weber's 'scientific objectivity' is a logical absurdity. In the remainder of this chapter, I propose to examine other central concepts of his technical methodology, in particular, the concepts of 'correct causal explanation', 'probability' and 'objective possibility' and of the historical judgement of 'causal significance'. This examination will show that Weber's technical methodology is intellectually worthless and that it cannot provide the basis for logically coherent theoretical investigations in the social sciences.

Weber distinguishes the 'sciences' of sociology and history in the following terms:

> 'The science of sociology seeks to formulate type concepts and generalized uniformities of empirical processes. This distinguishes it from history, which is oriented to the causal analysis and explanation of individual actions, structures and personalities possessing cultural significance.' (*Theory*, p.109)

One science seeks to establish general laws and uniformities and to formulate general concepts. The other makes use of these generalities for the causal investigation of singular events or singular concatenations of events. Whilst these sciences may confront rather different theoretical exigencies certain common epistemological concepts recur in Weber's discussions of sociology and history; in particular there recur the concepts of 'causal law', 'empirical uniformity', and 'probability'. Nevertheless his most extensive methodological discussions of these concepts takes place in *The Methodology of the Social Sciences*, which is primarily concerned with problems of historical explanation. The following discussion will therefore concentrate on that text.

1.3.1 Causal laws and causal explanation

A correct causal explanation is one which is both causally adequate and, since we are dealing with *action,* adequate at the level of meaning. The latter means:

> 'the subjective interpretation of a coherent course of conduct when and in so far as, *according to our habitual modes of thought and feeling,* its component parts taken in their mutual relations are recognised to constitute a 'typical' complex of meaning ... An example of adequacy on the level of meaning in this sense is what is, *according to our current norms of calculation or thinking,* the correct solution of an arithmetical problem.' (*Theory*, p.99 emphasis added)

The theoretical implications of Weber's definition of action in terms of non-empirical meanings have been examined above. It is enough to note here that the relations between meanings themselves or between meaning and behaviour is judged to be adequate according to '*habitual* modes of thought and feeling', according to '*current* norms'. The epistemological relativism of this position is apparent: as our norms and habits change so does our judgement of 'adequacy on the level of meaning'. Furthermore it is clear that the reference to habit or tradition in this context in no way elucidates the precise character of the relation of meaning to action which is so central to Weber's sociology. It is surprising therefore that Weber goes on to claim that in contrast to history 'sociological analysis can offer a greater precision of concepts' (*ibid.* p.109) precisely because its concepts are fully adequate at the level of meaning. 'Precision of concepts' is a matter of satisfying an obscure condition. There are good theoretical reasons for that obscurity: a rigorous theoretical formulation of the articulation of meanings and actions must encompass transcendent and phenomenal events. If transcendent meanings are beyond the realm of objective knowledge then so is the relation that obtains between an actor's meanings and his overt behaviour. Weber proposes to fill this gap by reference to habits and norms but his metaphysical conception of man precludes all theoretical justification of that proposal. There can be no theoretical grounds for accepting Weber's arbitrary notion of 'adequacy at the level of meaning'.[22]

So much for 'meanings'. Now consider the concept of causal adequacy.

'The interpretation of a sequence of events will on the other hand be called *causally* adequate in so far as, according to established generalizations from experience, there is a probability that it will always occur in the same way.' (*Theory*, p. 990)

In this definition two elements appear to be especially important: 'established generalizations from experience' and the judgement of the probability of an event or sequence of events. Probability is examined below. As for 'established generalizations' Weber also refers to these as 'causal laws' or ' "*nomological*" *knowledge* – i.e. the knowledge of recurrent causal sequences.' (*Meth.*, p.79) These 'laws' are essential for sociology and, as we shall see, for history. How are they to be established? Recall that Weber, following Rickert, insists on the absolute infinity of the world and all that appears within it:

> 'it presents an infinite multiplicity of successively and coexistently emerging and disappearing events, both 'within' and 'outside' ourselves. The absolute infinitude of this multiplicity is seen to remain undiminished even when our attention is focused on a single "object".' (*Meth.*, p.72)

This absolute infinity appears to be conceived, somewhat in the manner of J. S. Mill, as structured by an infinity of causal sequences between one phenomenon and another. These 'causal sequences' may be identified and validated 'by means of comprehensive historical induction' or they may be 'immediately and tangibly plausible according to our subjective experience'. (*ibid.*, pp. 72–3) While such 'laws' are not the principal object of history, in Weber's sense, they are nevertheless its essential tools. Now, the infinity of the world means that no *individual* event or phenomenon can be explained by causal laws. Since it is always the effect of an infinity of causes we must select the cause to be imputed through our selection of the 'essential' features of the event and our investigation of causal significance. In effect, value-relevance determines the finite class of causes that we choose to investigate in each individual case.

That aspect of Weber's position is well known: the infinity of the world means that causal laws alone can never suffice for the explanation of the individual fact. Unfortunately for Weber's methodology the infinity of the world must also imply that no discrete causal sequences can ever be identified – either through 'comprehensive historical induction' or through 'our subjective experience'. First, if the historian is compelled to select from the absolute infinity of phenomena then so is the sociologist. His 'established generalizations' will be a product of his selection criteria. Secondly, if each phenomenon is in fact the effect of an infinity of 'causes' then no finite process of induction can discover real causal sequences since the constant conjunction of phenomena in a finite number of cases may be entirely accidental. The absurdity of the doctrine of knowledge by induction is demonstrated in Chapter 4.[23] If the world of phenomena is infinite, as Weber's epistemology supposes, then induction is worthless and 'nomological knowledge – i.e. the knowledge of recurrent causal sequences' is nothing of the kind. Whatever their source Weber's 'causal laws' cannot be derived by induction or experience and they cannot perform their required role in sociological or historical proofs of 'causal significance', 'objective possibility', and the like.

Consider, for example, a 'law' which Weber introduces to account for the failure of rational administration to develop in China. He notes that a tendency toward rational administration was present in the period of the Warring States but that it dies out after political unification.

> 'Just as competition for markets compelled the rationalization of private enterprise, so competition for political powers compelled the rationalization of the state economy and economic policy both in the Occident and in the China of the Warring States. In the private economy cartellization weakens rational calculation which is the soul of capitalism; among states, power monopoly prostrates rational management in administration, finance and economic policy.' (*The Religion of China,* p.61)

This may be a vague analogy from a conservative economic platitude but it is hardly a 'causal law' nor even an 'empirical generalization'. The 'law of the rationalizing effect of competition' and the other 'causal laws' that may be abstracted from Weber's voluminous writings are not the product of any empiricist process of induction. While many such 'laws' have a definite theoretical place in relation to the concepts and theoretical positions elaborated in Weber's substantive discourse that place is not the one ascribed to 'causal laws' and 'empirical generalization' in his methodology. [24]

1.3.2 Causal significance, objective possibility, and probability

In Weber's epistemology the absolute infinity of the phenomenal world and of every object and event within it poses a problem of the causal explanation of any individual fact:

> 'Even with the widest imaginable knowledge of 'laws', we are helpless in the face of the question: how is the *causal explanation* of an *individual* fact possible – since a description of even the smallest slice of reality can never be exhaustive?' (*Meth.,* p.78)

The solution is given by the doctrine of value-relevance: 'We select only those causes which are to be imputed in the individual case, the "essential" feature of an event.' (*ibid.*) But the doctrine of value-relevance gives rise to another problem, namely, the problem of

the causal significance of a specific historical event with regard to subsequent, culturally significant historical developments. While there
may be causal laws, in the sense of determinate recurrent and sequential relations between one type of phenomenon and another, the real
movement of history cannot be subsumed under any such law. Laws,
in Weber's sense, refer only to regularities that may be observed
between determinate phenomena or classes of phenomena. The notion
that history itself is governed by a law of this kind is absurd: history,
for Weber, is a unique sequence of unique concatenations of an infinite
multiplicity of discrete phenomena. Thus the problem of the
significance of one particular event for subsequent historical conditions cannot be resolved by the application of any causal law.

Instead Weber proposes that we proceed by a series of abstractions.
Apart from the initial abstraction required by considerations of
value-relevance the most important of these is that:

> 'we *conceive* of one or a few of the actual causal components as
> modified in a certain direction and then ask ourselves whether ...
> the same effect or some other effect would be expected.' (*ibid.*,
> p.171)

In this way, for example, the battle of Marathon may be imagined as
effecting a 'decision' between two possible lines of development:

either

> 'development of a theocratic-religious culture, the beginnings of
> which lay in the mysteries and oracles, under the aegis of the Per-
> sian protectorate'

or

> 'The triumph of the free Hellenic circle of ideas, oriented towards
> the world, which gave us those cultural values from which we still
> draw our sustenance.' (*ibid.*)

Marathon decided in favour of the second alternative and thereby
made possible the development of the Western values which we know
and love. That 'is the only reason why we are historically interested in
it.' (*ibid.*, p.172)

The only serious complication in this procedure is that, having conceived the situation as different in some respect, say, a Persian victory
at Marathon, we must make a judgement of 'objective possibility' with
regard to the effects of that difference. The judgement that the situation would have been different must be more than a mere guess; it

must be causally adequate. Thus the judgement of the causal significance of the battle of Marathon for the development of Western civilization:

> 'rests, on the one hand, on the knowledge of certain "facts" (ontological knowledge), "belonging" to the "historical situation" and ascertainable on the basis of certain sources, and on the other, knowledge of certain known empirical rules, particularly those relating to the *ways* in which human beings are prone to react under given situations (nomological knowledge).' (*ibid.* p.174)

Consider, first, these *facts* 'belonging to the historical situation'. Why do we not investigate their 'causal significance' for Western civilization?'. It is all too easy to discover facts and events belonging to the situation which might be considered pertinent, for example, the wreck of the Persian fleet off Mount Athos in 492 BC or the revolt against the Persians by the Ionian Greeks from 499 to 494. Or again we might speculate, in the case of Marathon itself, what might have been the consequences had the Athenian commander, Miltiades, forgotten to blow his nose on the morning before the battle commenced.

The list of *facts* 'belonging to the situation' whose potential causal significance might be investigated is endless. Yet in order to arrive at our judgement of the causal significance of one fact, the Athenian victory, we have to hold these other facts constant. Our judgement of 'the decisive causal significance' of one thing requires that we choose not to investigate a mass of other things. In this respect, as so often according to Weber's methodology, our conclusions appear to be the product of an entirely arbitrary theoretical choice. We *choose* to investigate one feature of a situation, we *choose* to treat certain other features as given facts of the historical situation and considerations of value-relevance ensure that we ignore other features altogether.

Next, the 'known empirical rules' that Weber refers to, 'the *ways* in which human beings are prone to react under given conditions'. The general character and status of such rules or 'causal laws' has been outlined above. In the present case Weber has in mind rules such as 'the Persians establish the cooperation of and the domination by the priests whenever they get the chance'. It is true, as Weber admits in a later discussion of this same example, that this 'known empirical rule' rests on a very small number of instances, viz. 'the examples of the conduct of the Persians in cases where they were victorious, as in

Jerusalem, Egypt and Asia Minor, and even this verification must remain unsatisfactory in certain respects'. (*E & S,* p.98) No matter, we empirical scientists must do the best we can with the available materials, and further, 'the striking rational plausibility of the hypothesis must here necessarily be relied on as a support.' (*ibid.*)

Finally, let us consider the concepts of 'objective possibility' or 'probability'. Weber tells us that the judgement of objective possibility admits gradations of degree and that, in this respect, it involves principles similar to those of the calculus of probability. The only difference is that we cannot assign a numerical value to this 'probability' and the judgement cannot be perfectly unambiguous. Thus, apart from the fact that mathematical calculation and rigorously determined results are impossible, the procedure is identical to that of mathematical probability theory.

> 'When we carry through this comparison in our imagination ... then a considerable degree of certainty for a judgement of 'degree' of objective possibility is conceivable at least in principle – and it is only its conceivability in principle which concerns us here primarily.' (*Meth.,* p.183)

Such judgements are made all the time in daily life and in history. Indeed, without them:

> 'a distinction of the causally 'important' and 'unimportant' would simply not be possible.' (*Meth.,* pp.183–4)

Here the degree of 'objective possibility' or 'probability' is a matter of a 'feeling of certainty'.

It is this concept of 'probability' that appears in Weber's definition of causal adequacy and in his definitions of the concepts of social relationships and social collectivities:

> 'The social relationship *consists entirely and exclusively in the existence of a probability* that there will be, in some meaningfully understandable sense, a course of social action.' (*Theory,* p.118 emphasis added)

Similarly Weber insists that to talk of the existence of *friendship* or a *state* means:

> 'that *we, the observers, judge that there is or has been a probability* that on the basis of certain kinds of known subjective attitudes of

certain individuals there will result in the average sense a certain specific type of action.' (*ibid.*, p.119)

What is the logical character of such judgements of 'objective possibility' or 'probability'? Weber insists that such judgements are frequently made in history and in ordinary life but, even if we were to grant Weber that 'fact', its existence is no proof that these judgements are rational or logically coherent. A 'feeling' of certainty' is not a mathematical proof; it is not even unambiguous. Yet Weber insists on the *objective* character of judgements based on such feelings.

Weber's error is a simple one: he confuses the rigour of proof with a 'feeling of certainty'.[25] Thus the mere absence of the calculation and strict numerical determination of mathematical probability theory appears to make no essential difference. That error, all too common in subjectivist sociology, cannot even be attributed to Weber's neo-Kantian epistemology. Indeed, the Kantian distinction between the 'objectivity' of proof and the 'subjectivity' of feelings is stated very clearly in Kant's *Logic:*

'The reason of a holding-to-be-true can be *objectively* or *subjectively* greater than that of the opposite. Which of the two it is can be found out only by comparing the reasons of holding-to-be-true with the sufficient reasons; for then the reasons of holding-to-be-true are greater than the reasons of the opposite can be. In probability the reason of holding-to-be-true is therefore objectively valid; in verisimilitude, however, only *subjectively* valid. Verisimilitude is mere magnitude of persuasion; probability is an approximation to certainty. In probability there must always be a standard by which I can estimate it. This standard is *certainty*. For as I shall compare the sufficient with the insufficient reasons, I must know how much is required for certainty. Such a standard does not exist in verisimilitude, since here I compare the insufficient reasons not with the sufficient, but only with those of the opposite.' (Kant, *Logic,* p.89)

So much for Weber's 'objective possibility' and 'probability'. I have shown above how little value can be attached to his 'known empirical rules' or his 'causal laws'. But, even if we were to grant him his 'causal laws', the fact remains that no rigorous and unambiguous determination of the degree of 'objective possibility' is possible. Given all the causal laws you like we are still left with nothing but feelings of certainty. For all the pretentious chatter about theory, objectivity and the like in Weber's methodological writings 'causal adequacy' and 'causal significance' are matters of *verisimilitude* at best, of plausible and subjectively convincing stories. Weber's 'objective' and 'value-free' social scientist and historian are authors of plausible generalizations and plausible stories, nothing more.

1.4 Conclusion

In this chapter I have outlined Weber's metaphysical conception of man, which governs his distinction between action and behaviour, and his epistemology. Together these define the distinctive methodological problems confronting what Weber represents as the social and cultural sciences, the sciences of *action*. The essential role assigned to values in Weber's conception of knowledge entails an inescapable epistemological relativism – concepts, theories and explanations depend on the scientist's selection of the cultural values which govern his research. A further and distinct set of problems emerge as a result of the supposedly transcendent character of human meanings and values, the essential rationality and freedom of man with respect to all merely natural determinations. The attribution of meanings by the student of action is necessarily speculative and, since pure ideal type concepts are organized around meanings and relations between meanings, these concepts take on the character of models to be compared with and measured against the real. If concepts *are* models then any comparison with the real must be extra-conceptual; it is theoretically arbitrary. Finally, I have examined Weber's conceptions of proof and demonstration in sociology and history with particular reference to his concepts of 'causal adequacy', 'causal significance', 'objective possibility' and 'probability'. Even at this more technical level Weber's methodology utterly fails to escape the relativism and irrationalism of his more general epistemology and metaphysics. His technical canons of scientific objectivity are logically absurd; they are more appropriate to story-telling than to science. It says much for the character of sociology as a discipline that it regards Max Weber as one of its foremost practitioners.

2. The 'Phenomenological' Sociology of Alfred Schutz

The work of Alfred Schutz has become increasingly well known since the publication of the three volumes of his *Collected Papers (CPI, CPII, CPIII)* and the appearance of an English translation of *The Phenomenology of the Social World (PSW).* His attempts to provide an elaborated philosophical foundation for the social sciences has been particularly influential in the recent growth of 'phenomenological' sociology and of ethnomethodology. [1] In his Introduction to *The Problem of Social Reality,* Natanson refers to the following remarks of Alfred Schutz: 'of my results I am not so sure, others may do better; but of one thing I am deeply convinced. *Here* are the problems of the social sciences' *(CPI,* p.XLVII). In this chapter I argue that Schutz's conviction is entirely without foundation, that his problems are not the problems of the social sciences. I argue that, on the contrary, the very formulation of his problems is possible only on the terrain of an eclectic theoretical position in which no coherent theoretical discourse, and therefore no *science* of history nor of society, is possible and in which what is called 'history' or 'social science' is no more than a specialised form of story-telling. In that respect the various Schutzian propagandists, revisionists and more distant followers are in much the same position as Schutz himself. [2] The first section of this chapter contains a summary discussion of Schutz's account of how the social scientist should proceed. In the following section I examine the specific character of his phenomenology and the place it occupies in the foundation of his social science. I argue that his attempt to provide a phenomonological foundation for the social sciences and history is theoretically eclectic and logically incoherent. In the final section I examine in more detail his account of the social scientist and historian as two different kinds of story-tellers with particular reference to his conceptions first of 'meanings' and the situations in which they are effective and secondly of the time-structure of the social world.

2.1 Humanistic Puppets and Empiricist Monsters

For Schutz, as for Weber, the point of departure for any serious consideration of the social sciences is the notion that human action is governed by subjective meanings. These subjective meanings cannot be observed and they cannot be investigated according to the procedures appropriate to the natural sciences. This 'fact' has serious consequences for the methodology of the social sciences. The most important question methodology has to answer is: 'How is it possible to form objective concepts and an objectively verifiable theory of subjective meaning structures?' The answer, in Schutz's view, is given by 'the basic insight that the concepts formed by the social scientist are constructs of the constructs formed in common sense thinking by actors on the social scene' (*CPI,* pp.62–3).

The significance of that question and of that answer will become clearer if we consider Schutz's use of 'objective' and of 'subjective':

'I can, on the one hand, attend to and interpret in themselves the phenomena of the external world which present themselves to me as indications of the consciousness of other people. But I can, on the other hand, look over and through these external indications into the constituting process within the living consciousness of another rational being.' (*PSW,* p.37)

'[To] know the subjective meaning of a product means that we are able to run over in our minds in simultaneity or quasi simultaneity the polythetic Acts[3] which constituted the experience of the producer . . . Objective meaning we can predicate only of the product as such, that is, of the already constituted meaning context of the thing produced, whose actual production we meanwhile disregard. Objective meaning therefore consists only in a meaning context within the mind of the interpreter, whereas subjective meaning refers beyond it [i.e. beyond the mind of the interpreter — B.H.] to a meaning context in the mind of the producer.' (*ibid.*, pp. 133–4)

The world of objective meaning therefore contains a potential reference back to particular individual actors whose own subjectivity lies beyond the sphere of objectivity. The effects of conceiving objective meanings as constituted products in this way are clearly recognised by Schutz:

'[The] problem of subjective and objective meaning is the open door to every theology and metaphysics. [Thus] the search for the meaning of every object is so tied up with the idea that the object was once given meaning by some mind that everything in the world can be interpreted as a product and therefore as evidence for what went on in the mind of God.' (*ibid.*, p.136)

On a more mundane level it follows that 'what we call the world of objective meaning is abstracted in the social sphere from the constituting process of a meaning-endowing consciousness ... This results in the anonymous character of the meaning content predicated of it'. The world of subjective meaning on the other hand is never anonymous. Subjective meaning always refers to a determinate subject and his subjective, or intended, meaning 'remains a limiting concept even under optimum conditions of interpretation' (*ibid.*, pp.37, 38)

Strictly, then, it is not possible for the social scientist to comprehend the subjective meaning of the actor. In that case how is he to cope with the problem of the subjective meaning of action? The answer, of course, is by the use of Ideal Types. The 'constructs of the constructs formed in common-sense thinking' are typifications. In forming them the social scientist is only doing, rather more carefully and in a different context, what the ordinary actor on the social scene does all the time. With such constructs of the second level it is possible to develop theoretical systems embodying testable general hypotheses. [4]

'[The social scientist] observes certain facts and events within social reality which refer to human action and he constructs typical behaviour or course-of-action patterns from what he has observed. Thereupon he coordinates to these typical course-of-action patterns models of an ideal actor or actors, whom he imagines as being gifted with consciousness. Yet it is a consciousness restricted so as to contain nothing but the elements relevant to the performing of the course-of-action patterns observed. He thus ascribes to this fictitious consciousness a set of typical notions, purposes, goals, which are assumed to be invariant in the specious consciousness of the imaginary actor-model. This homunculus or puppet is supposed to the interrelated in interaction patterns to other homunculi or puppets constructed in a similar way ... sets of motives, goals, roles are distributed in such a way as the scientific problems under scrutiny require' (*CPI*, p.64)

The social scientist's model-building is constrained by the scientific problem at hand and, more generally, by three basic postulates. The postulate of logical consistency 'warrants the objective validity of the thought objects constructed by the social scientist'. (*ibid.*, p.43) The strictly logical character of scientific constructs is one of the most important features which distinguishes them from common-sense constructs. The postulate of subjective interpretation concerns what 'model of an individual mind . . . can be constructed in order to explain the observed facts as the result of the activity of such a mind' (*ibid.*). Finally, there is the postulate of adequacy which

'means that each term in a scientific model of human action must be constructed in such a way that a human act performed within the life-world by an individual actor in the way indicated by the typical construct would be understandable for the actor himself as well as for his fellow-men in terms of common-sense interpretations of everyday life' (*ibid.*, p.44)

Where Weber writes of 'our habitual modes of thought and feeling' (*Theory*, p.99) in his definition of adequacy at the level of meaning Schutz refers to 'common-sense interpretations' and adds:

'compliance with this postulate warrants the consistency of the constructs of the social scientist with the constructs of common-sense experience of social reality' (*CPI*, p.44)

Common-sense experience is the measure of the sciences.

Within these constraints the social scientist has considerable freedom of action. He may, for example, 'construct a model of a producer acting under conditions of unregulated competition, and another of a producer acting under cartel restrictions, and then compare the output of the same commodity of the same firm in the two models' (*ibid.*, pp.64-5). In this way it is possible to discover certain determinate relations between a set of variables, in terms of which empirically ascertainable regularities can be explained. It is possible, in other words, to produce something which has the appearance of the type of theory advocated by logical empiricist philosophy of science.

How does Schutz's 'theory' with its unobservable 'subjective meanings' differ from the more orthodox empiricist theories of action in sociology? A brief comparison of Schutz's puppets with Lazarsteld's monsters (a logical empiricist equivalent) should help to answer this question. Lazarsfeld introduces his monsters in the course of a paper on latent structure analysis in which he is concerned with the problem of 'how precisely inferences from concrete observations to underlying concepts are to be made'. (Lazarsfeld, 1954, p.354). Consider the simplest case, in which concrete observations refer to positive or negative responses to questions. A probability mechanism may then be defined as 'any kind of structure which, through repeated trials, yields results approximating more and more closely to a previously determined proportion of positive replies'. (*ibid.*, p.357) For example, a roulette wheel with black counting as positive is a mechanism with a probability of 0.5. Equivalent mechanisms are those which produce the same probability. In the case of physiological mechanisms we may not know the precise blueprint of the structure.

No matter: 'even in those cases, repeated and controlled tests may make us confident that, for all practical purposes, the structure does have a positive response probability of its own'. (*ibid.*, p.358)

The world of Lazarsfeld's model is not peopled by ordinary human beings. 'Instead, its inhabitants are monsters who have roulette wheels ... which provide answers to questions put to them. There is a separate wheel corresponding to each question that might be asked. ... Within an individual monster the wheel settings associated with different questions are likely to vary. ... But, in addition, the probability mechanisms associated with a particular question are likely to vary from individual to individual'. (*ibid.*, pp.359–60) The settings of the different wheels are determined by a relatively small number of underlying attitudes, traits or other characteristics. In Lazarsfeld's mechanical model this means that the settings of the wheels are centrally controlled by means of transmission devices.

Examples of central characteristics are given in the text: courage, prudence, ethnocentrism, political interest, morale. The social scientist proceeds by constructing appropriate monsters and endowing them with suitable central characteristics. By means of various statistical tests he examines the 'fit' between the wheel settings determined by those central characteristics and the observed facts – that is, question-naire responses and so on. If the 'fit' is a good one then the postulated 'underlying' characteristics may be said to explain or to cause the observed facts. In this way it is possible to discover statistical relationships between morale, political interest, etc., and other characteristics of the individuals concerned.

There is a clear formal correspondence between the two worlds. Puppets correspond to monsters; purposes, motives, goals and systems of relevance, correspond to probability mechanisms, systems of transmission and central characteristics. In both cases it is the task of the social scientist to construct a theoretical model to reproduce the observed facts, 'to save the phenomena'.[5] The best model is the simplest or the one that saves the most phenomena. In both cases the phenomena are to be saved by means of characteristics ascribed to individual actors.

It is in the character of the connection between observations and unobservables, the theoretical[6] constructs required to 'explain the observed facts', that the most significant differences between the two worlds appear. Lazarsfeld relies on statistical or mathematical constructs connected to observation terms by arbitrarily chosen but non-etheless precise and unambiguous probability functions. He operates with a well-defined mathematical theory, while the colourful and sometimes extravagant terminology is merely a convenient means of exposition to a mathematically unsophisticated audience. Thus the only theoretically significant characteristics of 'morale' or 'courage' are those which determine their statistical properties. The 'common-sense' meaning of such terms plays no theoretical role.

For Schutz, on the other hand, it is precisely the 'common-sense' meaning of his constructs that is important. The connection between theoretical and observational terms is supplied by 'common-sense interpretations of everyday life'. (*CPI*, p.64) Thus the social scientists' data are 'constituted in part by common-sense concepts ... [they are] the already constituted meanings of active participants in the social world'. They have 'while still in the pre-scientific stage, those elements of meaning and intelligible structure which later appear in more or less explicit form with a claim to categorial validity in the interpretive science itself'. (*PSW*, pp.9, 10) In a vague and confused way human behaviour is already intelligible at the level of daily life. It is that intelligibility which lies at the heart of the social scientific enterprise.

In Lazarsfeld's case clear and precise mathematical formulations allow for the production of data in standardised and readily manipulable forms – all based upon an essentially arbitrary choice of mathematical structure. With Schutz, on the other hand, a determinate system of theoretical constructs (notions, values, goals, etc.) is related in not too clear and not too precise ways to observation terms. In this case the general form of the relation between theoretical and observation terms purports to be not in the least arbitrary: it is determined by common-sense interpretations. The justification of that assertion is the result of 'a laborious philosophical journey, for the meaning structure of the social world can only be deduced from the most primitive and general characteristics of consciousness'. (*ibid.*, p.12) The puppet world can only be investigated using a style of research in which there is a premium on sensitivity to nuances of meaning. Studies of this type produce more insights and fewer tables per 1,000 words than the corresponding monster studies.

2.2 Alfred Schutz and Phenomenology

'In this work I have attempted to trace the roots of the problems of the social sciences directly back to the fundamental facts of conscious life. Of central importance for this investigation are the studies of Bergson and Husserl on the internal time sense. Only in the work of these two thinkers, especially in Husserl's transcendental phenomenology, has a sufficiently deep foundation been laid on the basis of which one could aspire to solve the problem of meaning'. (*PSW*, p.XXXII)

Schutz's work is frequently said to have laid the foundations of a phenomenological sociology. Schutz himself and many commentators maintain that his phenomenology is based on that of Husserl. This interpretation appears to be supported by the appearance of his *Collected Papers* in the *Phaenomenologica* series, published under the patronage of the Husserl Archives in Louvain, and even by certain remarks of Husserl.[7]

In fact Schutz's phenomenology involves a gross distortion of Husserl. Far from being phenomenologically founded, Schutz's sociology employs a phenomenological gloss to support its basic and

unquestioned premise that 'the world of objective mind' can be reduced to the actions of individuals. The specific form of Schutz's distortion of Husserl determines the general character of the
'phenomenological' sociology that may be derived from his work. This
is not the place to document these assertions in great detail. However,
in view of its alleged significance for his sociology, it is necessary to
briefly examine Schutz's phenomenology and its distortion of
Husserl's. The discussion will be organised around the following
headings:

2.2.1 the role of phenomenology in Schutz's foundations;
2.2.2 psychologism and the transcendental ego;
2.2.3 the *lebenswelt* and the world of everyday life;
2.2.4 the subject of science.

2.2.1 The role of phenomenology in Schutz's foundations

Schutz begins his attempt to 'trace the roots of the problems of the
social sciences directly back to the fundamental facts of conscious
life'. (*PSW*, p.XXXII) with an examination of Max Weber's
Methodological Concepts. He accepts that 'Weber's approach was
correct and that he had determined conclusively the proper starting
point of the philosophy of the social sciences'. (*ibid.*, p.XXXI) What is
this approach?

> 'Never before had the project of reducing the 'world of objective
> mind' to the behaviour of individuals been so radically carried out
> as it was in Max Weber's initial statement of the goal of inter-
> pretative sociology. This science is to study social behaviour by in-
> terpreting its subjective meaning as found in the intentions of in-
> dividuals. The aim, then, is to interpret the actions of individuals in
> the social world and the ways in which individuals give meaning to
> social phenomena.' (*ibid.*, p.6)

Unfortunately Weber's analysis suffers from severe theoretical
limitations.

> 'He breaks off his analysis of the social world when he arrives at
> what he assumes to be the basic and irreducible elements of social
> phenomena. But he is wrong in this assumption. His concept of the
> meaningful act of the individual – the key idea of interpretative
> sociology – by no means defines a primitive, as he thinks it does. It

is, on the contrary, a mere label for a highly complex and ramified area that calls for much further study' (*ibid.,* pp.7–8)

This further study which Schutz proposes takes up the analysis where Weber left off. While accepting the conception of sociology as a science of action in Weber's sense he believes that Weber's concept of the 'meaningful act of the individual' requires further analysis. It is at this point, and this point only, that Schutz proposes to make use of Husserl. Here certain conclusions and analyses of Husserl are to be located within an already defined Schutzian, or Weberian, 'science'. It is Schutz's initial conception of the nature and problems of the social sciences that defines the contributions required from Husserl's phenomenology.

'In order to be clear about the status of the following investigations from the point of view of phenomenology, it should be stated that: Our studies of the constituting process in internal time consciousness will be carried out within the "phenomenological reduction". Therefore they presuppose the bracketing of the natural world and therewith the carrying into effect of a complete change of attitude (the *epoche*) toward the thesis of the "world given-to-me-as-being-there (*als daseinde gibt*)" . . . However, our analysis will be carried out within the phenomenological reduction only so far as this is necessary for acquiring a clear understanding of the internal time consciousness.

The purpose of this work, which is to analyse the phenomenon of meaning in ordinary (*mundanen*) social life, does not require the achievement of a transcendental knowledge that goes beyond that sphere of a further sojourn within the area of the transcendental-phenomenological reduction' (*ibid.,* pp.43–4)

The place and function of Husserl's phenomenology in Schutz's foundations should now be entirely clear. These are prescribed and precisely determined by the nature of the basic project which Schutz finds in Weber, namely, to reduce 'the "world of objective mind" to the behaviour of individuals'.[8] That project is not questioned, founded or justified in any way in the work of Alfred Schutz. It is not derived from any investigation, phenomenological or otherwise, of anything at all.

In particular, Schutz makes no attempt to establish that the object of his proposed science is a possible or coherent object of investigation or that its definition is compatible with the fundamental concepts of Husserlian epistemology. He does not subject his basic project to any 'radical investigation of sense' which, according to Husserl, is necessitated by 'the present condition of the European sciences' (Husserl, 1969, p.5). Modern science has 'abandoned radicalness of scientific self-responsibility. No longer is its inmost driving force that radicalness which unremittingly imposes on itself the demand to accept no knowledge that cannot be accounted for by original first principles, which are at the same time matters of perfect insight – principles such that profounder enquiry makes no sense'. (*ibid.,* p.4) Such a 'radical investigation of sense' is essential if we are to transform a judgement that is a mere opinion, for example, that 'the world of objective mind' exists as a coherent field of scientific investigation, into a 'fulfilled' judgement in which we have either established that things are indeed just as we imagine them to be or discovered that they are not.

> 'Sense investigation signifies nothing but the attempt actually to produce the sense 'itself', which, in the mere meaning, is a meant, a presupposed, sense;
>
> or, equivalently, it is the attempt to convert the 'intentive sense [*intendierenden sinn*]', the sense 'vaguely floating before us' in our unclear aiming, into the fulfilled, the clear, sense, and thus to procure for it the evidence of its clear possibility.' (*ibid.,* p.9)

Schutz does not attempt to procure for his projected science any 'evidence of its clear possibility', i.e. to show that it is based upon 'principles such that profounder enquiry makes no sense'.[9] On the contrary the assumption of the clear possibility of Schutz's 'social science' provides the basis for his 'phenomenological' investigations. His conception of the nature and problems of the social sciences determines in advance the theoretical range and scope of the set of concepts produced by these investigations.

Whatever it is that Schutz founds, its foundations are not phenomenological. Furthermore, as the following sections will show, these foundations, and the basic project they involve, are incompatible with Husserl's phenomenology. Thus, when Schutz calls upon Husserl to do his turn, it is only the latter's words that are brought into play. Husserl's concepts cannot enter the space that Schutz provides for them.

2.2.2 Psychologism and the transcendental ego

'No longer am I the man who, in natural self-experience finds himself as a man and who, with the abstractive restriction to the pure contents of 'internal' or purely psychological self-experience, finds his own pure *'mens sive animus sive intellectus';* nor am I the separately considered psyche itself. Apperceived in this 'natural' manner, *I and all other men are themes of sciences that are Objective, or positive, in the usual sense: biology, anthropology and also (as included in these) psychology.* The psychic life that psychology talks about has in fact always been, and still is, meant as psychic life in the world.' (Husserl, 1970c, p.25, emphasis added)

'The Objective world, the world that exists for me, that always has and always will exist for me, the only world that ever can exist for me — this world, with all its Objects, I said, derives its whole sense and its existential status, which it has for me, from me myself, *from me as the transcendental ego,* the ego who comes to the fore only with the transcendental-phenomenological epoche.

This concept of the transcendental and its correlate, the concept of the transcendent, must be derived exclusively from *our* philosophically meditative situation. The following should be noted in this connection: Just as the reduced Ego is not a piece of the world, so, conversely, *neither the world nor any worldly Object is a piece of my Ego, to be found in my conscious life as a really inherent part of it,* as a complex of data of sensation or a complex of acts.' (*ibid.,* p.26, emphasis added)

For phenomenology, and for all forms of idealism, the question of the difference between the transcendental and its correlate is not just one question among other questions. It is a question of fundamental importance for the whole character of the philosophical and epistemological concepts that may be derived from its answer. Either the difference is denied or is blurred in some way or else this denial is a radical vice or perversion. This choice is decisive: it determines the possibility of a rigorous idealism [10] on the one hand or the inevitability of incoherence on the other. In the rigorous transcendental phenomenology of Husserl this perversion is called psychologism: an identification, for example, of the 'real', or psychological, Ego and the transcendental Ego; of what can and what can never be a theme of some positive science.

For the ego of the transcendental reduction, all that exists is and must be a constituted product. The constituting ego is not the ego of the positive sciences: the ego of the positive sciences cannot constitute.

Husserl does sometimes admit a different type of constitution. 'Conscious life is constituted necessarily as human in the constituted world, and as a human conscious life in which the world is intended, psychically constituted, and so forth'. (*ibid.,* p.52n) This psychical constitution takes place within a constituted, i.e. transcendent, conscious life.[11] It may, therefore, appear as a theme in 'sciences that are objective, or positive, in the usual sense; biology, anthropology and also ... psychology'. (*ibid.,* p.25)

Schutz appears to be concerned with the analysis of this latter, non-transcendental, constitution. 'In ordinary social life we are no longer concerned with the constituting phenomena as these are studied within the sphere of the phenomenological reduction. We are concerned only with the phenomena corresponding to them in the natural attitude.' (*PSW,* p.44) It is such 'corresponding' phenomena that appear to be involved when he talks of 'the meaning of each social relationship and structure, constituted as these are, in the last analysis, by the action of the individual in the social world' (*ibid.,* p.6), or of social phenomena as 'constituted in part by common-sense concepts'. (*ibid.,* p.9)

Such constitution is carried out by individuals living in the social world: that is, in the Objective world that exists *for* the transcendental Ego which is 'not a piece of the world'. (Husserl, 1970c, p.26) The concept of this constitution may well be a properly scientific concept and its explication a proper concern of the positive sciences. Schutz does not agree:

> 'It is within ... duration that the meaning of a person's experience is constituted for him as he lives through the experience. Here and here only, in the deepest stratum of experience that is available to reflection, is to be found the ultimate source of the phenomena of 'meaning' and 'understanding'. This stratum of experience can only be disclosed in strictly philosophical self-consciousness'. (*PSW,* p.12)

Or again:

> '(1) What does it mean to say that the actor attaches a meaning to his action?
> (2) In what manner is the other self given to the Ego as something meaningful?
> (3) In what manner does the Ego understand the behaviour of

others, (*a*) in general, (*b*) in terms of others' own subjective meaning?

These questions do not as such belong to the social sciences. They refer rather to that substratum of objects of the social sciences, [to] the level at which the social world is constituted in Acts of everyday life with others — Acts, that is, in which meanings are established and interpreted'. (*ibid.,* p.17)

Schutz conflates two constitutions, the transcendental and the psychical and two constituting Egos. The difference between the transcendental and its transcendent correlate, between philosophy and (positive) science, is transformed into a mere distance: the distance between the deep and the shallow. The social world and its component actors have hidden depths which are inaccessible to science.

This is psychologism with a vengeance. It enables Schutz to derive, for example, the basic structure of the social world, the world that exists for 'me as the transcendental Ego' from our ordinary everyday thinking about our fellow men. (*PSW,* pp.139–214; *CPII,* pp.20–63)[12] Thus:

'If the world of predecessors is completely fixed and determined, the world of consociates free, and the world of contemporaries probable, the world of successors is completely indeterminate and indeterminable. Our orientation toward our successors cannot amount to more than this: that we are going to have some. No key will open the door to this realm, not even that of ideal types. For the latter method is based on our experience of predecessors, consociates, and contemporaries, and there is no principle which permits us to extend it to the world of our successors.' (*PSW,* p.214, emphasis added)

The basic structure of the social world is given in common-sense experience.

2.2.3 The lebenswelt *and the world of everyday life*

'The intrinsically first being, the being that precedes and bears every worldly objectivity, is transcendental intersubjectivity: the universe of monads which effects its communion in various forms' (Husserl, 1970c, p.156)

The 'universe of monads' is the realm of direct experience of an immanently transcendent, primordial or lived world [13] (*Umwelt* or *Lebenswelt*). It is not enough merely to open one's eyes and live in order to find this world of original experience since what is given in the 'natural attitude' is always impregnated by logical and other cognitive operations. [14] Nor can it be revealed through a genetic psychological inquiry for that would lead only to mental processes or lived experiences as 'experiences of the world, of a world which, for this subject, is already given as complete; and this means that the world is there as that on which contemporary science has already done its work of exact determination' (Husserl, 1973, pp.47-8). [15] To return to the original, to pure experience, would be to strip the world of the idealizations with which it has been clothed by the determinations of science. Only then, in Husserl's view, could we hope to reach the 'pure universal nature' which for the concretely existing world of the natural attitude 'signifies an abstraction'. (*ibid.,* p.56) Bachelard notes that this is 'an abstraction in the sense that one must exclude all of the idealizations which impregnate the concretely existing world. This is enough to indicate that an existentialism cannot legitimately avail itself of Husserl's return to the life-world' (Bachelard, 1968, pp. 142–3). [16]

The concretely existing, objective, world belongs to 'a higher level than that of primordial transcendency'. (Husserl, 1970c, p.105) Husserl's *Lebenswelt* and *Umwelt* refer to this latter, the primordial realm of direct experience. They are not the concepts of any (positive) science and they play no part in the scientific investigation of the concretely existing world. They do, however, appear in the philosophical investigation of the origins of the sciences (and therefore of the 'concretely existing world'): that is, they appear in the tracing of the sciences back to their sources in antepredicative experience. [17] Such an investigation, in Husserl's view, is neither an alternative to, nor a denial of, science. It is not, nor do its concepts belong to, a sociology — of knowledge, of science, or of anything else. In particular, then, these concepts can play no part in a science which aims to 'see the world of social facts with an unbiased eye, to classify these facts under concepts in an honest and logical way, and to subject to exact analysis the material thus obtained' (*PSW,* p.4). If an existentialism cannot legitimately avail itself of Husserl's return to the life-world neither can a sociology.

It is clear that the *common-sense interpretations* of everyday life, which play such a crucial role in Schutz's projected scientific models of human action, refer to experiences of the world 'on which contemporary science has already done its work of exact determination' and which, one might add, is infected by the idealizations with which it has been clothed by the inexact determinations of philosophies, ideologies and pseudo-sciences. These common-sense interpretations do not, any more than scientific interpretations, refer to the original world of pure experience, the 'pure universal nature'. In Husserl's philosophy common-sense interpretations have no claim whatever to any priority over the interpretations of the sciences.

It is no surprise that Schutz's psychologism has its effects here in a confusion of these various worlds. In all of his writings, early or late, the 'original world of pure experience' reappears as the 'world of daily life', as the 'world of common-sense interpretations', or the 'world of everyday life.'

'[This] world of daily life is the archetype of our experience of reality. All other provinces of meaning may be considered as its modifications'. (*CPI*, p.233)

It reappears also as a specific sector of the social world: that is, as one sector among others.

'[The] social world is by no means homogenous but exhibits a multiform structure. Each of its spheres or regions is both a way of perceiving and a way of understanding the subjective experiences of others.' (*PSW*, p.139)

These spheres or regions are: the realm of directly experienced social reality, or realm of consociates, (*soziale Umwelt*); the realm of contemporaries; the realm of predecessors; and the realm of successors. These realms are differentiated on the basis of our (common-sense) experience of them. Of the differences between social science and history, he writes of 'the former being defined as the science of the world of contemporaries, and the latter as the science of the world of predecessors'. The world of contemporaries is 'the sole object of the social sciences'. (*ibid.*, pp.14–15)

Successors, as we have seen, and consociates are in a different position. Only in the realm of consociates, of face-to-face relationships, 'can the partner look at the self of the fellow man as an unbroken totality in a vivid present. All other manifold social relations are derived from the original experiencing, of the totality of the other's self in the community of time and space.' The We-relationship, or face-to-face relationship, is a 'basic structure of the world of daily life'. (*CPI*, p.221)

Thus one and the same social world contains: the original world of pure experience (the world of consociates); the world of everyday life, of common-sense interpretations; and the world of social science (contemporaries) and of history (predecessors). This social world is neither the primordial world nor the concretely existing world whose transcendency belongs 'to a level higher than that of primordial transcendency'. (Husserl, 1970c, p.105) Rather it is some union of the two worlds: they are merely experienced differently in ordinary social life.

So, too, are the provinces of history and of social science experienced differently: that is why they are distinct provinces. However, the constructs with which we interpret both realms – the course-of-action types, motivations, systems of relevance, and the rest – are derived from the same originary experiencing of the other in the realm of consociates. This fact assures the unity of the social world.

'In a sense history can be regarded as one continuous We-relationship from the earliest days of mankind to the present, a relationship of variegated content and ever-changing partners. This view of history is no mere metaphysics, although a metaphysics could no doubt be derived from it. Unless one accepts such a view, there is no reason to regard the world of our predecessors as one continuous world and, in fact, no reason to assert the unity of the social world. Indeed, our interpretation is the only one that leaves room for subjective meaning in history'. (*PSW*, p.214)

Thus the central core of the social world is forever opaque to objective knowledge. This central core provides the archetypes for both common-sense and scientific experience of reality. The continuity of the provinces of history and of social science is not assured by the system of concepts of these sciences, for they are quite distinct, but rather by an objectively opaque continuity within this central core. The continuous We-relationship thus serves, for Schutz, as the external condition of the possibility of history and of social science – and of the impossibility of social laws.

Schutz's psychologising of the transcendental ego produces a sociologising of 'the universe of monads which effects its communion in various forms'. The sociology of this sociologised nomadic sphere is heavily infected by a methodological individualism.

2.2.4 The subject of science

'Only a science clarified and justified transcendentally (in the phenomenological sense) can be an ultimate science; only a transcendentally – phenomenologically clarified world can be an ultimately understood world; only a transcendental logic [18] can be an ultimate theory of science, an ultimate, deepest, and most universal, theory of the principles and norms of all the sciences'. (Husserl, 1969, p.16)

The positive sciences are not genuine or ultimate sciences. They are only one-sided sciences, 'lost in the world'. (Husserl, 1970c, p.157) Thus Husserl writes of 'the blinders imposed by their method, as an inevitable consequence of the exclusive focusing of each [positive science] on its own particular province', and of 'the self-forgetfulness of the theorizer, who, in his theoretical producing . . . knows nothing of the inwardness of that producing – who lives in producing, but does not have this productive living itself as a theme within his field of vision.' (Husserl, 1969, p.4) The particular sciences, even the most theoretical of them, e.g. mathematics, are, for Husserl, only techniques, lacking 'insight into the *ratio* of [their] accomplished production'. (*ibid*, p.3) They are theoretical techniques.

'Thus modern science has abandoned the ideal of genuine science that was vitally operative in the sciences from the time of Plato; and, in its practice, it has abandoned radicalness of scientific self-responsibility'. (*ibid*, pp.3–4)

This position does not involve Husserl in any disavowal of science or denial of its accomplishments. On the contrary he was 'quite in earnest in admiring the great discoverers of classical and post-classical physics and their intellectual accomplishment, which, far from being merely mechanical, was in fact astounding in the highest sense. This accomplishment is not at all disparaged by the above elucidation of it as τέχνη [technique]' (Husserl, 1970a, p.53)

However, the scientist 'knows nothing of the inwardness of [his] producing'. The sense, or meaning, of a science, of scientific practice, is not determined by the attitude of the scientist towards his work, the meaning it has for him. The subject of the science, the transcendental correlate of its knowledge, is neither the individual scientist nor the community of scientists – neither the technician nor the community of technicians. The subject is transcendental intersubjectivity, the universe of monads that precedes and bears every worldly Objectivity – sometimes loosely referred to as humanity, or Western or European Man.

In contrast the subject of Schutz's science is the individual scientist, and only then, by extension, the community of scientists. The world of scientific theorizing is just one finite province of meaning amongst others.

> All these worlds – the world of dreams, of imageries and phantasms, especially the world of art, the world of religious experience, the world of scientific contemplation, the play world of the child, and world of the insane – are finite provinces of meaning. (*CPI*, p.232)

The world of scientific theorising is distinguished from other finite provinces of meaning – in particular, from the paramount reality, the world of daily life – by 'a specific tension of consciousness and . . . a specific epoché, a prevalent form of spontaneity, a specific form of self-experience, a specific form of sociality, and a specific time perspective'. (*ibid.*) The shift from one finite province to another is prompted by the experience of 'a specific *shock* which compels us to break through the limits of this 'finite' province of meaning and to shift the accent of reality to another one'. (*ibid.*, p.231)

Thus the scientist shifts the accent of reality from the world of daily life and adopts instead the role of disinterested observer. He 'detaches himself from his biographical situation within the social world' and enters a 'field of pre-organised knowledge, called the corpus of his science'. (*ibid.*, p.37) This corpus he must accept in his scientific work or else show cause why he does not. He thus operates with a stock of knowledge that has 'quite another structure than that which man in everyday life has at hand'. (*ibid.*, p.39)

The scientist, as scientist and not just another human being, has a specific attitude towards the world which he interprets with reference to a specific stock of knowledge at hand and to a specific problem which provides him with criteria of relevance. Given the problem, he is scientific if he has the appropriate attitude and uses the appropriate stock of knowledge. If not, not. The sense of a science, of scientific practice, is determied by the attitude of the scientist towards his work and by his conformity to the standards acknowledged by his colleagues. This scientist is an actor like other actors and his scientific activity may be studied by the social scientist in the same way as any other activity may be studied − in terms of the relevant attitudes, values, norms, etc. For Schutz, science, as a cultural objectification, is reducible to the most elementary forms of individual behaviour. Its meaning 'is precisely that which the individuals involved attach to their own acts'. (*PSW*, p.6)

Thus Schutz's social science is not founded or based upon a phenomenology. The 'foundational' role that phenomenology may play is precisely determined in advance by what is the true foundation of his thought: the unexamined basic project of reducing the world of objective mind to the behaviour of individuals. This basic project defines a role for phenomenology which (Husserl's) phenomenology is unable to play. In consequence Schutz produces a theoretically eclectic and ultimately incoherent conception of social science and history, a more or less complex psychologistic perversion of transcendental phenomenology which gives an appearance of 'radicality' to Schutz's idealist individualism. In the 'phenomenology of the social world' thus generated the correlative realms of the transcendental and the transcendent interpenetrate. In the cases of the actor and of the world in which he acts there is a sector which is accessible to knowledge and another sector which is not. The latter functions both as the primordial basis of the social world and as the forever hidden depths within it. These depths, in so far as they can be reached at all, are the province of philosophy. Scientific knowledge of the social world, and of the actor within it, is forever condemned to scratching around on the surface.

2.3 The Social Scientist as Puppet Master

The social scientist observes certain facts and events within social reality or, perhaps, he takes an interest in a certain type of situation. He then proceeds to set up models of puppet actors which he endows with a consciousness 'restricted so as to contain nothing but the elements relevant to the performing of the course-of-action patterns observed'. (1962, p.64) He thus brings together, in his (real) model of (imaginary) actors, circumstances, or situations on the one hand and puppets endowed with meanings, sets of motives, relevances, and so on, on the other. The social scientist has selected the appropriate set of meanings for his puppet-actors when these meanings can reproduce the behaviour observed in the situation. This account raises two issues in particular: the relation between the situation and the meanings of the actor who is in it; the problem of accounting for the situation. Examination of this latter issue will lead on to a discussion of the time structure of Schutz's social world.

2.3.1 Meanings and situations

If the actor acts in terms of meanings, of his definition of the situation, these meanings are never, as far as the social scientist is concerned, directly observable. Yet the scientist must refer to these meanings in order to account for the actions which he observes. The scientist observes things, actions, events to which he assigns objective meanings. The actors who populate the world he observes assign meanings to these also. In particular they assign 'subjective' meanings to their own acts.

Do these 'subjective' meanings belong to the 'concretely existing world'? Are they properties of objects in that world which just happen not to be observable? Are they non-observable properties of actors? A positive answer to such questions leads directly to Lazarfeld's problem discussed in the first part of this paper; the problem of 'how precisely inferences from concrete observations to underlying concepts are to be made'. (Lazarsfeld 1954, p.345)

If the problem of subjective meaning is of this kind then it must be answered, in general terms if not in precise details, in the way that Lazarsfeld answers it. We expose actors to well-defined stimuli in well-defined situations and carefully observe their reactions. In this way it is possible to establish precise relationships between stimuli and reactions; and, more generally, between situations and actors' reactions to them. There is no difficulty, in principle, in investigating the way an actor's biographical situation affects such relationships. There is no reason why such relationships should not allow for the 'unpredictability' of individual behaviour. They may, in the standard statistical terminology, be either probabalistic or deterministic in form.

It is easy to see that such an interpretation of the problem of subjective meaning leads to a formulation in which subjective meaning, the actor's interpretation, or what have you, functions as a mere intervening variable relating a more or less complex set of observable stimuli to an equally observable response.

Such, at least, is how a sociological empiricism must respond to any talk of subjective interpretation, of verstehen, of the actors' definition of the situation. That is how, for example, Lazarsfeld interprets Weber and how Kuhn or Bales interpret Mead.[19] No longer is there any imperative to refer back to subjective meaning or 'to the activities of the subjects within the social world and their interpretation by the actors'. (*CPI*, p. 35) On the contrary reference to subjective meaning is, at most, a theoretical convenience.

In general, it might seem that if subjective meanings affect action in the 'concretely existing world' it must be because they belong to that world and can therefore be studied and located within a network of relationships in much the same way as anything else. If they cannot be studied, they do not belong to the concretely existing world and can play no part in the explanation of anything that happens within that world. If the social scientist 'always can and for certain purposes must – refer to the activities of the subjects within the social world and their interpretation by the actors' (*ibid.*) then these interpretations are simply facts, difficult perhaps to establish, but nonetheless facts among other facts.

It is clear that, for Schutz, subjective meanings are not simply facts among other facts; that they do not just belong to the 'concretely existing world', of phenomena in the same way as other facts, events or situations do. As far as the social world is concerned they are determining but not determined, in it but not of it in the way that all other things are.

'He who lives in the social world is a free being: his acts proceed from spontaneous activity. Once the action has transpired, once it is over and done with, it has become an act and is no longer free but closed and determinate in character. Nevertheless it was free at the time the action took place; and if the question concerning the intended meaning refers, as it does in Weber's case, to the point in time before the completion of the act, then the answers must be that the actor always acts freely, and this is true even though I am able to know him only indirectly and in Ideal-Typical fashion. On the other hand, the personal Ideal Type that is correctly constructed, that is, one that is nontype-transcendent, is essentially unfree'. (*PSW*, p.277)

The actor on the social scene, unlike the puppet-actor in the social scientist's model, is essentially free and unknowable. What the social scientist, or indeed any social observer studies, 'is only a conceptual model, not a real person'. (*ibid.*, p.242) The realm of directly experienced social reality, the scientifically unknowable central core of the social world, is the source of the undetermined-determining subjective meanings, the home of human 'freedom'. It is the special character of his social world, combining the 'concretely existing world' of phenomena and the primordial, pre-phenomenal, pre-predicative world in a single structure, that enables Schutz to maintain the privileged status of the concept of subjective meaning. It is the conflation of the transcendent and its transcendental correlate that gives human freedom its central place in his social science.

This freedom produces the essentially problematic character of the relation between situation and actor's interpretation. Schutz's actor is not only 'unpredictable', he is essentially free and creative. In this respect Schutz's actor shares many of the characteristics of Mead's self and generates much the same kind of social science:

> 'Insofar as sociologists . . . are concerned with the behaviour of acting units, the position of symbolic interaction requires [him] to catch the process of interpretation through which they construct their actions. This process is not to be caught merely by turning to conditions which are antecedent to the process. . . . Nor can one catch the process merely by inferring its nature from the overt action which is its product'. (Blumer, 1967, p.145)

In its insistence on the need to refer back to the subjective meaning of the actor, on the essential incompleteness of the merely 'objective' meaning of an act, Schutz's account of social science is an affirmation of a particular notion of human freedom. Schutz's social science resembles Duhem's conventionalist astronomy: a saving of the phenomena, a science *ad majoram gloriam dei*. (Duheim, 1969) Where one science speculates in the name of an omnipotent and creative deity the other speculates in the name of a lesser but essentially similar creature: the sensible-supersensible free individual subject. It was shown in section 2 above that this subject was anathema to Husserl: it is precisely such beings that his transcendental phenomenology sought to abolish.

2.3.2 *Accounting for the situation*

The social scientist puts his puppets into situations characterised by, amongst other things, various more or less 'institutionalised patterns of behaviour'. The puppets themselves are endowed with relevant values, motives, interests and appropriate 'stocks of knowledge at hand' which form the basis of their interpretation of the world. 'All interpretation of this world is based on a stock of previous experiences of it, our own or those handed down to us by parents or teachers'. (*CPI*, p.7)

Thus, if he is to proceed at all along the lines laid down by Schutz, he must select situations, stocks of knowledge at hand, institutionalised patterns of behaviour, and much more. It is clear that some situations, institutionalised patterns of behaviour, stocks of knowledge at hand, will be of more interest to social scientists than others. Of particular interest, for example, would be those situations which the social scientist had observed within social reality, or which, for some reason, he feels are likely to appear there. How is he to account for those situations? What grounds could he have for asserting that certain types of situation seem likely to arise? Or that others, equally possible in the free play of his imagination, will not appear within social reality? Similar problems arise in the case of other notions. Why has precisely this stock of knowledge been handed down by parents or teachers? Why have those previous experiences been lost? And so on.

Consider the case of a puppet banker and part-time philosopher — we might call it Alfred Schutz [20] — forced by the coming Nazi occupation to leave Austria. He stays in France for a while and finally emigrates to the United States, arriving there in July 1939. Having observed these facts and events within social reality, how does the social scientist proceed? He constructs a model of the situation in which the banker finds himself. He endows the banker with a fictitious consciousness containing values, motives, sets of relevances and a stock of knowledge at hand. This fictitious consciousness notes certain changes in the situation, interprets them in terms of the given set of relevances, and tells the puppet that he ought to be going. He goes. Other puppets, with different, but equally fictitious consciousnesses, stay behind.

The social scientist proceeds by filling out such a sketch. Given the situation and the observed facts and events the social scientist has dealt with this problem as soon as he has discovered fictitious consciousnesses to fit the actions of his puppets. Given the fascism and the facts that some actors on the social scene get out while they can and that others do not the social scientist constructs consciousnesses to fit these actions.

But where does the fascism come from? How did this situation, which would have seemed so unlikely to our banker a few years earlier, come about? Those are questions which do not arise in the fictitious consciousness of the puppet social scientist that Schutz describes.

It is no accident that his account fails to provide for the posing of such problems. Certainly a glance at his work might suggest that his main interests lay in a social psychology: in particular his essays on 'The Stranger', 'The Homecomer', 'Making Music Together', 'The Well Informed Citizen', (all in *CPI*, p.11), or parts of his *Reflections on the Problem of Relevance* (1970). Such an interpretation leaves open the possibility that Schutz has provided the foundations for a social psychology; and either that other aspects of the social sciences could be built upon these same foundations, or that this social psychology is to be practised in situations provided, so to speak, by some other science. In the latter case the puppet master survives as a humble Punch-and-Judy man playing on a pier provided by the corporation, who perhaps provide his stall also, but nonetheless endowing his Mr. Punch with motives, goals, and all the rest, and relating him in interaction patterns to Judy, the policeman, and so on.

Schutz leaves no room for such interpretations. There is no possibility of any over-arching macro-discipline providing the situations in which the Punch-and-Judy man performs. Such a discipline would concern itself with various structural and historical features of the world. However, the conditions which assure the validity of the procedures adopted by the puppet social scientist render such a macro-discipline utterly meaningless. These conditions concern the structure of the social world and, in particular, the distinction between social science and history.

The structure of the social world has been discussed in section 2.2.3 above. History and social science are two quite distinct provinces of meaning. These provinces – that is, the realms of predecessors and of contemporaries considered in the context of scientific knowledge – are related in two ways. One is that the constructs with which we interpret both realms are derived from the same originary experiencing of the other in the realm of consociates. In other words, the course-of-action types, motivations, systems of relevance and the rest, which we use in interpreting the realm of contemporaries and the realm of predecessors are all derived from the same intersubjective, directly experienced, primordial reality – apart, of course, from the constructs derived from the stock of knowledge that has been handed down to us. This stock of knowledge in turn can be traced back to its origins in the same primordial reality. Ideal types based on these constructs enable us to establish purely external relations of similarity and difference between the two provinces.

The other relation is one that exists between any two finite provinces.

> 'The finite provinces of meaning are not separated states of the mental life in the sense that passing from one to another would require a transmigration of the soul and a complete extinction of memory and consciousness by death, as the doctrine of metempsychosis assumes. They are merely names for different tensions of one and the same consciousness ... experiences in various provinces can be remembered and reproduced. And that is why they can be communicated in ordinary language'. (*CPI,* pp.257-8)

Thus relationships between the provinces of history and of social science exist only in the consciousness of the knowing subject – or in books or papers that he may have written. Such relations are external to their objects: 'there is no possibility of referring one province to another by introducing a formula of transformation'. (*ibid.,* p.233) The 'continuity' of the social world (which ensures the possibility of history and of social science) is established in the realm of 'directly experienced social reality', the 'lived world', which is not available for scientific scrutiny but is pre-predicative, pre-scientific. History and social science are forever set apart. There is no possibility of an overall science, e.g. of history, which covers both the past and the present. In the absence of such a science the problem of the emergence of some present situation out of the past, say, the presence of fascism in Europe, cannot arise as a problem amenable to scientific study. The social scientist, then, when he puts his puppets into some situation or other, must take the situation as already given or as something dreamed up by himself.

2.3.3 The time structure of the social world

While the realms of predecessors and of contemporaries are quite distinct the line dividing the two is rather fluid. Some people were once contemporaries. '[I] remember that I was around at the time, that I was on the scene having my experiences as my partner was having his.' (*PSW*, p.207) In such memories the sense of the simultaneity of the experiences of the partners is preserved. Such memories overlay the boundary between the world of contemporaries and the pure world of predecessors which existed before I was born. 'Simply by looking at them in a different light'. (*ibid*) I can interpret these memories as belonging to the world of my predecessors.

Thus the stream of history appears as a continuous manifold of present moments, each one blurred a little at the edges and flowing into the succeeding present moment. In this respect the stream of history is similar 'to our own stream of consciousness. But in another respect the two are different, for history takes place in objective time, whereas consciousness takes place within the inner duration-flow of the individual. The stream of history includes anonymous events, it knows coexistence and fixed loci in time'. (*ibid.*, p.213) In the flow of this objective time consociates and contemporaries become predecessors, successors become consociates and contemporaries.

Each moment in objective time has its own social science and its own history. That social science is the science of the present moment viewed from the standpoint of the detached social observer. That history is the science of what precedes the present moment. As one moment flows into the next history gains the territory that social science loses. As the moment changes so do its sciences.

Each moment has its full complement of individual actors. As each moment flows into the next some actors drop out, others drop in. The remaining actors act. The product of this dropping in and out and of this acting is the next moment, in the course of which more dropping in and out and acting takes place. The acting, but not necessarily the dropping in and out, is free and undetermined. After the event, to the future historian, it appears unfree and determined. Such is the march of history: from one simultaneous product of the actions of a multiplicity of free individuals to another.

Given any fact or event within social reality the historian may trace a sequence of acts or events of which the fact in question may be said to be the result. At each step of this sequence he must single out a few of the multiplicity of preceding acts for attention. The present moment and all that it contains is the product of every one of the acts performed in the preceding moment. From the infinite multiplicity of paths leading backwards from the fact in question the historian creates his 'history' by singling out a few for special attention and relegating the rest to a more or less amorphous background.

'The main task of the science of history is to decide which events, acts, signs, and so on of all those found in the past are to be singled out for interpretation and systematised into something called history.' (*ibid*, p.211)

The 'history' of a given historian, or the 'social science' of a given social scientist, depends on the present moment in which he finds himself and on his attitude towards the time which is the object of his scrutiny.

'Just as the individual interprets his past experiences in different ways at different times, so the historian interprets past ages now in this way and now in that, looking at them from his own experience of the social world. This means that in the process of interpretation he will always be constructing new ideal types of both persons and actions, all in order to understand precisely the same facts.' (*ibid*, p.212)

History and social science are determinations of the present moment. As the moment changes so do its 'histories' and its 'social sciences'. But this does not mean that all of their categories are historical. The schemes we use to interpret the world of our predecessors are based on the characteristics of human experience in general: on 'the essence of human experience as such, something that necessarily transcends not only our own directly experienced and contemporary social worlds but the whole civilisation of our times as well'. (*ibid*, p.210) The supertemporal character of such categories is guaranteed by the view of history 'as one continuous We-relationship from the earliest days of mankind to the present . . .' (*ibid*, p.214)

Such supertemporal categories apart the historian is free to interpret the past 'now in this way and now in that'. Just as he singles out certain acts or actors for special attention so he organises the multiplicity of simultaneous background facts and events into a pattern. This pattern is the 'situation' which his puppet actors have to met. Just as the choice of actor is determined by the historians' interests or relevancies, so is the structure of the situation in which the actor has to play play his part.

The present moment has no intrinsic structure.[21] It contains individuals endowed with consciousnesses but the content of these consciousnesses comes into play only after the social scientist has picked his facts and events and has sorted out the actors who are going to generate these facts and the situation in which they are going to do it. He makes these selections on the basis of the interests and relevances that he happens to have at the time.

The movement of history is the movement from one intrinsically structureless moment to another. The facts and events that lie scattered across the fact of this history are connected to each other by an infinite multiplicity of temporal sequences. The historian and the social scientist make patterns out of these. There is no social structure and no structure of history beyond those determined by the interests of some social scientist or historian or other. In particular Schutz's 'phenomenological' sociology and history are the only social sciences: they are not dependent upon some other structural science. The effect of Schutz's humanism is a speculative empiricism of the surface phenomena of social formations in which social structures and historical events are reduced to givens which govern but do not appear in the analysis.

There can be no Schutzian politics and indeed no rational social action of any kind. The 'knowledge' of the social world upon which such action might be based consists merely of one set of stories about the world among a multitude of others. The fascism in Europe was nothing but a pattern that some storyteller or other happened to have made up about some facts and events that he happened to be interested in. Why then did our puppet banker/philosopher flee to America?

2.4 Concluding Remarks

From the many puppets with which Alfred Schutz populates his models this essay has been particularly concerned with the two puppet puppet-masters: the social scientist and the historian. They are both storytellers making sense of the mass of facts and events that lie before them. This mass is already given as organised into layer upon layer of present moments with a multiplicity of temporal sequences running from one layer to another. The social scientist is concerned with the top layer of the mass, the historian deals with the rest. Both work with a set of supertemporal categories, which have been uncovered in the course of a 'laborious philosophical journey, for the meaning structure of the social world can only be deduced from the most primitive and general characteristics of consciousness'. (*PSW*, p.12) They flit around applying the categories provided by the nice philosopher to their plasticene figures until they are able to reproduce the behaviour observed in the situations they happen to be interested in.

Their stories are constructed in such a way that each act 'would be understandable to the actor himself as well as to his fellow men in terms of common-sense interpretations of everyday life'. (*CPI,* p.64) The storyteller, in other words, must use categories and situations that are already familiar to his audience. His stories must appear plausible.[22] Schutz's preferred audience is given by the everyday world of his essays and the categories used in its description. This audience is drawn from the cultured middle classes of Western Europe and North America, sensitive academics and professional men. They are staid and rather conservative, rational economic men. Their story-book world is governed by the hidden hand of the margin.

That such an audience can recognise themselves in some of Schutz's accounts, and are familiar with the characters appearing in others is hardly sufficient to ensure the scientific status of his social science or his history. If some of Schutz's followers in sociology use the 'commonsense' categories of a somewhat more radical audience that in no way alters the general character or the scientific status of their stories.

In both cases social science and history are subordinated to the interests of a more general concern: that of reducing 'the world of objective mind' to the actions of individuals. These individuals are the true, and indeed only, subjects of history. Schutz's social science is no science. It is a complex product of his humanism, a theoretical ideology affirming in its 'results' its own necessary and unquestioned premise: that 'the world of objective mind' can be reduced to the behaviour of individuals. The cost of this humanism is a social world in which there are no social or historical laws; in which there is no possibility of rational political action. Far from posing the problems of the social sciences, Schutz was concerned with a rather different issue: that of subordinating these sciences to his conceptions of man. His answers show the social scientist his place and his procedural injunctions would keep him in it.

3. Husserl: Transcendental Phenomenology and the Problem of the History of Philosophy and the Sciences

3.1 Introduction

In his uncompleted last book, *The Crisis of European Sciences and Transcendental Phenomenology,* [1] and particularly in its second part, 'Clarification of the Modern Opposition between Physicalistic Objectivism and Transcendental Subjectivism', Husserl discusses the birth of scientific physics in Galileo's 'mathematisation of nature' and the theoretical effects in philosophy induced by this transformation of the field of objective knowledge. In this text and to a certain extent elsewhere [2] Husserl develops the elements of a theoretical history of philosophy and of the sciences. The object of the present chapter is to demonstrate the contradictory structure of the history attempted in this text and to show that its contradictions are inescapable effects of its fundamental concepts.

Husserl's *Crisis* and several other texts of his later years have been subjected to humanist readings and have been interpreted as evidence of a move towards existentialism in his later philosophy. [3] In fact, as will shortly become clear, all such interpretations are the product of gross and vulgar misrepresentations of what is, in reality, a profoundly antihumanist position. I have shown in chapter 2 that, far from being based on the work of Husserl, Alfred Schutz's alleged phenomenology perpetrates a specific humanist and psychologistic distortion of

Husserl's philosophy. The subsequent critique of the theoretical effects of Schutz's position with regard to history and the social sciences was therefore directed not against the phenomenology of Husserl but only against certain of its grosser misrepresentations. Thus that chapter might seem to leave open the possibility of a sociology and, more generally, of a science of history based on the rigorous transcendental phenomenology of Husserl. I argue that no such possibility exists, that no sociology or history based on the phenomenology of Husserl can be scientific and that a transcendental empiricism cannot escape the theoretical constraints of the empiricist conception of the knowledge process.

This chapter may be summarised as follows. It is concerned to analyse the theory of the nature and history of the sciences and of philosophy which governs the argument of Husserl's *The Crisis of European Sciences and Transcendental Phenomenology*. It will be argued that Husserl's position is structured around a central and inescapable contradiction between his theoretical objective on the one hand and the terms in which that objective is to be realised on the other. His objective is to demonstrate the possibility of a rational non-subjectivist history of the sciences and of philosophy and to present at least the outlines of such a history with respect to the birth of a scientific physics in the seventeenth century and the theoretical effects of that birth in philosophy. This attempted demonstration is governed by the problematic of a theory of knowledge which retains the essential structure of empiricism, in this case, of a transcendental empiricism. That structure is discussed immediately after this Introduction.

The effect of this contradiction between Husserl's problematic and what he attempts to achieve within it is to produce a discourse structured by a series of 'discrepancies' between its elements and by the presence of a denegatory play on words, a theoretical 'slide'. These last function so as to cover or gloss over the discrepancies or else to link the discrepant elements. The crucial discrepancies that may be identified in Husserl's text are indicated below.

First Discrepancy. Husserl maintains that Galileo's physics is grounded in a meaning which is taken for granted by Galileo and which he fails to recognise. Galileo's endowment of meaning upon his physics refers back to an earlier original endowment of the meaning of pure geometry. Thus the origin of pure geometry is thought as an original act of endowment of meaning taking place within the consciousness of a subject. Yet Husserl's analysis of the origins of pure geometry shows that its meaning cannot be located within the consciousness of an epistemological subject but that, on the contrary, it is the effect of a determinate system of concepts and theoretical instruments. There are thus two quite distinct concepts of 'meaning' at work in this portion of the text. Husserl's play on the word 'meaning' denegates this difference and functions so as to gloss over the discrepancy between the grounding of Galileo's physics in a presupposed meaning and the absence of any original embodied meaning in the pure geometry which this physics presupposes.

Second Discrepancy. The meaning assigned by Husserl's text to Galileo's natural science is of a character entirely different from that assigned earlier to pure geometry. The latter 'meaning' is embedded within the system of concepts and instruments of the science; it does not refer to the consciousness of any transcendental ego. The 'meaning' of natural science on the other hand functions as a very different concept. It refers to the consciousness of a specific subject, Galileo. Hence there are two quite distinct epistemologies. In one knowledge is conceived as the result of a process of production governed by a determinate system of concepts. In the other it is an effect of the practice of a unique type of subject confronted by a real world which he maps with the aid of mathematical instrumentalities.

Third Discrepancy. In the analysis of Galileo's mathematisation of the world the scientist is conceived as working on a real given externally to him – so that the idealities of, for example, pure geometry are said to reflect the essential form of the world that is immediately given to the knowing subject. In contrast Husserl's conception of the essential meaning of philosophy as consisting in the suppression of all forms of objectivism involves a subjectivisation of the world as an accomplishment of world-constituting subjectivity. Here the opposition of subject and object is superseded since both are now thought to be contained entirely within consciousness. Hence there is a discrepancy between his conceptions of science and of philosophy. The unconditional objectivity of scientific idealities that is an essential feature of the one is unthinkable in the other. Ultimately, philosophy is seen as representing a process without a subject, as the self-consciousness of a world-constituting subjectivity, that is, of a world that is essentially spiritual.

These discrepancies are essential to the theoretical structure of Husserlian epistemology. It follows that an Husserlian epistemology is impossible without these discrepancies and impossible as an epistemology because of them. The objective of the present chapter is thus to show that no Husserlian theory of knowledge is possible unless these contradictions are also present. As a consequence of this demonstration it must follow that there can be no 'positive' knowledges that are realisations of Husserl's theory of knowledge, that is, no Husserlian anti-psychology, no Husserlian histories (of the sciences, of philosophy, etc.), and no Husserlian sociology or science of history. This chapter therefore closes the gap left left by my discussion of Schutz, which might appear not to have eliminated either the possibility that Schutz's sub-Husserlian position was inadequate because it invited a rigorous Husserlian critique or the possibility of a Husserlian social phenomenology. The effect of the present chapter is to forestall any possible attempts at an Husserlian social theory.

The theoretical collapse of even the most rigorous transcendental epistemology is an inescapable effect of the essential structure of the empiricist conception of knowledge. No theoretical empiricism can avoid the contradictions that are the necessary result of this structure. At best those specific to one variant of empiricism may be displaced into the somewhat different contradictions specific to another. Before proceeding to establish these results in the analysis of Husserl's text it is necessary to situate his transcendental philosophy in relation to other variants of the empiricist conception of knowledge.

3.2 Transcendental Variants of the Empiricist Problematic

In the empiricist conception of the knowledge process as one that takes place between a given subject and a given object the result of this process is that the subject extracts from the object its essence. This essence is then called knowledge and its structure is thought to represent that of the object known. Here the subject is conceived as preceding any knowledge process in which it may happen to engage. If the process of knowledge takes place under appropriate conditions it results in scientific, or objective, knowledge, but if not the result is either a knowledge of some other kind (i.e. not objective, not scientific) or else it is not really a knowledge at all but a non-knowledge parading in the guise of knowledge.[4] If in these conceptions the subject of the knowledge process is also conceived as a possible object of knowledge then certain interesting and curious consequences follow. Knowledge in general, and scientific knowledge in particular, appears to be an effect of the conditions of the knowledge process and to be the product of whatever governs the habits of thought and modes of perception of the subject in question. In this way the theory of knowledge may be conceived as belonging properly to the province of whatever natural science is thought to investigate the functioning of the thinking apparatus. It follows that scientific knowledge must now appear to be subjected to natural determinations that are independent of the particular structure of the object known. This latter structure, therefore, can no longer be represented in knowledge in undistorted form and scientific knowledge cannot be considered objective in any worthwhile empiricist sense.

In the history of western philosophy the recognition of this consequence has provoked responses ranging from acceptance to various attempts at escape. The extreme of bland acceptance is represented by the varieties of subjective idealism, a tendency which reaches its highest development in the work of Hume and Berkeley, a systematic and reactionary anti-rationalism culminating in the doctrine that reason and objective knowledge are fictions. Social phenomenology and ethnomethodology are more recent examples of a similar tendency. Others, while recognising the effects of social and psychological influences, have appealed to the norms and conventions of the scientific community to save us from the dreaded relativism and subjectivism. The work of Popper and his associates and of logical empiricism represent two somewhat different attempts of this kind. All such attempts are doomed to failure. At most 'psychological' influences and problems may be replaced by 'sociological' ones, psychology by the sociology of knowledge. Scientific knowledge is then reduced to an effect of whatever produces the norms and conventions of the scientific community. In recent years Kuhn and those who follow him in sociology and philosophy have gone furthest in this direction.

More interesting and at first sight perhaps more successful is the response of transcendental philosophy in Kant and the neo-Kantians and later in a very different form in the transcendental phenomenology of Husserl. By representing the epistemological subject and certain of its properties as the condition of existence of phenomena, that is, by specifically excluding the transcendental subject from the phenomenal realm of objects of knowledge, Kantian epistemology appears to guarantee the autonomy of knowledge with regard to any determination by natural, that is, material, causes. The anti-naturalism of these positions ensures that the conditions of knowledge are not subjected to psychological, biological or other natural determinations. In thus establishing the autonomy of the sciences these positions would seem to guarantee the possibility of an empiricist knowledge process resulting in objective knowledge. In short, transcendentalism appears to escape from the theoretical trap of reducing objectivity to a fiction into which all non-transcendental, or naturalistic, empiricism must fall.

However the various theoretical devices whereby transcendental philosophy may attempt to preserve the objectivity of knowledge are inherently incapable of achieving their objective. In escaping from one theoretical impasse transcendentalism merely falls into another which, in the last analysis, is not too different from the first. If the existence of a realm of objects requires that of a non-objectifiable subject-correlate of knowledge then knowledge itself ceases to be an object, that is, it cannot be the proper object of any positive science. Thus a rigorous Kantian epistemology must distinguish the epistemological subject of the knowledge process from the merely animal subject whose several properties are to be quite properly investigated in the natural sciences. The double status of the subject and the peculiar status of knowledge in this conception raise immediate difficulties. For if knowledge is not to be subjected to natural determinations there nevertheless remains every appearance of a real history and a real development within knowledge, that is, within the realm of the transcendental. How is this history or this development to be investigated without sacrificing the autonomy of knowledge?

If the transcendental subject is not to be a phenomenal object it must follow that the activities of subjects in the world, producing knowledge, making choices, and the like, cannot be susceptible to naturalistic explanation. If the phenomenal effects of these activities are to be treated as phenomena in nature and therefore as susceptible to naturalistic explanation then, by definition, such explanation cannot proceed by reference to the transcendental attributes of free human subjects since these are transcendent objects. Naturalistic explanation is restricted to the phenomenal, sensible realm of nature while supersensible, transcendent objects are beyond both knowledge and explanation.

'Now where determination according to laws of nature ceases there all explanation ceases also, and nothing remains but defense, that is, the removal of the objections of those who pretend to have seen deeper into the nature of things, and thereupon boldly declare freedom impossible.' (Kant, 1949, p.76)

Since knowledge, *qua* knowledge, is a function of the operation of transcendental faculties it cannot be treated as an object in nature. Similar arguments apply to other cultural products in so far as they are conceived as dependent on the operation of transcendental faculties of free human subjects, for example, as products of aesthetic and ethical conceptions. In this way transcendental epistemology appears to leave the field of history, or at least of cultural history,[5] prey to the theoretical ravages of all kinds of humanism, free will, mysticism, and other irrationalist tendencies. In effect the very possibility of an objective knowledge of history has to be denied in the name of the free creative human subject. The pernicious theoretical effects of this dogmatic imposition of limitations to knowledge with respect to history and the social sciences are only too well known. They may be seen in the various subjectivist, irrationalist and romantic positions elaborated by the Geisteswissenschaften traditions of German philosophy and historiography, in particular, in the idealist distinction between the 'natural' and the 'human', that is, non-natural, sciences, and in the doctrine of a special hermeneutic method peculiar to the latter, a doctrine in which rationalist forms of proof and demonstration are systematically denegated in favour of the mysterious faculty of the understanding.[6] Positions of this kind have found their way into sociology through the works of Weber, Dilthey, Scheler, and of their later followers and interpreters.

The human subjectivity whose will, freedom, choice, and related humanistic appendages are defended by hermeneutics at so great a theoretical cost is anathema to the rigorous idealism of Husserl. In fact it is easy to see that the hermeneutic division between the natural and the human sciences merely reproduces in a specific romantic and irrationalist form the essential structures of the old 'naturalistic' accounts of knowledge. Where a naturalistic empiricism reduces objectivity to a fiction in the name of natural causes a hermeneutic empiricism calls in unnatural, that is, human, causes to achieve the same result. The arbitrary assignment of various human characteristics to the epistemological subject of the empiricist process of knowledge reduces the theory of knowledge to a hermeneutic psychology, history or sociology. If these consequences are to be avoided within the constraints of an empiricist conception of the knowledge process a more rigorous and systematic transcendentalism is required in which all *qualities,* natural or human, are ejected from the epistemological subject. The transcendental phenomenology of Husserl attempts precisely this displacement of all that is human into the realm of positivity so that neither the natural nor anything human is to be abitrarily excluded from the possibility of a rigorous and objective knowledge. [7] Thus in the transcendental subject of the knowledge process

'nothing human is to be found, neither soul nor psychic life nor real psycho-physical human beings, all this belongs to the 'phenomenon', to the world as constituted pole.' (p.183)

It will be argued below that this project is unrealisable and that in liberating the theory of knowledge from the fetters of theoretical humanism Husserl's empiricism can only reproduce in more rigorous, and therefore more acute, form the difficulties of the earlier, incomplete transcendentalism of Kant and the neo-Kantians, in particular, the problems resulting from the double status of the subject (epistemological and human/natural) and from the contradictory status of knowledge. The theory of the knowledge process and, in particular, of the history of the sciences and of philosophy consequently remains the site of acute contradictions. If the knowledge process of transcendental subjectivity is to be the object of investigation then that investigation itself requires reference to a higher subjectivity. Since the existence of its object requires that of a non-objectionable subject-correlate of knowledge the transcendental movement can only be repeated. Indeed it is clear that this movement must be repeated indefinitely if it is not to be brought to an entirely arbitrary halt. Cavaillès has insisted on this crucial point in his critique of Husserl's analysis of logic. If there is to be an absolute logic, if transcendental subjectivity is to be governed by the norms of logic in its argumentation, then

'a new transcendental investigation is necessary in order to relate its norms to a higher subjectivity, since no content but, rather, only consciousness has the authority to be posited in itself. If transcendental logic truly grounds logic, there is no absolute logic (i.e. logic subjecting the absolute subjective activity to its norms). If there is an absolute logic, it can draw its authority only from itself; it is not transcendental.' (Cavaillès, 1947, p.65)

In Husserl the empiricist theory of the knowledge process reaches its highest point of rigour and of theoretical honesty. It is this that gives his work its exceptional interest. If in his attempts too rescue the theory of knowledge from the ravages of a romantic and irrationalist humanism Husserl nevertheless produces a contradictory history of the sciences that finally collapses into a speculative philosophy of history then this collapse has an exemplary character with respect to the essential structures of the empiricist conception of knowledge. In its very rigour and purity it exemplifies the inherently contradictory character of empiricism, a theory of knowledge perpetually torn between the extremes of speculation on the one hand and of irrationalism and subjectivism on the other.

This chapter analyses certain texts in which Husserl discusses questions concerning the history of the sciences and of philosophy. It is concerned with his concepts and with the logical character of their relationships and it argues that Husserl's position involves fundamental and inescapable logical discrepancies and contradictions. It should perhaps be emphasised that this analysis is in no way concerned to elicit the views of the subject, Husserl, on these histories or on the supposed crisis of philosophy and contemporary science. To search the text for the view of its author is to impose a preconceived and possibly spurious coherence on to the structure of its argument.[8] It cannot be maintained that the order of, and relations between, the concepts of a text is a mere expression of the consciousness of its author, nor can it be maintained that this consciousness is, perhaps, more accurately represented in some portions of the text and less accurately in others so that, by judicious selection, it might prove possible to isolate what he 'really' thought. The theoretical structure of a text is a matter of the logical properties which obtain between its concepts[9] and not of some ghostly emanations originating, say, from the pineal gland or cerebral cortex of its author's body. An exposition of the views of an author has the effect of denegating the specificity of the theoretical structure of his text. It identifies various manifest statements as the views of its author, thereby separating these statements from the theoretical conditions of their appearance. That is, it denegates the specific theoretical character of the text, transforms it into an untheoretical discourse, and allows the reader to deal with specific identifiable positions in a piecemeal fashion.[10] The contradictory structure to be examined in this chapter is that of the concepts and the relations which obtain between them in Husserl's text. The crucial ambiguities of his text are necessary effects of that structure. To read the text for the views of its author is to denegate that necessity.

3.3 Science and Philosophy in Husserl's Conception of Knowledge

The empiricist conception of knowledge is characterised by the invariant structure of the subject-object relation. Variations in the precise characteristics assigned to the subject and correlatively to the object define the variants of the basic empiricist problematic. In all cases knowledge, if it is indeed a genuine knowledge, is thought to be based upon and reducible to the original experience of a knowing subject. It has been shown above that in Husserl's case this subject is to be one in which 'nothing human' can be found. Only if it can be reduced to the original experience of such a subject may what is alleged to be knowledge be accepted as genuine. In this respect the existence of the sciences and of philosophy poses an immediate and obvious problem. Scientific knowledge is never reducible directly to the immediate experience of a scientific subject. It always rests upon some existing and presupposed knowledges. Galileo, for example, makes use of a pre-given mathematics in the formulation of his theories. A similar situation prevails in fact in philosophy and in other non-scientific theoretical domains. Not even the most theoretical of the positive sciences can guarantee the epistemological status of their knowledges, that is, that they are indeed knowledges. Two aspects of this situation are especially significant for the present argument. First, the sciences must appear to be radically incomplete. Husserl can therefore claim that 'modern science has abandoned the ideal of genuine science ... and, in its practice, it has abandoned radicalness of scientific self-responsibility' (Husserl, 1969, p.3—4). It is this situation that Husserl refers to as the 'crisis of European sciences': not a crisis within the positive sciences but rather a disjunction between these sciences and their necessary grounding in original experience. This 'crisis' is an effect of the very success of the sciences, of the theoretical, formal and mathematical, techniques which they have developed and which can be used mechanically without reference to their true meaning. The scientist knows nothing of the meaning of his work, he 'lives in producing, but does not have this productive living as a theme within his field of vision' (p.15).

Nevertheless the knowledge produced by the sciences is always thought to be reducible to its basis in original experience.

> 'Science, and in particular geometry, with this ontic meaning, must
> have had a historical beginning. This meaning itself must have an
> origin in an accomplishment: first as a project and then in
> successful execution. This process of projecting and successfully
> realising occurs, after all, purely within the subject of the inventor
> . . . .' (p.356)

This reduction to original experience is a task that can be performed
only by philosophy. Thus it is the radical incompleteness of the
sciences that leads to the necessity of philosophy in which their supposed knowledges are to be judged and either guaranteed or found
wanting and their essential meaning, of which the scientists themselves
are ignorant, determined. In thus establishing philosophy as the final
arbiter of scientificity Husserl reflects the roles traditionally assigned
to the sciences and philosophy in the problematic of the empiricist
conception of knowledge.[11] In the absence of such a philosophy the
sciences can only appear as brilliant and successful theoretical
techniques that have no meaning for life in the world. In its absence
the crisis of European science must appear as a crisis of reason itself,
meaningless yet technically successful, as a general crisis of culture
and of mankind.

Secondly it should be noted that, for Husserl, when the scientist
makes use of some pre-given knowledge he is ignorant of its essential
meaning. It is because he fails to investigate the presupposed and
hidden meanings that he takes over that the scientist is ignorant of the
true meaning of his own work. In this conception theories, formal and
mathematical techniques, instruments, function as embodiments of the
true meanings with which they were supposed originally to have been
endowed. Husserl's philosophical history of the sciences and of
philosophy therefore consists in the re-establishment of the original
meanings of scientific knowledge and of philosophies, in the identification of what meanings were presupposed and what original meanings
were added in Galileo's work, and so on. This history is not and cannot be a merely empirical history of scientific products, a
chronological sequence of results, of theories, facts and discoveries.
Such a history would be as meaningless for Husserl as are the positive
sciences themselves. Husserl's philosophical history is a theoretical
history, a history which must weigh and judge the facts presented to it
and which, in particular, must seek the true meaning of a theory

beneath the conceptions and manifest statements of the theorists themselves.

Now this establishment of original and presupposed meanings, this tracing of knowledge back to its basis in some original experience, is possible only on condition that these original meanings, in spite of the fact that they go unrecognised, are indeed transmitted in the theories, techniques and instruments in which they are embodied. In effect it requires that there be a transcendental intersubjectivity which must precede any particular communication of meanings if that communication is to be able to function as the bearer of hidden and presupposed original meanings from one transcendental ego to another. It would seem then that the true subject of scientific knowledge is not so much the isolated transcendental ego in all its epistemological splendour but rather the transcendental intersubjectivity that is the indispensible condition of existence of the ego's scientific or philosophical practice. It appears, in other words, that scientific knowledge is strictly reducible to the original experience of one or more individual transcendental egos only on condition that the ego ceases to be conceived as the true subject of the knowledge process. But if transcendental intersubjectivity is the true subject of the knowledge process then there can be no necessity for maintaining that the possibility of reduction to the original experience of an individual ego is a condition of existence of all genuine knowledge. It will be shown that in practice Husserl's history must make use of 'meanings' that are not reducible to the original experience of any subject.

It is essential that the nature of this difficulty be clearly understood. The rigorous delimitation of knowledge to what conforms to Husserl's empiricist criteria must presuppose a transcendental intersubjectivity which functions as a bearer of embodied meanings. What is *presupposed* as a condition of existence of the empiricist knowledge process cannot be *established* by such a process. This difficulty is in no way reducible to that problem of vulgar existentialism, the existence of other human beings. For Husserl everything human belongs to the realm of positivity and is the proper object of the positive sciences. Whether the observed motions of some appropriately shaped lump of flesh are connected with any peculiarly human processes going on within is not a serious question for the philosopher. The existence of other transcendental egos is another matter entirely and it is certainly true that Husserl is continually troubled by that question. [12] However the problem that Husserl is confronted with by the existence of theoretical knowledges cannot be resolved by the mere presence of a multiplicity of transcendental subjects. They must also be able to communicate. But if the communication of determinate presupposed meanings is required as an essential precondition of the production of scientific knowledge then that knowledge cannot be reduced without residue to the original experiences of these subjects; they cannot be the true subjects of the knowledge process. Thus in his attempts to locate the sciences within the terms of an empiricist conception of the knowledge process with the individual transcendental ego as subject Husserl is forced into a quite different conception of the knowledge process. In this new conception knowledge still appears to be the embodiment of meanings but individual subjects are reduced to the status of functionaries of the knowledge process and can no longer appear therefore as its determinant elements.

The essential parameters of Husserl's epistemology and his history of philosophy and the sciences are given in the above sentences. On the one hand he produces a purely speculative philosophy of history in which the philosopher and the scientist appear as mere functionaries, as the bearers of the self-development of transcendental intersubjectivity. On the other hand knowledge is to be rigorously reduced to the original experience of a transcendental ego. But it seems that this reduction is possible for the sciences only on condition that it is incomplete. One index of this necessary incompleteness is the fact that Husserl's history requires the presence of knowledges that are not reducible to any original experience. Several commentators have observed the presence of a speculative philosophy of history in Husserl's later writings, notably in the *Crisis* itself and in the 'Hegelian' fragment 'Philosophy as Mankind's Self-Reflection: the Self-Realisation of Reason' (pp.335-342). [13] It is easy to see that this speculative philosophy must contradict the transcendental empiricism that is the dominant problematic of Husserl's work. Less obvious is the necessity of the coexistence of contradictory variants of empiricism in these texts. This chapter is intended to demonstrate that his collapse into a speculative philosophy is a final empiricist response to Husserl's production of problems that are insoluble within the terms of his dominant transcendental empiricism. The ambiguities and inconsistencies of his text are produced in the tension between a rigorous empiricist epistemology of the transcendental ego and a speculative philosophy of history. In the following discussion these effects will be demonstrated in the analyses of the pure geometry taken for granted by Galileo and of Galileo's 'mathematisation of the world'. These will be followed by the analysis of what is the true objective of Husserl's text, namely, the establishment of the meaning of modern philosophy and its origin in the transformation induced by the birth of a scientific physics. Finally this chapter examines the more general theoretical effects of the contradictory conceptions of the knowledge process at work in Husserl's text.

3.3.1 The 'meaning' of the pure geometry taken for granted by Galileo

The book of nature, in Galileo's conception, is written in mathematical characters and nature itself is conceived as a mathematical manifold, a rational infinite totality which can be systematically mastered by a mathematical natural science.[14] If we are to establish the meaning of this mathematisation of nature it is necessary that we examine the motivation of Galileo's thinking. Husserl finds that pure geometry, the mathematics of spatio-temporal shapes in general, is taken for granted by Galileo, it is pre-given as part of an already old tradition. With this relatively advanced geometry a hidden, presupposed meaning enters Galileo's physics. In order, then, to establish the meaning of this physics it is first necessary to determine the hidden meaning implicit in pure geometry.

Pure geometry is a science of pure idealities, that is, of ideal entities that are not to be found in the world. In this respect Husserl insists that it be distinguished from the practical art of surveying which knows nothing of the geometrical idealities, of dimensionless points, of ideally straight lines without width, and so on. Pure geometry is not, in Husserl's view, reducible to the practical art of surveying and its idealities are not derived from the surveyor's instruments. Instead they emerge

> 'out of the *praxis* of perfecting, of freely pressing toward the horizons of *conceivable* perfecting again and again, *limit shapes* emerge toward which the particular series of perfecting tend, as toward invariant and never attainable goals. If we are interested in these ideal shapes and are constantly engaged in determining them and in constructing new ones out of those already determined we are "geometers".' (p.26)

The ideal shapes do not fall ready made from the sky, they 'emerge' as limit shapes produced in an existing conceptual and theoretical practice. Thus the construction of the concepts of these limit shapes requires the concepts of the non-ideal shapes whose limits are to be the idealities and also the concept of limit and the related concepts which govern the practice of constructing the limit of a series. The birth of this geometry, far from being a pure endowment of original meaning in the consciousness of the first geometer, is dependent on an existing mathematical practice and on what is presupposed in that practice.

The offspring of this birth process is, according to Husserl, a scientific geometry in which we 'have an *ideal* praxis of "pure thinking" which remains exclusively within the realm of pure limit shapes'. (*ibid*) Once produced these limit shapes become acquired tools which, like all cultural acquisitions, 'remain objectively knowable and available without requiring that the formulation of their meaning be repeatedly and explicitly renewed'. (*ibid*) In this way geometry is able to develop a technique of calculation according to technical rules. These rules enable the geometer to achieve results which are valid but of whose genuine meaning and truth he may be completely ignorant. The technical development of a science leads to an emptying of the original meaning. The technical practice of mathematics therefore contains meanings that are present but unrecognised, 'significations which are, so to speak, sedimented in their embodiments'. (p.27) It would seem then that starting originally from the practical art of measuring there develops, through the change to a theoretical interest and a purely geometrical way of thinking, the science of 'all possibly *conceivable* ideal shapes'. (*ibid*) This science in turn is able to transform and to guide the practical art of measuring by means of an applied geometry based upon the technical rules for calculation with geometrical idealities. Now, the transformation of the methodology of surveying through the change to a theoretical interest and the development of a pure geometry plays a crucial role in Husserl's account of the meaning of modern physics and of its mathematisation of the world. The hidden meaning that enters into the new physics by means of the geometry taken for granted by Galileo is precisely the meaning of measurement that appears as a result of that transformation. I have just shown that in Husserl's account of the construction of pure geometry a pre-existing mathematical practice is required. In that case since pure geometry is thought to be the first of the sciences to appear this practice which precedes pure geometry must be non-scientific. Husserl locates it in the pre-scientific practice of surveying. He notes that the art of measurement, whether or not it is based on an applied geometry, necessarily involves much more than the actual technical process of making a particular measurement. The possibility of measurement requires a set of strictly determinable concepts (forms, magnitudes, positions) and the construction and practical determination of empirical standard measures and instruments. Any art of measurement therefore involves a practice of determination governed by a definite system of concepts and of instruments. Measurement is never reducible to the raw experience of a knowing subject, to the mere recognition of a given. In the case of a pre-scientific art of measurement the system of concepts and instruments cannot be the product of the application of any science. On the contrary it strictly precedes the process of 'idealisation' that results in 'the ideal praxis of pure thinking'.

The essential features of Husserl's theoretical history of the sciences are already present in this attempt to establish the meaning of pure geometry. Husserl describes the *original* endowment of meaning as a process in which an *existing system of emodied meanings* (the techniques and instruments of the pre-scientific art of measurement) is transformed by a determinate theoretical labour. This labour consists of the construction of limit concepts and the establishment of forms of proof and demonstration with respect to these concepts. It is precisely their character as limit concepts that enables the establishment of rigorous forms of demonstration with respect to these idealities. The properties of these geometrical idealities are related to those of the 'practical', 'non-ideal' concepts by the mechanism of construction of the limit. Since Husserl presents geometry as an exemplar of mathematics and as the first of the sciences we may conclude that the science of pure mathematics is the product of a determinate transformation of an existing impure mathematical practice. Generalising this result it appears that the original endowment of meaning of a science must be analysed as the product of a determinate theoretical labour of transformation of an existing system of embodied meanings. The 'original' endowment of meaning always refers back to *already endowed meanings*.

Nevertheless this concept of the endowment of meaning is not equivalent to the concept of the epistemological break developed by Bachelard and others to refer to the constitution of a scientific problematic in the transformation of existing theoretical but non-scientific problematics. [15] For the latter the determinant element in the production of knowledge is the problematic itself, a determinate articulated system of concepts, instruments and modes of theoretical labour. Here the scientist far from being a meaning-endowing epistemological subject is present solely as the bearer of certain functions in the process of production of knowledge. For Husserl on the contrary the endowment of meaning is the determinant element. The system of concepts and instruments is thought as the embodiment of original meanings, that is, of meanings originally produced in the consciousness of a knowing subject. It is these meanings alone that guarantee the truth of whatever knowledge may be produced with these concepts. If the development of technical means of calculation makes it possible to achieve valid results while ignoring these original meanings then there appears the possibility of unrecognised and 'dangerous shifts of meaning'. These dangers are to be avoided only by 'keeping always immediately in mind the original bestowal of meaning upon the method, through which it has the sense of achieving knowledge about the world' (p.47). Thus pure geometry and the preceding practical art of measuring are thought as the embodiment of meanings, significations, ideas, and so on. Yet these meanings are located within the system of concepts and instruments and not in the consciousness, mind, soul, or what have you, of some epistemological subject. The meanings are not therefore to be found in the consciousness of any geometer, in particular, of Galileo. It is only on this condition that an essential element in Galileo's mathematisation of the world can appear in the relatively advanced pure geometry that he takes for granted.

The 'dangerous shift of meaning' that may appear as a result of the technical development of geometry or of other sciences obviously refers to a shift away from the meaning originally bestowed by the consciousness of an epistemological subject, of a transcendental ego. We have just seen that in the case of pure geometry the original bestowal of meaning is not strictly original. The system of concepts in which the meaning is embodied is itself the product of a determinate transformation of an existing system of embodied meanings. It is not the simple product of some original act of bestowal. A shift in meaning, then, can refer only to some further transformation of an existing system of concepts and of instruments. The 'dangerous shift' referred to in Husserl's text is therefore a shift from a non-existent origin.

These last points may be taken as a first index of the contradictory structure of Husserl's theoretical history of the sciences. The question of the origin of geometry must be posed in terms of the original endowment of meaning by a transcendental ego. This original endowment gives the meaning of the pure geometry taken for granted by Galileo. It is with respect to this original endowment that 'dangerous shifts of meaning' can appear. In fact it has been shown that Husserl's text gives the answer to a somewhat different question, namely, in what does the process of constitution of pure geometry consist? The answer to that question is indicated above. The scientist constitutes pure geometry on the basis of an existing system of embodied meanings by means of a determinate theoretical labour of transformation. This answer ensures that the transcendental ego cannot appear to be the true subject of the knowledge process and that his endowment of meaning cannot be original. The scientist, as will be shown below, far from being the subject of the process is a mere functionary, a bearer of the activity of transcendental intersubjectivity.

3.3.2 Galileo's mathematisation of the world

The existence of a pure geometry and of a pure mathematics in general provides the conditions of a specific manner of objectifying that may 'be practiced on one abstract aspect of the world'. (p.33) With regard to this aspect pure mathematics allows in principle for an exact measurement, i.e. 'for empirical measuring with increasing precision, but under the guidance of a world of idealities – such a world having been objectified in advance through idealisation and construction'. (p.34) Geometry provides, that is to say, a universal form of the world. Unfortunately there is only one geometry, the geometry of spatio-temporal shapes. It follows that a direct mathematisation of the specifically sensible qualities of bodies is impossible since the limit 'shapes' of these qualities are not themselves idealisable in the same way. Thus 'measurement of them cannot be related to corresponding idealities in a constructible world already objectivised into idealities' (p.35).

If that is not to appear an entirely arbitrary conclusion it is necessary to examine the specific character of the objectivity of the idealities of pure geometry. Otherwise it might seem that 'ideal' concepts relating to other sensible qualities could be constructed in the same way as geometrical idealities. Husserl examines this question in 'The Origins of Geometry' (pp.353–378) where he argues that geometry must have its origin in an accomplishment which occurs 'purely within the *subject* of the inventor and thus the meaning, as present, *originaliter* with its whole content, lies exclusively, so to speak, within his mental space. But geometrical existence is not psychic existence; it does not exist as something personal within the personal sphere of consciousness; it is the existence of what is objectively there for "everyone".' (p.356)

In the problem of the origins of geometry is posed the problem of the emergence of the unconditional objectivity that is neither relative nor time-bound of scientific idealities. The ideal constructions of pure geometry, as opposed to the non-ideal constructions of the art of surveying, are products

'arising out of an idealising, spiritual act, one of "pure" thinking, which has its materials in the designated general pre-givens of this factual humanity and human surrounding world and creates 'ideal objects' out of them.' (p.377)

The idealities of pure geometry reflect the essential form of the world that is immediately given to the knowing subject and pure geometry itself represents a direct mathematisation of that world. Here the objectivity of geometrical idealities is reduced to an effect of the conditions of the confrontation of the knowing subject and its known object: geometry is objective because it really does reflect the essential form of the real world that is really given to the consciousness of the subject. It may be noted that this 'objectivity' specifically precludes the account examined above of the 'meaning' of pure geometry. If this latter meaning emerges only on the basis of an existing system of embodied meaning then the world is not immediately given to the consciousness of the first geometer. Instead it is given in and through the system of embodied meanings that he takes for granted.

In the discussion of Galileo's mathematisation of the world, however, it appears that the subject is confronted with a given world one aspect of which may be directly mathematised by pure geometry. Other aspects must be mathematised indirectly. Galileo's achievement consists precisely in producing an indirect mathematisation of the non-geometrical plena. Since geometry, or rather mathematics, is the only universal form of the world Husserl is now confronted by the problem of how Galileo could have hit upon the following conception:

'That everything which manifests itself as real through the specific sense qualities must have its *mathematical index* in events belonging to the sphere of shapes? (p.37)

What, in other words, was the motive for taking an analytical attitude towards the network of intuitively given events in respect of their dependencies on events in the sphere of shapes? Husserl is content to note that the men of the Renaissance were inclined to bold generalisations. It seemed reasonable, then, to assume that qualitative occurrences were mathematisable if only an appropriate method of measuring could be worked out. Thus the mathematisability of nature, the conception of nature as a realm of universal exact causality, is a given for Galileo. What was lacking was the means of establishing exact causal determination with regard to both aspects of the world, to spatio-temporal shapes and to sensible qualities. This 'was a matter of *discovery* in physics . . . for the passionate *praxis of inquiry* and not a matter for prior systematic reflection upon what is possible'. (p. 40) This can hardly be considered a satisfactory solution but it appears to be sufficient to enable Husserl to return to the question of the meaning of Galileo's mathematisation of the world.

Galileo, it seems, is the inheritor of a pure geometry which was founded upon a practical art of surveying which itself knew nothing of idealities. Since Galileo fails to inquire back into the original meaning of this geometry it must appear to be a self-contained science producing self-sufficient objective truths which could be applied without further ado. In other words the existing technical forms of proof and demonstration in this geometry appear to stand in need of no further guarantee. Nevertheless the real world is not inhabited by geometrical idealities.

> 'Yet this triviality has been buried precisely by exact science; indeed since the days of ancient geometry, through that substitution of a methodically idealised achievement for what is given as actually presupposed in all idealisation, given by a verification which is, in its own way, unsurpassable.' (p. 50)

In this way a well-fitting garb of ideas has been surreptitiously substituted for the life-world, for the world that is originally given.

> 'Mathematics and mathematical science, as a garb of ideas, or the garb of symbols of the symbolic mathematical theories, encompasses everything which, for scientists and the educated generally, *represents* the life-world, *dresses it up* as 'objectively actual and

true' nature. It is through the garb of ideas that we take for *true be-ing* what is actually a *method.*' (p. 51)

It follows that the true meaning of their theories had to remain hidden from the physicists, even from Galileo himself. If natural science 'can only be and remain meaningful in a true and original sense if the scientist had developed in himself the ability to *inquire back* into the *original meaning*' (p. 56) then the true meaning of natural science has *never been recognised by any scientist*. The natural scientist is at best a brilliant technician. He is unable to ensure that the knowledge he produces is indeed 'true knowledge of the *world itself, of nature itself*'. (p.57) Thus what Husserl calls the 'crisis of European science', the disjunction between the sciences and their necessary grounding in original experience, is co-extensive with the very existence of the sciences. The 'crisis' appears at the very beginning of natural science in Galileo's ignorance of the true meaning of his work – and before then with the technical development of a pure geometry in which the meaning is merely sedimented.

It has been shown in the preceding section that in Husserl's account of the meaning of pure geometry there is no original meaning for Galileo or anyone else to inquire back into. There is, in other words, no original meaning in the sense of a meaning endowed by the consciousness of a transcendental ego that corresponds to and is embodied within the system of concepts and instruments of a science. In that case the 'crisis' of Husserl's title consists precisely in the existence of the sciences, in the production of knowledge by means of a determinate theoretical labour governed by a system of concepts and instruments, in the existence, that is to say of a knowledge that is never strictly reducible to the original experience of a transcendental ego. The crisis consists in the production of knowledge independently of the category of the individual epistemological subject. Yet it is in the name of this category that all scientific knowledge has been declared by Husserl to be radically incomplete.

It is clear that the meaning assigned by Husserl's text to Galileo's natural science is of a character entirely different from that assigned earlier to pure geometry. This latter 'meaning' as we have seen, is embedded within the system of concepts and instruments of the science. It does not refer to, and is not constituted within, the consciousness of any transcendental ego. The account of the origin of that meaning is an account of the process of production of a new system of embodied meanings, a process which has no transcendental ego as its subject. The former 'meaning', that of natural science, functions in Husserl's text as a very different concept. It refers to the motivation, that is, to the consciousness, of a specific subject, Galileo – a consciousness in which there are admittedly the hidden, presupposed meanings of pure geometry. Once this motivation has been established the accomplishment of the new physics, the production of the new system of concepts, is left to look after itself.[16] It is a matter 'for the passionate praxis of inquiry' (p.40), for the ego to discover in its given object. The presence of these different and opposed senses of 'meaning' in different sections of Husserl's text may be taken as a second index of the inherently contradictory structure of his attempted theoretical history of the sciences.

3.3.3 The birth of scientific physics and its effect in the transformation of philosophy

These preliminary investigations of the meaning of Galileo's 'mathematisation of the world' provide the requisite foundations for what is the true objective of Husserl's text, his investigation of the meaning of modern philosophy. This philosophy is seen as the result of a transformation induced by the new developments in science beginning with Galileo's mathematisation of nature. The effect of the new science is that 'the world and, correlatively, philosophy take on a completely new appearance'. (p.61) This transformation is not to be interpreted as the establishment of a new philosophy alongside existing philosophies but rather as a transformation of the whole theoretical field within which individual philosophies take their place. With the birth of the new physics the philosophical field takes the form of a struggle between transcendentalism and objectivism. The objective that Husserl sets for his historical investigation is to elicit the unity of these opposing philosophical projects and thereby to establish the meaning and the teleology of the historical development of philosophy. In this way, he suggests, it is possible to achieve clarity about ourselves 'who are the bearers of this teleology, who take part in carrying it out through our personal intentions'. (p.70)

In Husserl's view the unity of this development is the unity of the epistimological structure of this subject-object relation.

'The whole transcendental set of problems circles around the relation of *this,* my I – the 'ego' – to what it is at first taken for granted to be − my soul − and, again, around the relation of this ego and my conscious life to the *world* of which I am conscious and whose true being I know through my cognitive structures'. (p.98)

It seems however that the knowledge of this unity must be of a very special and privileged kind. It is a knowledge that cannot be supported by documentary proof:

> 'it is not to be gained through the internal exposition and comparison of the individual systems. Rather, it is a concept acquired by pondering the coherent history of the entire philosophical modern period . . .' (*ibid.*)

Thus the existence and form of the unity of the modern philosophical field is not to be established by means of any rational forms of proof and demonstration, by the marshalling of evidence. It will be necessary to return below to the significance of this appeal to a faculty of judgement at the heart of Husserl's rationalism.

Before doing so we must examine Husserl's account of the effects of the presence of the new science on the structure of the philosophical field of the theory of knowledge. It seems that these effects are of two kinds. The first concerns the transformation of knowledge that is effected within the domain now occupied by the new science. In this connection it must be emphasised that the 'science' in question here is a science recognised and duly accredited by philosophy, that is, its knowledges are recognised as genuine knowledges appearing in the consciousness of an epistemological subject. Thus the knowledge recognised by the empiricist theory of knowledge always appears to be the result of a process of abstraction by some subject. In that respect the philosophical theory of knowledge always involves a specific distortion of the theoretical mode of production of knowledge by the sciences.[17] In Husserl's conception it is such 'sciences', already transmuted so as to conform to his empiricist reading, that appear to transform the structure of the field of knowledges that form the subject matter of the theory of knowledge. Thus, for example, he is able to represent Galileo's physics as the mathematisation of a 'nature' that is given in immediate experience. The mathematisation of this nature is thought to result in a separation between the world that is given in sense experience and the world that is given in scientific knowledge; between the 'merely subjective' sense qualities and an objective nature 'that is itself mathematical; it is given in formulae and can only be interpreted in terms of the formula' (p.58); or between the 'real' elements of experience and the 'merely conventional' constructs built up out of these elements; and so on. These and many other variations are just so many different forms of realisation of the one determinate opposition between the knowledges produced in the sciences and those produced in immediate experience.

Secondly there is the effect of the new science, that is, of what is recognised as such, which functions as an exemplar with regard to the forms of proof and of demonstraton developed within other theoretical domains. This effect consists in the external application of theoretical forms developed in one domain to other domains. Of particular significance for the history of philosophy is the development of a naturalistic psychology (for example Hobbes, Locke) in which relations between mental things are thought to be modelled on the relations established by physics between physical things and in which, for example, forces of attraction and of repulsion may be thought to exist between ideas. Having noted the existence of this examplar effect Husserl observes

'it is something else to ask *how far* the exemplary character of these sciences [mathematics and physics – B.H.] should be stretched and whether the philosophical reflections which were said to be responsible for the new conceptions of the world and of world sciences, were at all adequate.' (p.66)

Thus the philosophical theory of knowledge appears in Husserl's conception to be a field of discursive forms in which the following oppositions are realised:

  (i) subject – object;
  (ii) experience – scientific knowledge;
  (iii) naturalistic/physicalistic domains – other domains.

Any theory of knowledge in the field of modern philosophy must specify what, if anything, occupies each of the notional categories defined by these oppositions. The following brief examination of two cases from Husserl's exposition will show that the first of these oppositions is dominant since the form in which it is realised determines the manner in which the remaining oppositions can appear.[18] It will then be possible to consider Husserl's account of the meaning of modern philosophy and of the teleology of its development.

(a) Descartes

Husserl's examination of Descartes is concerned with 'extracting what was really involved in his thinking and then separating what he became conscious of from what was concealed from him, or rather what was smuggled into his ideas, because of certain things taken for granted'. (p.75) It can be seen here that the opposition noted above between a 'meaning' which exists only as a function of the system of concepts and instruments in which it is embodied and a 'meaning' which exists in and by means of the consciousness of a subject is displaced on to an opposition between a conscious meaning and one that is taken for granted, one which could have been conscious but as it happens was not. Thus the 'meaning' of Descartes philosophy is conceived as one which could have been endowed by a single consciousness.

In Cartesian philosophy the place of the subject appears to be doubly determined. In the first place the method of the radical skeptical *epoché* places the subject in opposition to all possible objects. While the existence of the the latter may be doubted that of the former may not; 'I am necessary as the one carrying it out'. (p.77) Secondly the subject appears as the legitimate subject matter of one of the sciences, that is, of psychology. Thus 'in wonder over this ego, fiirst discovered in the *epoché*, he himself asks what kind of ego it is'. (p.79) The subject that precedes and is opposed to all possible objects is transformed by Descartes himself into an object. For him the soul becomes the 'residuum of a previous abstraction of the pure physical body' (p.80).

Thus the ego appears both to be the condition of existence of all things and to be a thing that can be known like other things. The object pole of the subject-object relation therefore divides into two distinct realms (called substances), matter and thought. It is thought that subjects belong to the latter realm and that they can be known by an objective psychology. Scientific knowledge is then conceived to be the result of an abstraction from the experience of the subject. Knowledge of thought is the result of a corresponding abstraction.

(b) Hume and Kant

Hume's achievement is to reduce to an absurdity the double determination of the subject in Cartesian philosophy. If the knowing subject is also a known object (belonging to psychology) then the theory of knowledge must become a province of psychology. Thus in Husserl's view 'the world in general, nature, . . . and accordingly also objective science are transformed into fictions. To be consistent, we must say: reason . . . is fiction'. (p.87) As soon as a naturalistic psychology includes the rational knowing activity of scientists and philosophers the whole of knowledge becomes completely incomprehensible to empiricism. Hume's arguments appear to demonstrate this bankruptcy of objective knowledge. However, according to Husserl, there is a hidden motif underlying the absurdity of Hume's skepticism. It consists in the 'revelation of a *completely new way* of assessing the objectivity of the world'. (p. 90) Thus, in spite of appearances, Hume's attack has the effect of clearing the way for a transformation of the philosophical problematic with regard to the position of the subject as a knowable object and also to the opposition between the objective knowledge of the sciences and the merely subjective. In the new transformed philosophy made possible by Hume the subject is to become the foundation of all objective and subjective meanings. All thing-like qualities are to be ejected from the transcendental subject.

'nothing human is to be found, neither soul nor psychic life nor real psycho-physical human beings, all this belongs to the 'phenomenon', to the world as constituted pole.' (p. 183)

In this new transformed philosophy the sciences and the objectivity of scientific knowledge must appear to be accomplishments of the life of consciousness.

Kant, unfortunately, fails to respond to the hidden motif of Hume's philosophising and he fails, therefore, to effect the requisite transformation of the philosophical theory of knowledge. In his philosophy the subject-object polarity takes the form of an opposition of the transcendental subject to the transcendent object. While the former can never be an object for scientific knowledge the latter can never be known in itself. In this case the opposition between sense experience and scientific knowledge is realised as follows. Experience or sense data given to the subject are brought together into things through *a priori* forms. Since these forms determine the necessary structure of objective knowledge the necessary form of the world is presented as a construct of the faculties of the subject, of 'pure reason' and of 'pure intuition'. In Husserl's view, then, the critical philosophy of Kant replaces the earlier objectivist treatment of the subject as an object that can be known by a partial insertion of the object into the subject. All knowledge is represented by Kant as a combination of *a priori* forms coming from the subject and of raw experience coming from the 'thing-in-itself'. Things-in-themselves must therefore be inaccessible to objective knowledge. Since, furthermore, the transcendental subject cannot be a phenomenal object it necessarily follows that the activities of subjects in the world cannot be susceptible to naturalistic explanation. Thus history and culture are established as domains for which the new physics and mathematics cannot serve as exemplars. The 'freedom' of the human subject is thereby preserved at the expense of the possibility of objective knowledge. The theoretical consequences of this result have been indicated above and are, in any case, only too well known.

Thus in Husserl's account the emergence of a new science has the effect of imposing a division within the field of knowledge which is the recognised subject matter of the theory of knowledge between the scientific knowledge of an object and the subject's pre- or non-scientific experience of the same object. More generally it imposes a division between scientific and non-scientific forms of knowledge and therefore between domains in which these different forms of knowledge are appropriate. The unity of the different and opposing philosophies, of the varieties of 'physicalistic objectivism' and 'transcendental subjectivism', consists in the fact that they are just so many different forms of realisation of the same essential structure. They are all variants, it is tempting to conclude, of the same fundamental system of concepts. However this temptation is one that must be resisted. Husserl does not represent the unity of modern philosophy as that of a set of fundamental *concepts* but rather as the unity of a meaning and a teleology. If for Husserl modern philosophy has the unity of a structured whole the form of this structuring is that of an expressive totality. It is a totality in which each component part, each individual philosophy, is a *pars totalis,* [19] an expression of the essence of the whole, that is, of its meaning or teleology. Thus, however complicated it may appear, the unity of modern philosophy consists in its expression of the same basic meanings. It is essentially simple.

It is clear that, for Husserl, the meaning of modern philosophy is to be found in the invariant structure of the whole rather than in the consciousness of any philosophical subject. The history of philosophy is represented in the form of a teleology, of the realisation of an historical task. The investigation of the historical becoming of philosophy is necessary in order that we may achieve clarity about ourselves 'who are the bearers of this teleology, who take part in carrying it out through our personal intentions'. (p.70) Since the teleology is realised through the personal intentions of philosophers it must be distinct from those intentions. Its meaning cannot be located at the level of the intentions themselves. It follows that the truth of the teleology cannot be deduced from nor refuted by the personal testimony of philosophers. Nor is it to be gained 'through the internal exposition and comparison of the individual systems'. According to Husserl it can only be acquired by 'pondering the coherent history of the entire philosophical modern period'. (p.98)

What is the meaning of this teleology that can be recognised only by a subject endowed with a suitable faculty of judgement? How does it differ from the meanings of the particular philosophies that are the moments of this teleology? These latter meanings can and indeed must be demonstrated through the analysis of documents, through 'the internal exposition and comparison of the individual systems'. Husserl's own exposition gives several examples of such demonstrations, however sketchy and incomplete they might be. The meaning of the teleology on the other hand involves the suppression of all forms of objectivism through the achievement of a level of reflection in which all opposition of subject to object is dissolved and in which, therefore, all questions of proof and demonstration must vanish. Two forms of this objectivism were identified in the examples discussed above: the double determination of the subject in Descartes and in British empiricism as that which knows and as an object to be known; the partial identification of subject and object in the critical philosophy of Kant and the neo-Kantians. Both forms must lead to the limitation of knowledge and the devaluation of reason. The first implies the bankruptcy of objective knowledge by reducing all categories of knowledge to fictions while the second denies the possibility of objective knowledge of things-in-themselves. These limitations on reason are effects of the different forms in which the subject-object opposition is realised in the different philosophies. Wherever this opposition appears, wherever the subject is indeed confronted by an object that is essentially foreign to it, the conditions of the confrontation determine precisely what may or may not be known. It follows that these conditions themselves must be essentially unknowable, knowledge is turned into a mystery and reason must require the support of something beyond reason. Thus all forms of objectivism must end in a doctrine of the limitation of reason, that is, in irrationalism.

The meaning of modern philosophy, in Husserl's view, and the task which its teleology imposes on the true philosopher is to supersede the limitations on reason imposed by objectivism. It is the defence of reason against all limitation while preserving, in a certain sense, the category of the subject. This radical suppression of objectivism, the task of a genuine philosophy, is to be achieved in the demonstration that all phenomena without exception, that is, everything that is given, are accomplishments of the constituting activity of consciousness. The apparent giveness of an object, then, is an effect of consciousness' mis-recognition of its own activity, that is, of itself. In this problematic of the alienation of the subject the world is represented as a 'universal mental accomplishment', as

> 'the construct of a universal ultimately functioning subjectivity. It belongs essentially to this world-constituting accomplishment that subjectivity objectifies itself as human subjectivity, as an element of the world.' (p.113)

Here the subject-object opposition is preserved and also superseded since it is now contained entirely within consciousness. All the limitations that objectivism imposes on reason and knowledge are therefore overcome in principle. The task that Husserl finds in philosophy, it seems, is to achieve that variant of empiricism which allows the most consistent and thoroughgoing rationalism. This glorification of reason in the recognition of the teleology underlying the history of philosophy in the modern period is not something to be gained by means of exposition and comparison of different systems.

> 'Rather, it is a concept acquired by pondering the coherent history of the entire philosophical modern period.' (p.98)

Strictly speaking each philosopher is a mere functionary of this teleology and expresses its meaning in his work. If, therefore, this functionary is to become conscious of the meaning of the teleology he expresses it can only be because the world-constituting subjectivity chooses to represent itself to itself, that is, to become conscious of itself, through his work.[20] But that condition can never be shown to be satisfied. It can only be asserted by those functionaries who believe it to be the case and denied by those who do not. In the last resort the privileged character of Husserl's final solution to the problem of knowledge rests on an act of faith and in this respect his history of philosophy is merely speculative. In recognising itself as the ideal solution to the problem of knowledge that it poses Husserl's philosophy is no different from those other representatives of modern philosophy that it claims to supersede.

Now this variant of empiricism is quite distinct from that identified above in the discussion of Galileo's mathematisation of the world. In the latter the idealities of, e.g. pure geometry, far from being accomplishments of world-constituting subjectivity, reflect the essential form of the world that is immediately given to the knowing subject. If that world is itself a mental accomplishment, that is to say, not in fact given, what happens to the alleged unconditional objectivity of geometrical idealities and of scientific idealities in general? If everything is an accomplishment there are no unconditional objectivities and the specific difference of the sciences, those producers of unconditional objectivities, collapses. The difficulty that the recognition of the existence of the sciences poses throughout Husserl's work is exemplified in this combination of two contradictory variants of the empiricist problematic, an extreme subjectivism and a scientific objectivism.[21] The suppression of objectivism proposed by the former suppresses also the specific difference of the sciences. The final glorification of reason is achieved at the cost of the denegation of the products of reason.

3.4 Conclusion: from Transcendental Objectivism to a Speculative Philosophy of History

The movement of Husserl's text may be schematically represented as starting from a rigorous transcendental empiricism in which the idealities of the sciences are thought to represent the essential form of the world that is immediately given to the transcendental subject, that is, they represent an 'apodictically general content, invariant throughout all conceivable variation'. (p.377) The absolute givenness of this content is the condition of the objectivity of scientific knowledge. It is not the construct of a freely constituting subjectivity. Rather the subject is confronted with absolute and invariant structures of the given and the objectivity of the sciences consists in the fact that their idealities reflect these invariant given structures. Scientific knowledge is therefore free from all relativity; it is neither time nor culture bound. Cultural differences with regard to scientific knowledge are reducible to differences in the recognition of what is always already there. An immediate difficulty appears in the form of the inescapable circularity of any attempt to demonstrate these assertions concerning the objectivity of the sciences. The epistemological structure of transcendental empiricism must refer these assertions to a higher level subjectivity which relegates the original subject to the level of an object. An analogous difficulty emerges, as Cavaillès has shown, with regard to Husserl's account of the objectivity of logic. In addition certain positions emerge in the course of Husserl's analysis of the meaning and the origins of the sciences which cannot be reconciled with this variant of empiricism.

In the above analysis of Husserl's account of the meanings of pure geometry and of Galileo's mathematisation of the world it was shown that there is a certain tension between two quite different senses of the word 'meaning'. One 'meaning' is represented as originally endowed within the consciousness of an individual subject while the other is thought to be embodied in a determinate system of concepts and of instruments. Husserl attempts to maintain that the latter 'meaning' is reducible to the former so that the user of existing concepts and instruments may be represented as taking their meanings for granted. Thus his examination of Descartes' philosophy seeks to establish both what meanings he was conscious of and himself endowed and what meanings he took for granted and failed to become conscious of. The presumption that, in principle, he could have become conscious of these latter meanings clearly depends on their being originally endowed by some other individual. With Descartes, then, as with Galileo the analysis refers back to some earlier original endowment of meaning. However when we turn to consider such an original endowment in the case of pure geometry we find that it is analysed as a process depending on already existing embodied meanings. The apparent origin is not really an origin at all. In Husserl's text the endowment of a meaning is represented as a process in which a subject labours to transform an existing set of embodied meanings. Such meanings cannot be analysed as originally endowed entirely and without residue within the consciousness of any one individual subject. To be truly original a meaning would need to be endowed in the absence of any pre-existing embodied meanings. But in Husserl's text no individual ego appears to be capable of such a feat. It must be concluded, in effect, that there are no true origins in the process of knowledge described by Husserl. If there are no origins then the analysis of objectivity sketched in the previous paragraph must collapse.

These difficulties in Husserl's theoretical history result from a conception of the existence and the objectivity of the sciences, that is, of a form of production of knowledge, that cannot be reduced to processes occurring in any individual consciousness. All attempts at such reduction either reduce the sciences to the level of ideology, to fictions, or else, as with Kant, save certain sciences at the expense of imposing limitations on others and on reason.

We have seen that the radical suppression of all forms of objectivism that is the task of genuine philosophy is to be achieved in the demonstration that anything that is given is itself an accomplishment of the constituting activity of consciousness. The apparent givenness of an object is an effect of the world-constituting subjectivity's misrecognisation of itself, in other words it is an effect of its alienation. In this conception the structure of the subject-object relation is retained yet also denegated by its insertion within an all-embracing subjectivity. It has been shown above that each individual subject (philosopher, scientist, or whatever) must be conceived as a mere functionary of the alienated spiritual totality which expresses itself in his work. In Husserl's conception one such functionary, namely, the true philosopher, is the means whereby the world-constituting subjectivity becomes conscious of itself. Philosophy is not therefore conceived simply as one mode of expression of world-constituting subjectivity: it is the highest of all possible modes of expression. Philosophy is the self-consciousness of the world. It follows that the history of philosophy must be conceived as the history of the development of the self-awareness of the world. In this conception it must appear also that history consists in the world-constituting subjectivity recalling its own past to consciousness. Thus the practice of history is a philosophical activity and philosophy itself is identical to the philosophy of history, that is, to subjectivity's self-conscious reflection upon its past and its present.

In his apparent attempts to save reason and objective knowledge from the ravages of empricism Husserl's text finally culminates in a fullblown speculative philosophy of history, a position in which the subject-object relation is both preserved and denegated by its insertion within a larger subjectivity. The world then appears to be an ideal or spiritual whole in which the subject and its object are effects of the world-constituting activity of consciousness. Subjects, the world, and the objects within it are all alike effects of the mode of self-alienation of the spiritual whole. Thus the tension noted above between the two 'meanings' vanishes since both are referred to this larger subjectivity within which the object is no longer essentially foreign to the subject.

This final solution to the problem of objectivism posed by the recognition of the existence of the sciences is achieved through the displacement of the subject to the level of an element or expression (these two concepts are now identical [22]) of the whole. Individual subjects (scientists, philosophers, and the rest) now appear to be the bearers of specific functions in the process of development of the world-constituting whole. No longer can they appear to be autonomous consciousnesses busily abstracting knowledges from the world around them. It is this denegation of the epistemological autonomy of subjects that finally legitimises Husserl's mode of analysis of the history of modern philosophy and, in particular, his refusal to reduce the meaning of a text either to its concepts or to the personal testimony of its author. The text is no longer conceived as an expression of the consciousness of its particular author but rather as an expression of the present moment in the movement of the whole. [23] This distinction is easily misrecognised and it may appear arbitrary to other empiricist readings of Husserl. Thus Ricoeur complains that he

> 'systematically sacrifices each philosopher's particular set of problems to a single problem-set which is termed the 'true' problem, the 'hidden' problem, ... the aspects of a philosopher which do not lend themselves to this unifying reading of history are omitted.' (Ricoeur, 1967, p.170)

This complaint is registered in the name of the importance of 'the character peculiar to each philosopher' (*ibid.*), that is to say, precisely in the name of the epistemological autonomy of the individual creative subject that Husserl's analysis has forced him to reject. Ricoeur's complaint is addressed to what is in fact a necessary effect of the concepts at work in Husserl's text.

At the same time Husserl's solution involves him in the systematic denegation of all origins. We have seen that neither Galileo's physics nor Descartes' philosophy represent any true origin. Both refer back to the origin of the science of pure geometry but that origin too has its conditions of existence in a pre-existing process. Since Husserl conceives of origins as internal to the consciousnesses of individual subjects it is clear that the denegation of all origins is the necessary correlate of his displacement of the subject.

In these respects, in its denegation of origins and in its displacement of the subject, Husserl's conception of history corresponds to what Althusser, in another context, has called a process without a subject, [24] a process that is neither initiated by nor governed by the consciousness of a subject. For Husserl subjects, their consciousnesses and activities, are so many subordinated elements in the world-historical process of the self-realisation of consciousness. What remains of the empiricist category of the subject in this process is the particular form of unity of the ideal or spiritual totality. It is a unity of meanings in which each component part of the whole is an expression or embodiment of one essential meaning. Thus the movement of world-constituting subjectivity is governed by the mode of expressive, teleological causality. In this way Husserl's text reproduces the essential structures of those other great speculative system builders of modern philosophy, Leibniz and Hegel.

In spite of their apparent glorification of reason these speculative systems can only result in a denegation of the sciences. All things, the objectivity of things, all human qualities, are conceived as accomplishments of subjectivity. The subject-object relation of the empiricist conception of knowledge then becomes a relation internal to subjectivity itself, a relation between one of its constructs and another. The positive sciences provide a knowledge of objects as already constituted while ignoring their conditions of existence as expressions of the alienated structure of the whole. Scientific knowledge must therefore be conceived as necessarily distorting its object and as misrecognising the real nature of the world. In this speculative philosophy of Husserl subject, object, and knowledge of the object are all conceived as just so many expressions of the present moment in the development of the alienated process of world constituting subjectivity. Transcendental inquiry is itself conceived as a further moment in this process. Thus in the discussions of psychology in part 111B of the *Crisis* we are informed that

transcendental inquiry is itself a world-historical process insofar as it enlarges the history of the constitution of the world, not only by adding a new science to it but also by enlarging the content of the world in every respect; everything mundane has its transcendental correlates, and every new revelation of the latter adds, for the investigator of man, the psychologist, new determinations of man and the world. (p.264)[25]

The effect of conceiving the totality as being governed by the mode of expressive causality is that knowledge, whether or not it is called objective, is reduced to a mere expression of the present state of the whole. In particular, then, any knowledge which represents its object as having a determinate structure and any analysis of the possible future states of that object in determinate conditions is nothing more than an expression of the present state of alienation of the whole. Hence, for example, there can be no rational Husserlian politics since the conditions for the determination of rational action to produce a determinate specific effect cannot be realised within the expressive totality. Similarly it is clear that there can be no Husserlian science, in particular, no science of history, which produces in its theories and its objects a determinate theoretical knowledge of the real. In the last analysis Husserl's speculative philosophy resolves for empiricism the problem of objectivism posed by the production in the sciences of objective knowledge of the real by eliminating the cause of all the trouble, that is, by the traditional idealist denial of the existence of any reality independent of subjective activity.

To conclude, Husserl's rigorous transcendental empiricism attempts to save the objectivity of the sciences from the theoretical ravages of all forms of psychologistic empiricism. However the cost of this anti-psychologism is an epistemology that can cope neither with the history of the sciences and philosophy nor, as Cavaillès has shown, with the objectivity of logic and mathematics. Husserl resolves these problems by collapsing into a speculative philosophy of history which with its mode of expressive causality and the consequent necessary denegation of the sciences is the last theoretical refuge of the empiricist category of the subject.

4. Positivism: Fact and Theory

Non-subjectivist methodology in the social sciences is dominated by systematic empiricism and by the self-styled critical rationalism of Karl Popper and his acolytes. These positions are derived from more or less sophisticated forms of positivist epistemology, from more or less elaborated versions of the thesis that, in the last resort, all knowledge is reducible to the facts of experience and that all claims to knowledge must be measured against those facts. In this chapter I outline the basic features of positivist epistemology, indicate something of the range of epistemological positions that may be taken up within positivism, and, finally, demonstrate the inescapable circularity and ultimate dogmatism of even the most sophisticated positivist epistemology. Popper's position is discussed in a later chapter. We shall see that it is neither rational nor critical and that, despite its extravagant pretensions, its conception of testing denegates the conditions of rigorous theoretical argument and debate. The most significant varieties of systematic empiricism, on the other hand, have already been the subject of a devastating and most effective critique by David and Judith Willer in *Systematic Empiricism: critique of a pseudo-science*. Their argument involves first an internal critique of empiricist methodologial doctrines to show that, even in terms of empiricist epistemology, these doctrines have no coherent foundation, and, secondly, an epistemological argument to establish that empiricism and science are quite distinct forms of knowledge. I argue in chapter 7 that their epistemology merely counterposes a complex and sophisticated positivistic empiricism to the crude and simplistic versions current in the social sciences. Nevertheless, the weakness of the Willers' own epistemology in no way detracts from the effectiveness of their thorough and systematic demolition of many of the dominant positivistic methodological doctrines. In that respect their work cannot be too highly recommended and I shall not attempt to repeat their arguments here. My critique of *Systematic Empiricism* in chapter 7 is concerned exclusively with their epistemology, in particular, with their contrast between science and empiricism as distinct forms of knowledge which, by representing empiricism as a real process, falls into the fundamental problems of the positivist conception of knowledge.

4.1 Positivist Epistemology [1]

The term 'positivism' is used in a number of senses in the social sciences and in philosophy. In this book it is used to refer to a distinctive type of epistemology, a theory of the possible forms and conditions of knowledge, that is perhaps best characterised by its adherence to a fundamental doctrine of phenomenalism. This doctrine asserts that we can know reality only on the basis of experience and, further, that the object of knowledge can only be what is given or what can be given in experience. There is no real difference between the object of knowledge and the phenomena of experience. Positivism is thus concerned not only to assert the claims of experience as the ultimate foundation of human knowledge but also to deny the possibility of knowledge of supersensible objects, that is, of objects whose very definition precludes their being given in sensory experience. For positivism, then, there can be no essences lying beyond the realm of phenomena and no 'ideal' objects corresponding to universal terms such as square, circle, triangle, and so on; there are particular triangles but there is no essence of triangle of which each particular triangle is a phenomenal realization. To admit even the possibility of such an object is to admit the possibility of objects of knowledge that do lie beyond the realm of sensible phenomena. But if there are no such objects of knowledge then there can be no meaningful discourse concerning them. Positivism is thus a form of subjective idealism; that is, it is a doctrine according to which the objective world cannot be regarded as existing independently of man's cognitive activity and means of cognition. Metaphysics, which does lay claim to a knowledge of objects beyond the realm of sensible phenomena, is therefore meaningless. The claim that the world consists of 'spirits' or 'matter in motion' would be meaningless on this view since 'matter' or 'spirit' would then be something different from and underlying the phenomena of experience. Similarly value judgements and normative statements would not count as knowledge since 'justice', 'goodness', etc., are not phenomena of experience, nor, for that matter, is 'truth'.

Positivism is completely opposed to the epistemological bases of the subjectivist methodologies examined in the preceeding chapters. The force and the significance of that opposition can be seen if we consider the first section of the Introduction to Kant's *Critique of Pure Reason.* Kant does not doubt that all our knowledge begins with experience:

> 'But though all our knowledge begins with experience, it does not follow that it all arises out of experience. For it may well be that even our empirical knowledge is made up of what we receive through impressions and of what our own faculty of knowledge (sensible impressions serving merely as the occasion) supplies from itself. If our faculty of knowledge makes any such addition, it may be that we are not in a position to distinguish it from the raw material, until with long practice of attention we have become skilled in separating it.
>
> This, then, is a question which at least calls for closer examination, and does not allow of any off-hand answer:– whether there is any knowledge that is thus independent of experience and even of all impressions of the senses. Such knowledge is called *a priori*, and distinguished from the *empirical*, which has its sources *a posteriori*, that is, in experience' (*Critique of Pure Reason,* B, pp. 1–2)

Positivism provides precisely such an 'off-hand answer' to Kant's question, namely, that there can be no knowledge that is independent of experience. Kant's answer, namely, that a pure *a priori* knowledge is indeed possible, requires the existence both of knowledge that does not depend on experience and of objects that do not belong to the realm of sensible phenomena and it admits the possibility of rational and meaningful discourse concerning at least some such objects. The neo-Kantian, subjectivist, conceptions of the cultural and historical sciences are predicated on Kant's answer.[2] They presuppose a 'knowledge' of man as a supersensible (i.e. extra-phenomenal) object whose meanings, actions, etc., receive phenomenal expression in the objects investigated in the cultural and historical sciences. The neo-Kantian sciences of culture and of history are therefore predicated on a theoretical position that is strictly precluded by positivist epistemology.

But the positivist repudiation of all objects that in principle cannot be given in sensory experience has a further and in many respects a more significant implication. I cannot discuss Kant's conception of knowledge here but it should be clear even from the passage cited here that the notion of *a priori* knowledge is dependent on a definite conception of the conditions of obtaining knowledge on the basis of experience, namely, that 'empirical knowledge is made up of what we receive through impressions and of what our own faculty of knowledge supplies from itself'. Knowledge of the conditions of obtaining knowledge allows one to determine which forms of knowledge are in fact possible and what constraints any claim to valid knowledge should conform to. Kant's conception of these conditions allows him to conclude that a pure *a priori* knowledge is indeed possible and it allows him, further, to castigate the bulk of 'pre-critical' metaphysics for failing to respect the constraints on such a knowledge.

Now, any doctrine of the formation of knowledge on the basis of experience would seem to depend on some conception of the conditions in which experience takes place and of the processes in which knowledge is formed out of experience. We shall see that positivist epistemology is certainly no exception. Yet the conditions in which experience takes place can hardly be conceived as given in experience itself. The peculiar and distinctive feature of positivist epistemology is therefore this: that while it is logically dependent on a conception of the conditions in which knowledge is produced it must insist that those conditions cannot be an object of knowledge and, in consequence, that there can be no rational discourse concerning those conditions. Positivism's insistence that knowledge must be restricted to what is or may be given in experience must therefore take the form of a dogmatism; it is a conclusion that can be supported by no meaningful argument.[3] I return to this point in a later section. For the present it is sufficient to note that positivist epistemology does depend on a conception of the conditions in which knowledge takes place but that it prefers not to talk about them.

4.2 A Positivist Methodology: J. S. Mill's *A System of Logic*

If epistemology involves a definite conception of the possible forms and conditions of knowledge than methodology goes further and attempts to elaborate a definite system of rules and protocols for the formation of knowledge in general and of scientific knowledge in particular. A methodology is positivist to the extent that its rules and protocols are derived from and in conformity with positivist epistemology. Propositions that are methodological in this sense may be found in the works of any positivist philosopher but few have troubled to elaborate a systematic methodology. One of the earliest and still perhaps the most comprehensive of all systematic positivist methodologies is elaborated in J. S. Mill's *A System of Logic*. Mill's 'logic' concerns the rules of valid or correct reasoning and his book contains a lengthy and systematic exposition of the canons of experimental inquiry, that is, of the methods of the empirical sciences. The following brief examination of Mill's logic will serve to highlight some of the fundamental problems of positivist epistemology and methodology.[4]

Mill's methods of experimental inquiry are derived from a definite conception of the regularity of nature and from a 'law of universal causation'.

> 'The course of nature in general is constant, because the course of each of the various phenomena that compose it is so. A certain fact invariably occurs whenever certain circumstances are present, and does not occur when they are absent; the like is true of another fact; and so on. From these separate threads of connection between parts of the great whole which we term nature a general tissue of connection unavoidably weaves itself, by which the whole is held together. If A is always accompanied by D, B by E, and C by F, it follows that AB is accompanied by DE, AC by DF, BC by EF, and finally ABC by DEF; and thus the general character of regularity is produced, which, along with and in the midst of infinite diversity, pervades all nature' (p.206)

The law of universal causation affirms that every phenomenon which has a beginning has a cause.[5] That 'law' and the conception of the regularity of nature are arrived at by induction. The regularity of nature consists in the coexistence of an infinity of separate uniformities called 'laws of nature'. The objective of the empirical sciences is to discover these laws by identifying and sorting uniformities such as 'A is always followed by D'. Mill gives the following as examples:

> 'the law that air has weight, the law that pressure on a fluid is propagated equally in all directions, and the law that pressure in one direction, not opposed by equal pressure in the contrary direction, produces motion, which does not cease until equilibrium is restored.' (*ibid.*) [6]

In Mill's view the so-called deductive sciences, logic and pure mathematics, are also based on experience. Thus the 'necessity' that is sometimes attributed to logical or mathematical propositions is an illusion for the deductive axioms referred to in logical or mathematical reasoning are really the products of experience. The ubiquity of experience in both the experimental and the deductive sciences suggests a certain basic continuity between the methods of the sciences and those of everyday life. This point is given a concise formulation in Mill's table of contents: 'The Logic of Science is also that of business and life'.

But what are phenomena? The law of universal causation and the doctrine of the uniformity of nature are both expressed in terms of phenomena. Unless we know exactly what defines a phenomenon we can hardly proceed to a serious investigation of the laws of nature. Mill's account, such as it is, is given in Book III, chapter xiv, 'Of the Limits to the Explanation of the Laws of Nature and of Hypotheses':

> 'It is therefore useful to remark that the ultimate Laws of Nature cannot possibly be less numerous than *the distinguishable sensations or other feelings of our nature* – those, I mean, which are distinguishable from one another in quality, and not merely in quantity or degree. For example, since there is a phenomen *sui generis* called colour, which *our consciousness testifies to be not a particular degree of some other phenomenon,* as heat or odour, or motion, but intrinsically unlike all others, it follows that there are ultimate laws of colour; ... The ideal limit, therefore, of the explanation of natural phenomena ... would be to show that *each distinguishable variety of our sensations, or other states of consciousness,* has only one sort of cause; that, for example, whenever we perceive a white colour, there is some condition or set of conditions which is always present, and the presence of which always produces in us that sensation' (pp. 318–9 – emphasis added)

In the last analysis, then, phenomena are to be conceived as distinguishable sensations or states of consciousness or else distinguishable combinations of these. 'Laws of Nature' therefore describe relations which obtain between one state of consciousness and another. Yet those 'laws' discussed by Mill do not at first sight appear to relate states of consciousness to each other at all. Consider the examples cited above:

> 'the law that air has weight, the law that pressure on a fluid is propagated equally in all directions, . . .'

To which distinguishable states of consciousness or sensations do those laws refer? How is the concept of 'pressure on a fluid' to be translated into a rigorous statement of determinate sensations and states of consciousness? Unless we can answer such questions we remain confronted by the awful possibility that 'pressure on a fluid' may not be a properly scientific concept at all, that it may not be reducible without residue to the contents of experience, in short, that it may be metaphysical and our exemplary 'law of nature' the product of a metaphysical presupposition.

Now, while these problems clearly arise out of Mill's attempt to conceive of scientific discourse as reducible to the contents of experience it can hardly be claimed that he makes any serious attempt to deal with them. For that we must consult more recent positivist philosophers. Some examples of attempts to achieve a rigorous positivist conception of the phenomena of experience and of the relation between those phenomena and scientific concepts are considered below. If a relatively simple concept such as 'pressure on a fluid' poses problems for Mill's position the problem faced by later positivist philosophy seems even more serious. Contemporary scientific theories appear to arrive at knowledge of electromagnetic fields, electrons, protons, the geometrical structure of relativistic space-time continua, and other such entities which can hardly be considered to be objects of direct experience. If it is not to dismiss those sciences as meaningless rubbish, positivism must maintain that assertions referring to objects inaccessible to immediate perception only appear to refer to objects that transcend experience. In effect we shall see that it has to maintain that these assertions are only a complex shorthand which, correctly interpreted, translate into, or at least make possible, statements referring to sensible phenomena. For positivism, therefore, a great deal turns on the precise manner in which the relation between theoretical shorthand and observational phenomena is conceived.

To return to Mill's 'Logic of Science' it is clear that his 'Four Methods of Experimental Inquiry', namely, the methods of agreement, difference, joint agreement and difference and the method of residues (there is in fact a fifth method, concomitant variation), are intended to uncover Laws of Nature, the regularities which are supposed to pervade the infinite diversity of nature. The methods are sorting procedures designed to elicit laws by means of systematic observation or, at least, to test hypotheses concerning such laws. For example, Mill's first canon states:

'If two or more instances of the phenomenon under investigation have only one circumstance in common, the circumstance in which alone all the instances agree is the cause (or effect) of the given phenomenon' (p.255)

The method of agreement follows directly from the doctrine of the uniformity of nature. If nature were not in fact pervaded by regularities such that AB is accompanied by DE, AC by DF, and so on this method and all of the others would be entirely worthless.

It is perhaps unfortunate for Mill's 'Logic' that if nature were indeed regular and governed by the law of universal causation then its 'infinite diversity', which Mill also affirms, must render the operation of his methods of experimental inquiry practically impossible. For example, the method of agreement evidently requires a complete listing of all the circumstances of each instance of the phenomenon under investigation; otherwise it would be impossible to identify one circumstance as the cause (or effect) of the phenomenon in question. No such complete listing is even conceivable except in a finite universe that is composed of a small number of distinct parts. Even as little as a few million parts would render all four or five methods of inquiry practically inoperable. In an infinite, or even just a large, universe Mill's methods of inquiry would be impossible to operate.

In practice, of course, neither Mill nor the many social scientists who use his own or related sorting procedures to investigate their supposed regularities are at all disturbed by mere logical difficulties of this kind. But Mill himself is not totally unaware of the problem here for he comes close to citing it in his argument that the social sciences can never be *exact*. First, the use of the canons of proof in the social sciences is never entirely satisfactory since, although we may be able to identify the major causes in operation it is difficult to eliminate the effects of minor causes. A second argument is more interesting:

> 'But the impressions and actions of human beings are not solely the result of their present circumstances, but the joint result of those circumstances and of the characters of the individuals; and *the agencies which determine human character are so numerous and diversified,* (nothing which has happened to the person throughout life being without its portion of influence), that in the aggregate they are never in any two cases exactly similar. Hence even if our science of human nature were theoretically perfect, that is, if we could calculate any character as we can calculate the orbit of any planet, *from given data* [Mill's emphasis]; still, *as the data are never all given, nor ever precisely alike in different cases, we could neither make positive predictions, nor lay down universal propositions'* (p.554 emphasis added)

If we ignore the element of special pleading in favour of the distinctive character of the social sciences it is clear that the difficulty Mill refers to is in no way peculiar to any group of sciences and, further, that it must render the attainment of theoretical perfection in any science by the application of Mill's methods practically impossible. It is only because he already knows what circumstances are pertinent to each particular science – he does not tell us how – that Mill can imagine that his canons of proof have any practical or logical effectivity.

More generally, for Mill's methods to be rendered practicable it would be sufficient simply to select for consideration only those circumstances already known or considered likely to be pertinent to the phenomenon in question. Once it has been established that all but a finite class of circumstances are not pertinent then Mill's methods can be relied on to reveal nature's regularities – on the assumption that nature is indeed pervaded by them. Thus the practicability of viability of Mill's and related methods must presuppose a knowledge that can only be established in some other fashion, *viz.,* the knowledge that only certain types of phenomena need be considered pertinent. The validity of those methods must therefore presuppose the validity of some quite different form of knowledge. Thus, if nature is regular as Mill supposes then his methods are totally impracticable and can never be relied on to produce valid knowledge. If, on the other hand, they are made practicable they must become logically bankrupt since their practicability can only depend on the validity of a knowledge gained by other means, a knowledge which Mill's epistemology would rule out of court.

Finally, let us consider the status of the law of universal causation and of our belief in the uniformity of nature. In Mill's view they are based on induction:

> 'the belief we entertain in the universality, throughout nature, of the law of cause and effect, is itself an instance of induction, and by no means one of the earliest which any of us, or which mankind in general can have made. We arrive at this universal generalisation from many laws of inferior generality. We should never have had the notion of causation (in the philosophical meaning of the term) as a condition of all phenomena, unless many cases of causation, or, in other words, many partial uniformities of sequence, had previously become familiar. The more obvious of the particular uniformities suggest, and give evidence of, the general uniformity, and the general uniformity, once established, enables us to prove the remainder of the particular uniformities of which it is made up. As, however, all rigorous processes of induction presuppose the general uniformity, our knowledge of the particular uniformities from which it was first inferred was not, of course, derived from rigorous induction, but from the loose and uncertain mode of induction *per enumerationem simplicem;* and the law of universal causation, being collected from results so obtained, cannot itself rest on any better foundation' (pp.371–2)

Is it necessary to comment on the implications of this extra-ordinary passage? Mill's inability to distinguish between the question of the origin of our 'belief . . . in the universality . . . of the law of cause and effect' and the question of its *validity* (logically presupposed by his methods of experimental inquiry) is well known; and he does not explain how it is possible for us to be familiar with 'many cases of causation' in the absence of 'the notion of causation'. For the rest it is sufficient to repeat the Willers' caustic remark:

> 'To justify individual inductions, Mill argued from an induction based on them. He justified induction by induction.' (*Systematic Empiricism,* p.35)

4.3 The Elements of Experience

In Mill's view the ultimate limits to the laws of nature are determined by the distinguishable 'sensations or other feelings of our nature' and again by 'sensations, or other states of consciousness' (p.318). In principle, therefore, all phenomena are conceived as being reducible to sensations, states of consciousness, or combinations of these. Any so-called phenomenon that is not so reducible in fact cannot be given in experience, it is not a phenomenon at all. To treat of such 'phenomena' in the sciences is thus to deal with objects that are not definable in terms of the elements of experience. Statements or 'laws' concerning such objects are, if not strictly meaningless, certainly less than completely meaningful. If we are to establish laws of nature it is necessary to expunge such meaningless or metaphysical elements from the realm of scientific discourse. There is, then, in Mill's conception of the laws of nature an implicit programme of reduction of all phenomena to the irreducible elements of experience. That programme is not systematically elaborated by Mill and he does not attempt a rigorous specification of how precisely the irreducible elements of experience are to be conceived. I discuss the problems of reduction in the following section. As for the irreducible elements of experience, there can be no question here of surveying the variety of more or less sophisticated conceptions advanced by different positivist philosophers. For the purposes of the present argument it is sufficient to consider two relatively systematic positivist epistemologies in order to establish the inescapable dependence of positivist epistemology on a metaphysical conception of the world that is both surreptitious and meaningless on any strict positivist criterion.

Consider first the position of Ernst Mach, a leading physicist of the late nineteenth century and one of the most significant figures in the development of contemporary positivist thought. [7] Mach's epistemology is most clearly set out in *The Analysis of Sensations* whose tone is set in the first chapter, 'Introductory Remarks: Antimetaphysical'. That book sets out to eradicate all metaphysical notions by means of a conception of the basic elements of experience that appears to dissolve the question of the 'existential' status of experienced reality. All objects, physical or psychological, may be broken down into complexes of elements (sensations), ultimate component parts that cannot be further subdivided. Science is to be concerned with relations between these elements.

For example, let *A,B,C,* ... denote 'those complexes of colors, sounds, and so forth, commonly called bodies'; *K,L,M,* ... 'the complex known as our body'; and α,β,γ, 'the complex composed of volitions, memory-images, and the rest' (p.9). Now these apparent unities such as 'body', 'ego', etc.,

> 'are only makeshifts, designed for provisional orientation and for definite practical ends (so that we may take hold of bodies, protect ourselves against pain, and so forth)' (p.13)

However, in advanced scientific investigation it is necessary to dispense with these makeshift unities:

> 'The antithesis between ego and world, between sensation (appearance) and thing, then vanishes, and we have simply to deal with the connection of the elements $\alpha,\beta,\gamma\ldots A,B,C,\ldots K,L,M,\ldots$ of which this antithesis was only a partially appropriate and imperfect expression' (p.14)

For Mach there are only these elements. While it may be *practically* convenient to group them together into relatively permanent unities it is a *theoretical* error to treat those unities as real physical or psychological entities which cause sensations in us.

> 'We see an object having a point *S*. If we touch *S*, that is, bring it into connexion with our body, we receive a prick. We can see *S*, without feeling the prick. But as soon as we feel the prick we find *S* on the skin. The visible point, therefore, is a permanent nucleus, to which the prick is annexed, according to circumstances, as something accidental. From the frequency of analogous circumstances we ultimately accustom ourselves to regard all properties of bodies as "effects" proceeding from permanent nuclei and conveyed to the ego through the medium of the body; which effects we call sensations. By this operation, however, these nuclei are deprived of their entire sensory content, and converted into mere mental symbols. The assertion, then, is correct that *the world consists only of our sensations. In which case we have knowledge only of sensations,* and the assumption of the nuclei referred to, or of a reciprocal action between them, from which sensations proceed, turns out to be quite idle and superfluous. Such a view can only suit with a half-hearted realism or a half-hearted philosophical criticism' (p.12, emphasis added)

Sensations are not a means to knowledge of something else; they are the irreducible elements of the world. To postulate anything beyond sensations and causing them is to lapse into metaphysics, into a realm of pseudo-problems. Similarly, there is no such thing as an 'I' or 'ego' that receives sensations.

> 'The primary fact is not the ego, but the elements (sensations) . . . The elements constitute the I. *I* have the sensation green, signifies that the element green occurs in a certain given complex of other elements (sensations, memories). When *I* cease to have the sensation green, when *I* die, then the elements no longer occur in the ordinary familiar association. That is all.' (pp.23–4)

There exists nothing other than sensations and the whole of science consists of the analysis of the various relations that obtain between them. Physics deals with one kind of relation and psychology with another but both, in the final analysis, deal with the same fundamental elements.

Unfortunately the effect of reducing the observer and what he observes into the plane of sensations is to produce a conception of the world as a network of sensations, a conception that can only be regarded as metaphysical in Mach's own sense of the term. Two points here are absolutely crucial. First, consider the notion of relatively stable complexes such as 'ego', 'body', 'object'. If there is no 'I' or 'ego' to observe those complexes but only the elements themselves then how is the existence, let alone the relative stability over time, of complexes to be established? How is it possible for certain complexes to be recognised and admitted to the corpus of knowledge, however 'makeshift' or 'provisional' such knowledge may be? Mach himself answers a rather different question, namely, why are certain particular types of complex delimited and others not?

> 'The delimitation of the ego, therefore, is instinctively effected, is rendered familiar, and possibly becomes fixed through heredity. Owing to their high practical importance, not only for the individual, but for the entire species, the composites 'ego' and 'body' instinctively make good their claims, and assert themselves with elementary force' (p.23)

Here complexes are delimited because of their 'practical importance' – presumably for certain complexes – and that delimitation is effected through the agency of instinct and heredity operating, no doubt, on the elements themselves. It is clear that this account supposes some distinct entity, affected by practical considerations and instinct and formed by heredity, which does receive and organise elements into complexes. But, on Mach's own account there are only the elements themselves. We must therefore conclude that the formation and recognition of complexes requires that certain complexes are endowed with a wondrous capacity both to recognise themselves and to recognise other complexes. That 'capacity' is clearly a metaphysical notion since it is a property of a complex of elements that is not an element itself.

Secondly, Mach's position requires that elements occur in various combinations: 'when *I* die, then the elements *no longer occur in the ordinary familiar association'* (pp.23–4). But the elements themselves persist! The content of the ego is not confined to the individual. Indeed:

> 'Contents of consciousness that are of universal significance break through these limits of the individual, and, attached of course to individuals again, can enjoy a continued existence of an impersonal, superpersonal kind, independently of the personality by means of which they were developed' (*ibid.*)

The religious and spiritualist character of this position is evident. We must learn to 'renounce *individual* mortality' (p.25 – emphasis added) in the name of the immortality of the elements. At other points in the text (e.g. pp.32–6) Mach's exposition clearly requires that the same physical bodies (A,B,C, etc.,) are associated with different human bodies (K,L,M, . . .) and egos ($\alpha,\beta,\gamma, . . .$). The same sensations are experienced by different human observers. In both cases the essential problem remains the same, namely, that if Mach is to avoid an overt and systematic solipsism he must maintain that the same elements may persist from one person to another. Elements that are defined at the level of individual experience are required to possess a supra-individual, intersubjective character that, since it cannot be given in individual experience, can only be regarded as metaphysical. Thus Mach's antimetaphysical reduction of the world to sensations requires a surreptitious metaphysical grounding in an intersubjective domain of experience.

A further and equally fundamental problem for Mach's position arises from the fact that knowledge, whether scientific or 'only makeshift', consists not of complexes of elements but of statements.

Not only must complexes manifest themselves, they must also be described. The problem of the relation between language and the alleged elements of experience is not considered by Mach, but it is taken up in various forms in more recent positivist philosophy. Early logical positivism maintained that it is not so much the content of experience (e.g. the elements) that is represented in knowledge but the formal structure or relations of the given. Knowledge as such does not begin until we recognise relations of similarity or dissimilarity between experiences. Thus the essence of, say, 'red' lies not in the experience itself but in its unique set of relations to other qualities.

The most radical and systematic elaboration of this conception is given in Carnap's *The Logical Structure of the World*.[8] Carnap attempts to show that all concepts of empirical science can be constructed by purely logical operations on a single primitive relation and the primitive elements between which it holds. The relation and the elements are logically irreducible and indefinable; they can only be shown or pointed to. The primitive elements are total momentary experiences, cross-sections of consciousness[9] and the primitive relation that holds between them is 'remembrance of similarity'. Thus, it is argued, any proposition of the empirical sciences can be completely translated into a complex list of propositions which express the relational structure of the given as represented in the fundamental relation and elements. Knowledge expresses the structure of the given and points to its content. The propositions of the empirical sciences express the formal structure and not the content of the given. The formal sciences (logic, pure mathematics), in contrast to Mill's conception, have no empirical significance whatever and their propositions are tautologies, they say nothing.

Knowledge therefore consists in communicable statements and propositions in a language whose primary function is to express the structure of the given. Language, or at least its elementary propositions, express the structure of the world by virtue of a structural similarity between propositions and given facts. It is a mirror of the world. The truth or falsity of an elementary proposition is ascertained by comparing it with the given facts. The truth or falsity of more complex propositions may be ascertained by reference to that of the elementary propositions into which it translates. Knowledge communicates the structure of the given but is based upon the content since its elementary propositions are definable only through pointing to the content.[10]

However, while logical positivism has at least the merit of recognising a problem in the relation it proposes between knowledge statements and the content of the given it cannot avoid its dependence on a surreptitious metaphysics. First, the content of the given can hardly be relied upon to point to itself nor can it judge its own similarity to or its difference from the content of some other given. Each act of pointing to or judging similarity is thus a function of something that is not itself a given content of experience. That entity, since it is not in principle reducible to the immediately given, cannot be the subject of meaningful empirical discourse. It is logically presupposed but it cannot be discussed except in metaphysics – which is meaningless. It should be emphasised that the problem here does not concern the status of 'other minds' or of psychological concepts within Carnap's programme.[11] Even if it were possible to construct concepts of 'minds', one's own or others, on the basis of experience there could still be no warrant in the content of the given for identifying such constructs with what is logically presupposed in the notions of 'pointing to' the content of experience. The content of what is pointed to can hardly contain the pointer and the act of pointing. Thus, for logical positivism to identify the construct of 'mind' or 'ego' with what has experiences is to go beyond the given into metaphysics. Furthermore, if language does communicate the structure of the given then that structure must be the same for all users of the language. If it were not the same then language could communicate nothing. Once again, the antimetaphysical programme of reduction of the world to the content of immediate experience requires a surreptitious metaphysical grounding in an intersubjective realm of experience. In its conception of the relation between language and the world logical positivism clearly presupposes a definite conception of the conditions in which experience takes place and of the processes in which knowledge is formed out of experience but those conditions and processes cannot themselves be the object of empirical knowledge or of meaningful discourse.[12] Like all positivism, logical positivism represents a dogmatism, a conclusion unsupported by rational argument.

Finally, it should be clear that logical positivism does avoid the patent solipsistic tendencies of Mach's position with its conception of knowledge as communicable. Knowledge is not reducible to the experience of any one human subject. But the relation between the content of the given and the content of knowledge, even of its elementary propositions, remains problematic. Since the content of the given can only be pointed to there is an irreducible discrepancy between proposition and the given itself. How, for example, is it possible to establish that an elementary proposition does indeed correspond to the given facts? Does the structure of the given determine a unique totality of true elementary propositions? Conventionalism is a variant of positivist epistemology that denies the existence of elementary propositions in the sense of logical positivism. [13] Descriptions, even elementary descriptions, always have a certain conventional character. For example, it may be argued that the geometrical structure of space is a function of the measuring techniques we use to determine it and that the choice of elementary geometrical terms is to some extent a matter of agreement among scientists. I will discuss the effects of the conventionalist rejection of elementary propositions in connection with Popper's 'critical rationalism' but one consequence of conventionalism is worth noting in the present context. If all empirical knowledge is constituted in part by convention among scientists then there can be no question of identifying the structure of the real with the structure of our empirical knowledge. This fact induces a crucial modification of the anti-metaphysical stance adopted by other varieties of positivist epistemology since, in explicitly recognising a discrepancy between the world and our empirical knowledge of it, conventionalism opens a space for metaphysical discourse and for religion. [14] Popper has always taken a tolerant view of metaphysics: it is not science but it may well be meaningful and it may even be necessary for the development of science.

4.4 Theory and the Phenomena of Experience

The most elementary solution to the problem of the relation between scientific concepts and the phenomena of experience is to treat the former as strictly definable in terms of the latter. That, in effect, is Mill's solution when he considers the fundamental laws of nature as pertaining to the distinguishable sensations and states of consciousness. For Mill all legitimate scientific propositions are either strictly translatable into a finite conjunction of statements of actual or possible observations or else they are universal generalisations from such statements. Now, the latter, for example, the proposition 'All Ravens are Black', cannot be translated into any finite number of observation statements since it refers to *all* ravens and not to any finite number of them. Such universal statements are called 'laws of nature' and they are to be established by means of the canons of experimental inquiry discussed above. Thus all scientific terms and propositons are strictly definable in observation terms and propositions coupled in certain cases with the universal quantifier. In this view there is a scientific method and it consists in the application of various sorting devices to the phenomena of experience. This crude and simplistic conception of science which admits no systematic distinction between concept and observation still dominates positivist methodology in the social sciences. [15]

Carnap's book, *The Logical Structure of the World,* represents one of the first attempts to establish on a systematic basis the strict definability of scientific concepts in terms of elementary propositions which, as we have seen, describe the essential structure of the given. Those elementary propositions refer to 'cross-sections of consciousness' and 'remembrance of similarity' but Carnap maintained that propositions formulated in a 'physical object language' were methodologically equivalent in the sense that the propositions of one kind were definable in terms of propositions of the other. Thus the physical object language could be treated as the basic observation language and the criterion for legitimacy of scientific terms and propositions could be formulated in relation to that language. All legitimate scientific concepts are therefore definable in 'physicalistic' terms. In this sense all empirical discourse, including psychology, may be interpreted as pertaining to observable features of physical objects.

Now, it is an easy matter to show that numerous concepts of the sciences or other empirical discourse cannot be given strict definition in any 'physicalistic' or 'sensationalistic' observation language. In 'Testability and Meaning' (1936) Carnap argued that an important class of predicates indispensible to empirical science cannot be explicitly defined in observation terms. For example, the disposition predicate 'soluble in water' may be used to assert that a given class of objects, say, lumps of sugar, will, as a matter of general law, respond to specific conditions in a certain characteristic manner — sugar will dissolve in water. Thus the attribution of a disposition to a given object is inextricably bound up with the assertion of a general law, e.g. that sugar dissolves in water. Neither 'soluble in water' nor any other disposition predicate can be given explicit definition in observation terms alone. More complex concepts of the natural sciences pose a similar problem. Carnap therefore maintained that the interpretation of theoretical terms in observation language is always incomplete and that theoretical sentences are not in general translatable into the observation language.

What then remains of positivism's insistence that all empirical knowledge is reducible to the phenomena of experience? Short of dismissing the natural sciences as metaphysical rubbish positivism must somehow reconcile the reducibility of scientific concepts to observable phenomena with the impossibility of explicit definition of the former in terms of the latter. The task of reconciliation entailed a considerable 'liberalization of empiricism'.[16] A more liberal form than explicit definition for the legitimate introduction of concepts was given by the so-called reduction sentences in 'Testability and Meaning' and a further, more systematic liberalization of the status of scientific concepts was outlined in 'The Methodological Character of Theoretical Concepts'. This latter involves the introduction of concepts through theoretical postulates and correspondence rules which connect some theoretical terms with observation terms. Theoretical terms can still have an empirical interpretation but it is an interpretation that is necessarily incomplete. The essential difference between theoretical terms and explicitly defined terms is that only the latter have a complete observational interpretation. In Carnap's view the concepts of theoretical physics and of other advanced sciences are best considered to be theoretical terms in this sense. Scientific theory is therefore regarded as a 'freely floating system' of primitive theoretical concepts connected with one another by axioms. Further theoretical concepts are defined by means of the primitive concepts and eventually some are related to observation terms by means of explicit correspondence rules. In this way the freely floating network is finally 'anchored to the solid ground of observable facts' (Autobiography, p.78).

Thus, while retaining the fundamental positivist doctrine of the reducibility of empirical knowledge to the given phenomena of experience Carnap's 'liberalization' also allows the sciences 'the great advantages of the theoretical language, *viz.* the great freedom of concept formation and theory formation, and the great explanatory and predictive power of a theory' (*ibid.*, p.80). In his view:

> 'the prodigious growth of physics since the last century depended essentially upon the possibility of referring to unobservable entities like atoms and fields. In our century, other branches of science such as biology, psychology, and economics have begun to apply the method of theoretical concepts to some extent' (*ibid.*). [17]

Finally, what remains of the anti-metaphysical impetus of logical positivism and, in particular, of its attempted rigorous demarcation between the meaningful and the meaningless? Quine and Hempel have maintained that it is no longer possible to make a clear distinction between meaningful and meaningless terms so that the distinction must be taken as, if anything, a matter of degree. The exclusion of 'metaphysical' discourse from the realm of science must therefore be a matter of degree also.[18] Carnap does not agree. In 'The Methodological Character of Theoretical Concepts' he formulates criteria for the significance, i.e. the meaningfulness, of theoretical terms based on the operation of explicit correspondence rules and on the introduction of theoretical terms in serial order. The correspondence rules connect theoretical terms of science to observational terms such as 'blue', 'hot', 'cold', 'heavier than'. For example:

> 'a rule might refer to two materal bodies u and v (i.e. observable at locations u and v); they must be neither too small nor too large for an observer to see them and to take them in his hands. The rule may connect the theoretical term 'mass' with the observable predicate 'heavier than' as follows: "if u is heavier than v, the mass of u' (i.e. the mass of the coordinate region u' corresponding to u) is greater than the mass of v' " ' (Meth., p.48)

Notice that this rule does not directly connect the mass of, say, the earth with observable predicates. To be meaningful the mass of the earth must be related to other, already significant, theoretical terms by means of the postulates of the pertinent scientific theory. The procedure is as follows. Theoretical terms must be examined in serial order. Some terms are rendered significant by the correspondence rules. Other terms can be shown to be significant provided that for each such term, M, say, the mass of the earth, there is a definite proposition involving that term and others already known to be significant such that it is possible to derive with the help of the postulates and correspondence rules an observational sentence that cannot be otherwise derived. 'The mass of the earth' is significant if it is possible to derive the prediction of an observable event from a proposition concerning the magnitude of that 'mass' and if that prediction cannot be derived without reference to 'the mass of the earth'. Here the significance of theoretical terms is necessarily relative to the postulates of a theory.

If the significance of theoretical terms and propositions can be established in this way then perhaps the old anti-metaphysical doctrines may be preserved. The admission of theoretical terms must not be understood as entailing the acceptance of:

> 'certain "ontological" doctrines in the traditional metaphysical sense. The usual ontological questions about the "reality" (in an alleged metaphysical sense) of numbers, classes, space-time points, bodies, minds, etc., are pseudo-questions without cognitive content. In contrast to this there is a good scientific sense of the word "real", *viz.,* the common-sense use and the scientific use' (*ibid.,* pp.44–5)

But what of the theory itself in terms of which the significance of particular terms may be established:

> 'For an observer to accept the postulates of *T,* means here not simply to take *T* as an uninterpreted calculus, but to use *T* together with specified rules of correspondence, *C,* for guiding his expectations by deriving predictions about future observable events from observed events with the help of *T* and *C*' (*ibid.,* p.45)

Now the fact that terms are significant only relative to a definite theory must leave the choice of that theory entirely arbitrary and undetermined by any positivist criteria of meaning provided only that concepts may be articulated on observation by means of correspondence rules and the postulates of the theory. Only propositions may be tested against the phenomena of experience, the basic postulates of the theory are quite immune. It is difficult to see why the rational theology of, say, Aquinas or Duns Scotus could not be adapted to satisfy that rather weak condition. [19] To accept the postulates of such a theology would mean then to use it, together with appropriate correspondence rules, for guiding one's expectations. 'Gods', 'spirits', the 'exorcism of spirits', and other such entities would be no less real than 'numbers, classes, space-time points, bodies, mines, etc.'. In this sense rational theology, suitably adapted, may well be perfectly meaningful in the new 'liberal' era of positivism. Where early logical positivism excluded certain terms and propositions as meaningless the 'liberal' doctrine can do so only in relation to a given body of theory. Thus Carnap's 'legitimization' of scientific theory opens the way for the possible legitimization of theoretical discourses that are patently not scientific.

4.5 Critique of Positivist Epistemology

In the preceding sections of this chapter I have given a brief and very schematic outline of a number of distinct positivist epistemologies. The level of rigour and theoretical sophistication within positivism varies considerably: the later position of Carnap is clearly the most rigorous and systematic of those considered here. It is easy enough to establish the incoherence and downright absurdity of the crude positivism of, say, Mill or Mach and I have indicated a number of arguments that may be advanced against their positions. It is now necessary to examine the general structure of positivist epistemology and to consider whether, within the limits of its fundamental 'rule of phenomenalism', any logically coherent and rationally defensible epistemological position can be established.

Positivism is an epistemology. It represents a particular form of the general empiricist conception of knowledge in which knowledge is conceived as resulting from a process that takes place between a subject and something that is given to or confronts that subject, phenomena, objects, the world, etc. The 'subject' and the 'object' from which it extracts knowledge may be variously conceived but in all cases the structure of the empiricist conception of knowledge establishes some form of fundamental opposition between, say, 'theory' and 'fact', 'men' and 'world', 'subject' and 'object', 'transcendental subjectivity' and 'transcendent facticity', and so on. All epistemology, and all its derivative discourses, in particular, methodology and philosophy of science, takes some such opposition as constitutive of its theory of knowledge, the aim of which is to lay down the conditions in which valid knowledge is possible. In all cases, and however the opposition is conceived, epistemology confronts a fundamental problem of circularity in that its theory of knowledge logically presupposes a knowledge of the conditions in which knowledge takes place, that is, of the terms of the opposition, 'subject' and 'object', and of the character of the relation between them. Thus the specification of the criteria of the validity of knowledge must presuppose the validity of the 'knowledge' from which that specification is derived.

Positivism differs from the epistemologies of, say, Kant and Husserl in its conception of precisely what is given to the knowing subject, in its refusal to assign any transcendental attributes to the subject and in its negative 'off-hand answer' to Kant's question, 'whether there is any knowledge that is independent of experience and even of all impressions of the senses?'. I argue that positivism is indeed subject to the strictures just outlined and, further, that its 'knowledge' of the 'subject'-'object' relation from which its epistemological doctrines are derived is specifically precluded from the realm of meaningful discourse by those doctrines. In that respect positivist epistemology and its secondary discourses on methodology and philosophy of science are logically incoherent and rationally indefensible.

We have seen that positivism maintains that all knowledge, with the possible exception of that provided by the formal sciences of logic and pure mathematics, is reducible to the phenomena of experience. Knowledge is either 'empirical', in the sense of being so reducible, or it is analytic and tautologous. A proposition that is not reducible to phenomena can have no empirical significance; it is either analytic, that is, true or false by virtue of its meaning alone, or else it is meaningless. Positivist epistemology therefore must logically presuppose that there are indeed knowing subjects with the appropriate capacities, that they do indeed experience phenomena of the approved kind and that those phenomena consist of the sole and irreducible elements of the world or combinations of those elements. In addition, positivism supposes that the essential structures of experience are intersubjectively valid and that knowing subjects are also endowed with language and the capacity to communicate facts. Thus early logical positivism treats the content of the given as essentially private yet, by happy chance, its structure is intersubjective and mirrored in the elementary propositions of language. But what is the status of these logically necessary presuppositions of positivist epistemology? If they are to count as knowledge then positivism lapses into the circularity indicated above: the validity of its doctrine of the conditions of valid knowledge depends on the validity of its own presuppositions. If they are not knowledge then positivist epistemology is at best an empty dogmatism, a doctrine with no possible foundation in rational proof or argument.

Now, if we restrict ourselves to positivism's own conception of knowledge then it is easy to show that the second alternative must apply. Consider the knowing subject fully endowed with various wondrous attributes. No such entity is an irreducible phenomenon of its own experience, a 'cross-section of consciousness', 'element' or 'sensation'. But, it may be suggested, propositions concerning knowing subjects are reducible to elementary propositions concerning irreducible phenomena. It may, for example, be possible to construct concepts of human subjects, oneself and others, by means of Carnap's primitive 'cross-sections of consciousness' and 'remembrance of similarity' or in his 'physicalistic' observation language. In this sense it may be argued that discourse concerning knowing subjects is, at least in principle, consistent with positivism's criteria of meaningfulness. Unfortunately no argument along those lines can save positivism from incoherence. For the sake of argument let us admit that a meaningful concept of human subject is possible in positivist terms. Nevertheless there could be no warrant in the content of the given itself for the claim that what is experiencing this content is indeed such a 'subject' nor that other 'subjects' experience givens of their own. In either case an inference is called for that can hardly avoid going beyond the evidence of the senses. In that respect the concept of the knowing subject endowed with all the attributes required for the positivist theory of knowledge has no empirical significance, it is metaphysical. Thus positivist epistemology is the product of an ontology, a doctrine of what there is, that on its own terms is metaphysical and therefore meaningless.

It only remains to consider the effects of the treatment of language and of concepts as a result of the 'liberalization' of positivism's criteria of meaningfulness and, in particular, of its later conception of theory as a 'freely-floating system' ultimately 'anchored to the solid ground of observable facts' (Autobiography, p.78). There can be no escape from the circularity of epistemology but perhaps some of the other problems of positivism may be avoided with this more 'liberal' treatment of language.

It is clear that the crude positivism of Mill and of Mach must presuppose an intersubjectivity of the world, so that its ultimate constituents and the relations between them are basically the same for all human subjects, and a language in which knowledge may be stated and communicated. The relation between language and the irreducible elements of the given is treated as unproblematic. In particular, the problem of the articulation of empirical propositions onto the content of the given receives no serious consideration. In that respect the epistemologies of Mill and Mach are manifestly inadequate. They may be interesting historical curiosities and they may provide forceful statements or systematic elaborations of positivist dogma but as theories of knowledge they have little to recommend them.

The picture theory of language elaborated in the early work of Wittgenstein and early logical positivism has at least the merit of recognising the necessity of articulating propositions on to the content of the given. Knowledge communicates the *structure* of the given but it cannot express the *content*. The latter cannot be stated, it can only be pointed to and seen or not seen as the case may be. Elementary propositions therefore represent the point at which reason and argument must cease, where knowledge is confronted by the raw given which it may recognise or fail to recognise but which it cannot dispute. This conception of a naked confrontation between an observation language or a picture language and the world poses a problem for positivist theory to which I return below. For the present notice that the picture theory must strictly confine knowledge to propositions expressing the structure of the given. Universal propositions, for example, Mill's 'laws of nature' or even 'All Ravens are Black', cannot be represented as finite combinations of elementary propositions. Thus the positivist conception, accepted by Popper, that science aims at the formulation of universal propositions requires that science goes beyond the content of the given. Where positivism sees here an inference to be justified, i.e. the problem of induction, Popper and his acolytes maintain that universal propositions can only be falsified by the given. But in both cases the conception of science as aiming at universal propositions entails a necessary discrepancy between scientific theory on the one hand and statements of observation on the other.

I am not concerned here with the positivist problem of induction but with its conception of language. Once scientific discourse is conceived as containing the tautologies of elementary logic and both universal propositions and descriptions of observations then it must also contain concepts that cannot be given complete definition in observation terms. Elementary logical operations on universal propositions, which cannot be fully translated into statements of observation, suffice for the definition of concepts that are not definable in observation terms alone. The simplest possible case of such a concept would be the so-called disposition predicates, e.g. 'soluble in water', analysed by Carnap in 'Testability and Meaning' but there is no reason why the formation of theoretical concepts should be restricted to dispositionals. If universal propositions are a legitimate and meaningful part of science then so are the concepts formed from them. Thus the division of the language of science into a theoretical and an observation language and the conception of scientific theory as a 'freely-floating system' in relation to observable facts are logically necessary consequences of a conception of knowledge that combines a picture theory of language, with logic and pure mathematics as tautologies, and the doctrine that science formulates universal laws. For all its rigour and sophistication Carnap's 'liberalization' of positivism's meaning criteria involves little more than a systematic elaboration of the effects of logical positivism's conception of language and of science while his strict specification of the conditions for the legitimate introduction of 'theoretical' terms is designed to ensure the primacy of the ultimate positivist dogma of phenomenalism. I have suggested that it would be difficult to exclude rational theology from the realm of meaningful discourse under the new 'liberal' dispensation.

We can now return to the effects of 'liberalization' and of the logical positivist theory of language. I have argued that positivist epistemology is the effect of an ontology that is meaningless in terms of its own criteria of validity. Does the 'liberal' version escape that absurd consequence? Since the knowing subject and its language are neither 'cross-sections of consciousness' nor 'physical objects' their concepts can have no place in any strictly conceived positivist observation language. Perhaps the concepts of 'knowing subject' and 'language' belong to the theoretical language instead. At first sight this proposal seems quite promising. Given the character of the criteria of empirical significance it would be sufficient for the concepts of 'language' and 'knowing subject' to be necessary conditions for the derivation of empirical predictions for them to be admitted to the corpus of meaningful concepts. Thus, it seems, 'liberal' positivism may be saved from incoherence if not from circularity and dogmatism. But this 'solution' reckons without the effects of the primacy of the doctrine of phenomenalism. To admit certain concepts to theoretical discourse is not to be understood as accepting 'certain "ontological" doctrines in the traditional metaphysical sense'. (Meth. pp.44–5) On the contrary, the questions of the 'reality' or 'existence' of entities designated by these concepts 'are pseudo-questions without cognitive content' (*ibid.*). The following proposition is therefore without cognitive content:

> the existence of at least one knowing subject is a necessary condition of there being any *content* of the given and the existence of language is necessary for the communication of its *structure*.

Knowing subjects can hardly be less real than the content of the given which they make possible nor language less real than the structure of the given which it expresses. But to make that assertion is to assert an 'ontological' doctrine 'in the traditional sense'. Thus 'liberal' positivism remains a product of an ontology that is meaningless in terms of its own criteria. It is no more successful than the more primitive forms in avoiding incoherence.

Finally it is necessary to comment on the logical positivist conception of the articulation of language on the irreducible elements of the given. In effect this involves the conception of a point where reason and argument must cease, where elementary propositions in some alleged observation or picture language are confronted by irreducible givens. The observation language performs a double role in the positivist conception of science. On the one hand it belongs to science: its terms are, at least in principle, the terms of scientific observation and all 'theoretical' terms are reducible to, if not strictly definable in, observation terms. On the other hand it designates the elementary constituents of the real and it expresses the structure of their interrelations. Only on condition that the observation language performs this double role can scientific theory, in any positivist conception, be rigorously articulated on the irreducible givens that science is supposed to know. The observation language represents the very frontiers of theoretical knowledge, the ultimate point beyond which theory cannot go. But there can be no *demonstration* that an observation language does indeed designate the irreducible elements of the real and express its relational structure, that there is not, perhaps, some 'finer' structure of the given which the observation language in question cannot discriminate. Thus although any particular observation statement can be disputed, by reference, for example, to errors of observation or the competence of the observer, no amount of pointing at or showing can ever establish that the language in question does indeed express the relational structure of what is pointed at. Any such demonstration would of necessity prove circular: it would require reference to an observation language with respect to which the same problem would arise. There can be no proof that a proposed observation language is an observation language in the strict sense and that it does not include a hidden strain of metaphysics and meaninglessness. Thus, even if its criteria of meaningfulness and empirical significance are accepted logical positivism is condemned to dogmatism in practice. It must assume, without hope of demonstration, that a particular theoretical terminology, say, that of physics, is indeed meaningful and then judge others by its standard. But, if there can be no proof that any given language is an observation language then there can be nothing but positivist dogma, *viz.,* its meaningless ontological conception of the world, to show that an observation language is even possible. In fact, as I argue in the next chapter, it is impossible to provide a positivist demonstration of the possibility of an a-theoretical observation language.[20]

Now Popper has always denied the existence of an observation language in the strict positivist sense and, with the 'liberalization' of logical positivism's meaning criteria, many authors (e.g. Quine, Hempel, Kuhn) have disputed the possibility of maintaining a rigorous distinction between theoretical and observation languages. Nevertheless these authors maintain some allegiance to the positivist position that knowledge is reducible to the phenomena of experience and that therefore theory is to be tested against the facts of observation. Others have tended to assign what can only be called a 'transcendental' function to language maintaining, in effect, that the elements of the world and our knowledge of it are essentially structured by language so that the investigation of the structure of the world is best conducted, in the first instance, by means of an investigation of language itself. This tendency has been most clearly developed in the work of Wittgenstein and in the so-called analytic philosophy. This position would take us beyond the limits of positivist epistemology and it need not be considered here. It is however necessary to comment on those positions which appear to retain a residual positivism while denying the possibility of a strict observation language. If all observation is to some extent theoretical how is it possible to maintain that all knowledge is reducible to observation and that theory is to be tested against the 'facts' of observation? In the work of Carnap it is clear that the doctrine of the reduction of theoretical propositions to statements of observation and the related doctrine of testability are effects of the concept of a strict observation language. Theory must be tested against observation statements because these latter, at least in principle, really do designate the given and they really do express its relational structure. If, on the other hand, there is no strict observation language then observation statements do not strictly designate the given nor do they strictly express its relational structure. Why then test theory against observation statements? If observation statements do not express the structure of the real then why should we accept a theory if it conforms to them or reject it as false if it fails to conform? The doctrines of reduction and of the testing of theory against the 'facts' of observation are defensible only within a strict positivist epistemology by reference to its strict observation language. If the possibility of an observation language is denied — and it cannot be defended — than these doctrines have no possible rational foundation. I argue this case at length in relation to Popper's epistemology in chapter 6.

I have argued then that positivist epistemology in all its forms, however crude or sophisticated its formulations, is logically incoherent and rationally indefensible. The secondary discourses of positivism such as philosophy of science and methodology are therefore untenable. It follows that the sciences and other empirical investigations, for example, social surveys, cannot be represented as either testing or measuring theory against the template of the real. [21] The protocols of positivist methodology therefore have no pertinence for any substantive 'empirical' investigations. Furthermore, since positivist methodology is logically impossible, they cannot be realised in practice. I return to the significance of this point in my final chapter.

5. Model-Building and Positivist Semantics

The epistemology of model-building is an epistemology in which scientific knowledge is said to be produced through the construction and manipulation of models. Given an empirical domain, in which facts have been 'carefully observed and described, without allowing any theoretical preconception to decide whether some are more important than others' (Lévi-Strauss, 1968, p.280), the scientist is supposed to construct models to account for the observed facts. Models are reconstructions of the order of the facts; the validity of the model is determined by its 'fitting' the order of the facts. For the epistemology of model-building 'facts' are taken as given. Their observation and collection does not require any theoretical activity on the part of the scientist. Thus science has a theoretical and a non-theoretical moment. The latter is the moment of observation, the former that of model-building. Models are obtained through a double process of abstraction and simplification and they may be subject to an 'experimental' manipulation. This last refers to 'the set of procedures aiming at ascertaining how a given model will react when subjected to change and at comparing models of the same or different types' (*ibid.*). According to Lévi-Strauss, then, and according to other advocates of knowledge through models, knowledge may be produced through the experimental manipulation of formal systems. It is for this reason that the branch of mathematical logic known as the Theory of Models assumes a particular importance for this epistemology. A number of theorems, especially that first demonstrated in Gödel's paper, 'On Formally Undecidable Propositions in *Principia Mathematica* and Related Systems', have often been interpreted as establishing the inherent limitations of formalisation as a means to knowledge: 'since Gödel we know that the axiomatic method has certain inherent limitations'. (Piaget, 1971a, p.33) Again, the editor of a recent collection on the use of models in scholarly thought (with contributions from workers in physics, biology, mathematics, sociology, theology, . . .) tells us that the awareness of the limitations of formalised procedures:

> 'is reflected today in the conclusions of theoreticians right across the disciplinary boundaries from Heisenberg's 'uncertainty principle' in physics as far as to the discussion of 'theories of the middle range' in sociology with Gödel's theorem in mathematics as a further extension of it' (Shanin, 1972, p.5)

'Modern science' strikes again: in Gödel's proof, in the Copenhagen interpretation of quantum theory,[1] we appear to have the clearest possible proof of the intrinsic limitations of human knowledge. Shanin's volume represents yet another instance of the perennial attempts to use advances in the sciences in support of idealist epistemologies.[2] In fact this recourse of the epistemology of model-building to quantum mechanics or to mathematical logic is totally illegitimate. To interpret them as establishing the ineluctible limits to knowledge involves a gross distortion of the sciences in question. In the first section of this chapter I show that models in mathematics and the natural sciences do not function in the way suggested by the epistemology of model-building.

The second section of this chapter examines positivist semantics and the semantic concept of truth which, as we shall see, plays a central, if fundamentally ambiguous part in Popper's theory of science. In many respects positivist semantics reproduces the structure of the mathematical theory of models with the crucial difference that where the mathematical domain of semantic interpretation has a determinate theoretical structure which plays a crucial role in the theory of models the positivist domain of interpretation has no theoretical structure of its own – in effect it is a surrogate for the given phenomena of experience. In this respect positivist semantics involves little more than a more or less sophisticated elaboration of the fundamental logical positivist conception of language discussed in the previous chapter. I argue that positivist semantics cannot establish a rigorous distinction between analytic and synthetic expressions, between formal sciences (logic, mathematics) and factual sciences. It follows that no rigorous demarcation of theoretical and observational languages can be maintained and that, therefore, Carnap's insistence on that demarcation is impossible to defend on positivism's own terms. The significance of the breakdown of that demarcation for the coherence of positivist epistemology has been shown in the previous chapter.

Finally, I return to the epistemology of model-building. It could hardly be further removed from the rigour of mathematical logic or even of positivist semantics. On the contrary, in the epistemology of model building an essential arbitrariness in the selection of the facts to be modelled is further compounded by an arbitrary relation of 'resemblance' between the model and the facts it is supposed to represent. This epistemology is often supplemented by attempts to reduce this arbitrariness of knowledge by reference to the social, psychological, or biological determinations of the elements of perception and the structures of thought or else to some alleged essential organisation of the world itself. We shall see that such doctrines merely add a dogmatic and speculative dimension to a conception that is already so vague and imprecise as to be almost vacuous.

5.1 Models in Mathematics and the Natural Sciences [3]

Mathematical logic is a paradigm case of a theory in which the concept of model has a definite and rigorously defined function in theoretical discourse. Elsewhere, with few exceptions, the word 'model' is used in a loosely defined and analogical sense with little strict theoretical pertinence. Accordingly the following discussion will be limited primarily to the place of models in mathematical logic, a subject whose peculiar significance for the epistemology of model-building has already been indicated, and to a few additional remarks on the model in other sciences. In mathematical logic the concept of a model relates two mathematical domains, namely, a formal system on the one hand and its domain of interpretation on the other. 'Syntax' concerns the structure of the formal system while 'semantics' is concerned with relations between the formal system and its domain of interpretation. We shall see below that positivist philosophy of science involves a concept of semantics that is in many respects analogous to the mathematical concept. Where mathematical semantics is concerned with relations between two mathematical domains positivist semantics is concerned with relating scientific theory (the formal system) with the givens of observation (the domain of interpretation). The positivist concept, in effect, displaces intra-mathematical relations on to the relation between theory and the real.[4]

Very schematically we can say that a formal system involves a set of marks, finite strings of these marks, and formation and derivation rules. For example, an elementary formal system might contain the following types of mark: constants ($a, b, c, a', b', c', \ldots$); variables ($x, y, z, x', y', z', \ldots$); predicates ($P, Q, R, \ldots$); connectives of negation and implication ($-$ and $\rightarrow$); and universal and existential quantifiers (U and E). Informally the constants may be interpreted as designating objects, the predicates as designating properties of objects, and variables as 'unknown' constants, places where any constant may be written. Quantifiers may be read according to the following schema:

$(Ex)P(x)$: there is an x with the property P;

$(Ux)P(x)$: all x have the property P.

A formal system is governed by two sets of rules. Formation rules divide all possible strings of marks into those that are well-formed (e.g. '$x=y$') and those that are not (e.g. '$xy=$'). In effect the well-formed strings are grammatical expressions of the system. To continue the above example we might say that $P(a)$, $P(x)$, etc., are well-formed expressions and that, for any well-formed expressions A and B, $-A$ and $A \rightarrow B$ are well-formed. These, together with rules for the use of quantifiers, would be sufficient to define the well-formed expressions of a first-order predicate calculus containing only unitary predicates. Derivation rules operate on the well-formed expressions of the system. They allow one to deduce theorems from a set of axioms. For example, if A and B are well-formed and if :$-$ indicates that the expression which follows has been derived then we may have the following deductive schemata:

$$\text{generalisation:} \quad \frac{:- \quad A}{:- \quad (Ux)A}$$

$$\text{separation:} \quad \frac{:- \quad (A \rightarrow B)}{\frac{:- \quad A}{:- \qquad B}}$$

Informally these may be read: if A then, for all x, A; and, if A implies

B and if *A*, then *B*. These derivation rules may appear to be obvious from the informal readings. For example, an 'intuitive' or 'common-sense' reading of the sign-→(implication) leads directly to the rule of separation. However, such informal readings are no more than crude illustrations and they are frequently misleading. The formal system with its set of marks and its rules of formation and derivation cannot be interpreted as providing merely a neat expression of what is 'intuitively' clear or evident. In logic, as elsewhere in mathematics, what is alleged to be intuitively clear is frequently false. It seems clear, for example, that 'the whole is greater than the part', yet there are no more integers (i.e. 1, 2, 3, 4, . . .) than there are squares of integers (i.e. 1,4,9,16, . . .). In the present example there are 'intuitively clear' deductions that cannot be made. Consider the following sequence:

$$
\begin{array}{ll}
:- & (A \rightarrow B) \\
:- & -B \\
\hline
:- & -A
\end{array}
$$

Informally this would read: if *A* implies *B* and if not—*B*, then not—*A*. It corresponds to an intuitive rendering of implication. Nevertheless the conclusion, —*A*, cannot be deduced from the axioms, *A*→*B* and —*B*, by means of the rules introduced above without the use of further axioms.[5]

The formation and the derivation rules define the syntax of the formal system. A theorem is any well-formed expression that may be deduced from the axioms of the system. A formal system in which there is at least one expression that is not a theorem is said to be *coherent*. In a system that is not coherent the derivation rules are redundant: any expression, say; *A*=*B*, and its negation, —(*A*=*B*), are both theorems of the system. A formal system, in which every expression is either a theorem or the negation of a theorem is said to be *decidable*. Many of the most important formal mathematical systems are not decidable in this sense.

Formal systems may be constructed, for example, in order to isolate the deductive structure of an existing mathematical domain, arithmetic, geometry, set theory, etc. If we are to establish that a formal system does indeed express the structure of, say, elementary set theory, then it is necessary to establish a correspondence between the elements and expressions of the two domains. The rules of this correspondence define the semantics of the formal system. In the case of set theory and the formal system illustrated above this would require a function which assigns to each constant or predicate of the formal system an element or set. In addition, since our formal system contains variables and quantifiers it is necessary to establish a procedure for interpreting expressions containing variables or quantifiers in terms of set theory. For example, $(Ux)P(x)$ and $(Ex)P(x)$ might 'translate' into 'all elements, u, are contained in the set V' and 'there is an element, u, contained in the set V' respectively. With such a correspondence it would be possible to evaluate all expressions of the formal system in terms of propositions of set theory: an expression of the formal system is *valid* for this interpretation if the corresponding expression in set theory is correct. For example, the expression $P(a)$ is valid if and only if the correspondence assigns an element $f(a)$ to a and a set $f(P)$ to P so that $f(a)$ is contained in the set $f(P)$. Validity, in this sense, is defined relative to a determinate correspondence between the formal system and its domain of interpretation.[6] Now, if the correspondence is such that the deduction rules conserve validity (e.g. if A is valid then $(Ux)A$ is also valid) and the axioms of the system are valid then all theorems of the formal system are valid for that interpretation. In that case the domain of interpretation provides a model of the formal system. If, in addition, there corresponds to each true sentence of the model a theorem of the formal system, then the system is *complete* for the model. Since the concept of validity is defined relative to a determinate interpretation of the formal system the concept of model also presupposes the establishment of determinate rules of correspondence. Without such rules there is no model.

A formal system may or may not have a model. It is possible to establish that any formal system containing the first-order predicate calculus is coherent if and only if it has a model. Coherence means that some expressions of the formal system are not theorems, i.e., that there is at least one expression that cannot be deduced from the axioms using the derivation rules. With this result it is possible to show that the first-order[7] predicate calculus (as above but with n-ary predicates) is a complete formal logic. In other words every formula that is valid for all models of first-order formal systems is a theorem of the calculus.[8] In addition this formal system is decidable since every formula is either a theorem or the negation of a theorem.

This property of decidability is frequently used to define an 'ideal' in terms of which logical and mathematical theories are judged. Husserl's concept of 'formal system' is defined in terms of this property. It has an axiom system:

'distinguished by the circumstance that any proposition that can be constructed, in accordance with the grammar of pure logic, out of the concepts occurring in that system, is either 'true' — that is to say: an analytic (purely deducible) consequence of the axioms — or false — that is to say: an analytic contradiction — *tertium non datur*' (Husserl, 1959, p.96)

Now, a theorem established in Gödel's paper, 'On Formally Undecidable Propositions of *Principia Mathematica* and Related Systems', demonstrates that any formal system capable of generating elementary recursive arithmetic contains an expression that is undecidable: that is, neither the expression nor its negation is a theorem of the system.[9] The formal system of arithmetic must therefore be judged to be 'inadequate' in terms of Husserl's ideal concept of 'formal system'. Indeed, we have seen that Gödel's theorem is frequently interpreted as establishing limitations to mathematical thought. But Gödel's result can only be interpreted in this way by reference to some extra-mathematical norm of decidability.[10] In fact it means simply that the partition of well-formed expressions into those that are theorems and those that are not theorems places at least one expression and its negation in the same category (non-theorems). The formal systems of arithmetic and therefore the vast bulk of mathematical formal systems are undecidable in this sense. Decidability, coherence, completeness, etc., are properties that any given formal system may or may not possess. These properties are investigated by the theory of models. Gödel's theorem demonstrates that certain 'strong' formal systems (capable of generating elementary recursive arithmetic) do not have the property of decidability.

It should now be clear that the function of models in mathematics bears absolutely no relation to the function assigned to them in the epistemology of model-building. For the latter, in effect, it is the formal system that is the model for its domain of interpretation. In mathematics the domain of interpretation provides the model for the formal system. In the epistemology of model-building the domain of interpretation is external to theory: semantics is reduced to a relation of *similarity* between theory (the model) and non-theory. For mathematics the domain of interpretation is itself theoretical: semantic rules are theoretically defined relations between theoretical domains. It is only the erroneous placing of the domain of interpretation (in this case recursive arithmetic) as external to mathematics that appears to legitimize the ideological reading of Gödel's theorem as demonstrating yet again the inherent limitations of human knowledge. [11] This reading can now be seen to be entirely without foundation.

In this schematic account of the function of models in mathematical logic the essential points for the present argument are the following. First, both the formal system and its domain of interpretation are mathematical structures. The model relates theory to theory, it is not a bridge between theory and some reality external to theory. Secondly, the semantics of the formal system is governed by rigorously defined mathematical functions: the model is a theoretical relation between theoretical domains. In so far as models have any strict theoretical pertinence in other branches of mathematical and in the natural sciences their use retains these essential features. The model is able to function by means of a rigorously defined correspondence between elements and relations of one theory and those of another. It is only the presence of that correspondence which allows certain conclusions established in one to be carried over into the other. For example, the flow of electricity in a metal plate may serve as a model for the horizontal component of certain hydrodynamic phenomena. This transfer of results is made possible only by rigorously defined transformations between the theoretical structures of the two distinct orders of phenomena. It is precisely such rigorously defined correspondences that must be denied by the epistemology of model-building.

Where such correspondences have not yet been established we have nothing but a rough physical analogy which serves, at best, to illustrate relations of one science by means of another. [12] Despite the claims of von Bertalanffy and others [13] the use of mechanical or electronic models in biology remains largely at the level of illustration. If it has been possible, by way of illustration, to construct analogical models which replicate certain gross characteristics of, say, the performance of organs these analogies do not rest on rigorously established correspondences between elements and elementary functions in the two fields brought together in the model (i.e. between biology and mechanics or electronics). Such correspondences can only be established at the level of theory. In the absence of rigorously established correspondences 'explanatory' models in biology are a myth. Here as elsewhere the epistemology of model-building finds no support in scientific practice.

5.2 Positivist Semantics and the Semantic Concept of Truth

For mathematical logic the domain of interpretation is a mathematical structure: its properties are used in the investigation of the properties of semantic systems. In positivist epistemology the domain of interpretation consists effectively of the given facts. It is external to theory, by definition, and has no theoretical properties. Thus logical positivism identifies the formal or theoretical dimension with the syntax of the language of science. The real or empirical facts supply the domain of semantic interpretation. In science, therefore, propositions are subject to a double constraint: syntactic (theoretical consistency and deducibility); semantic (the facts of experiment or observation). Observation and measurement are essentially semantic operations; deduction and computation are essentially syntactical (theoretical). [14]

Carnap, for example, explicitly poses the difference between the formal sciences (logic and mathematics) and the empirical or factual sciences in these terms. There are no formal or 'ideal' objects of the formal sciences corresponding to the 'real' objects of the empirical sciences:

'The formal sciences do not have any objects at all; they are systems of auxiliary statements without objects and without content' (Carnap, 1953, p.128)

The value of the formal sciences is that they enable us to supplement the language of pure observation with 'theoretical' terms. A scientific theory may contain terms that have no direct empirical referent but which are nevertheless related to observation terms by the formal structure of the theory: that is, 'observable' consequences can be deduced from statements containing 'theoretical' terms. In 'The Methodological Character of Theoretical Concepts', discussed in the previous chapter, Carnap proposes to divide the language of science into two parts: the observation language (L_O) and the theoretical language (L_T).

'The L_O uses terms designating observable properties and relations for the description of observable things or events. The L_T, on the other hand, contains terms which may refer to unobservable events, unobservable aspects or features of events, . . .' (p.38)

This distinction poses the fundamental problems of positivist semantics which is concerned, for example, with relations between 'expressions of a language and their designata' (Carnap, 1958, p.79): how may new theoretical terms be introduced legitimately into the language of science?; what are the criteria for the significance (i.e. meaningfulness) of theoretical terms and sentences?; etc. All of Carnap's semantic analyses culminate in the problem of the relations between the observation language, L_O, and the various 'artificial' languages of the formal sciences. The notions of 'empirical science', 'formal science', 'semantic analysis', 'reducibility', 'the method of intension and extension', etc., serve both to represent the initial difference between the formal and the factual sciences and to conceptualise the relationship between them. I argue that the distinction is essentially arbitrary, that is, that it cannot be justified in any strict positivist epistemology. Carnap's position is, of course, disputed by exponents of other variants of positivist philosophy. For example, Quine effectively reduces the distinction between theoretical and observational languages to a matter of arbitrary choice (so that any set of propositions may be treated as observational) while Hempel appears to retain a form of this distinction but doubts whether a sharp distinction between meaningful and meaningless can be drawn. [15] It should be clear that if the rigorous demarcation of theory and observation is effaced in any way then the residual positivist notion of the testing of theory against the facts of observation can have no rational justification. Thus to deny the possibility either of a rigorously determined a-theoretical observation language or of a strict positivist criterion of meaningfulness is to destroy whatever coherence there is in the positivist doctrine of science as reducible to the phenomena of observation.

In Carnap's rigorous positivist epistemology scientific theory may be subjected to a double evaluation: syntactic – deducibility and consistency; semantic – measurement, experimentation, testing. This double constraint on the language of science is reflected in the title of Carnap's *Meaning and Necessity*. In that book he proposes an approach to semantics which he call the method of extension and intension. The meaning of every expression is analyzed into two components: the intension, which is apprehended by the understanding of the expression, and the extension, which is determined by empirical investigation. He begins by outlining a semantic system for an object language, S, and develops the semantic concepts of *truth* and *L-truth* (logical truth). We shall see that this construction reproduces the structure of the mathematical theory of models with the exception that the domain of interpretation has no theoretical properties. A semantic system for S requires four kinds of rules. First, the rules of formation determine the admissible form of sentences. Secondly, rles of designation for the non-logical constants and predicates translate atomic sentences in S into some metalanguage. Carnap proposes to use 'a suitable part of the English language' and offers the following examples:

> '1.1 *Rules of designation for individual constants*
>   *'s'* is a symbolic translation of 'Walter Scott',
>   *'w'* ..   .. '(the book) Waverly'
> 1.2 *Rules of designation for predicates*
>   *'Hx'* – *'x* is human'
>   *'RAx'* – *'x* is a rational animal'
>   *'Axy'* – *'x* is an author of *y'* (p.4)

Thus, *S* corresponds to 'formal system' and the meta-language to its domain of interpretation.

Thirdly, there are rules of truth for atomic sentences and for logical connections and quantifiers. For example,

> 'An atomic sentence in *S* consisting of a predicate followed by an individual constant is true if and only if the individual to which the individual constant refers possesses the property to which the predicate refers.' (p.5)

This rule presupposes the rules of designation. It produces, for example, the following result:

> The sentence *'RAs'* is true if and only if Walter Scott is a rational animal.

Finally, there are rules of ranges. These are defined in relation to the concept of *state-description*

> 'A class of sentences in S which contains for every atomic sentence either this sentence or its negation, but not both, and not other sentences, is called a *state-description* in *S,* because it obviously gives a complete description of a possible state of the universe with respect to all properties expressed by predicates of the system. Thus the state-descriptions represent Leibniz' possible worlds or Wittenstein's possible states of affairs' (p.9)

An atomic sentence is one that is irreducible in *S*. It, or at least its translation in the metalanguage, can be checked against the actual state of the universe by observation. It is easy to specify rules which determine whether a given sentence holds in a given state-description. An atomic sentence holds if it belongs to the state-description and other sentences in S may be dealt with by means of appropriate rules for logical connectives and quantifiers. Such rules are called rules of ranges because they define the ranges of state-descriptions in which a given sentence holds.

The necessity for a distinction between rules of truth and rules of ranges is not at first sight too clear since they involve equivalent procedures for treating atomic sentences on the one hand, *viz.*, determining whether they are 'true' or whether they 'hold in a given state-description', and logical connectives, quantifiers, etc., on the other. 'A sentence is true if and only if it holds in the true state-description' (p.10). However, since state-descriptions represent possible worlds the rules of ranges permit a definition of logical truth, that is, of a truth which can be established without reference to extra-linguistic facts. The definition is suggested by Leibniz' conception that a necessary truth must hold in all possible worlds. Thus:

'A sentence S is L-true (in S)$=_{def.}S$ holds in every state-description (in S)' (*ibid.*)

A sentence is factual, that is synthetic or contingent, if it is true but not L-true. The rules of ranges therefore determine whether a given sentence is analytic or synthetic.

Now, in spite of certain differences of detail the first three sets of rules reproduce the basic structure of the semantic theory of truth presented in Tarski's paper, 'The Concept of Truth in Formalized Languages', which, as we shall see, is of considerable importance for Popper's epistemology and methodology. I return to the rules of ranges in a moment. Although I have given a rather simplified and illustrative exposition the basic structure of the semantic theory of truth should now be clear. In particular, the construction of the semantic concept of truth for a given formal language involves the construction of an appropriate metalanguage (e.g. Carnap's 'suitable part of the English language' together with various symbols) containing the following kinds of primitive expression:

'(1) expressions of a general logical kind; (2) expressions having the same meaning as all the constants of the language to be discussed or which suffice for the definition of such expressions; (3) expressions of the structural-descriptive type which denote single signs and expressions of the language considered, whole classes and sequences of such expressions or, finally, the relations existing between them' (Tarski, 1956, p.211)

The necessity for the first group is evident. The second group allow us to translate expressions of the formal language into the metalanguage and the third provide for the assignment of a name to every such expression.

The semantic definition of truth certainly avoids the difficulties of the more simplistic interpretations of the classical definition: *Veritas est adaequatio rei et intellectus* – the truth of a thought consists in its agreement with reality. For if the concept 'dog' does not bark and the concept 'circle' is not round then the precise nature of what is required for a thought to agree with reality is problematic. [16] The semantic definition does not require that the concept 'dog' should bark nor that the concept 'sun' be larger than the concept 'earth' but, if S represents the proposition 'the sun is larger than the earth' then 'S is true' means that the sun is larger than the earth. [17]

But while the semantic definition of truth avoids the logical absurdities entailed in the simplistic attempts to formulate a definition in terms of the 'agreement' or 'correspondence' of a thought with reality by means of rigorously defined relations between one language and another it cannot avoid the problems of the positivist conception of knowledge. The semantic concept of truth must presuppose some version of positivist epistemology for to prove that 'S' is true is to prove a sentence in the metalanguage having the same meaning as S. Positivist semantics appears to reproduce the structure of the mathematical theory of models with the formal or object language corresponding to the formal system, the metalanguage to the domain of interpretation, and the concept of truth to the concept of validity. But there remains one crucial difference. In mathematical logic the domain of interpretation is itself a mathematical structure. Validity for expressions of the formal system may therefore be investigated by means of the theoretical structure of its domain of interpretation. In positivist semantics however only the formal languages are conceived as theoretical. The metalanguage, the domain of semantic interpretation, has no theoretical structure. On the contrary it serves as an extra-theoretical surrogate for the (unknown) structure of the real itself. For all the technical rigour of its formulations positivist semantics reduces the 'truth' of its atomic sentences to a question of observation. In the last resort the 'truth' of an expression is not a matter of theoretical demonstration. At this point the parallel between 'truth' and 'validity' breaks down. To investigate 'truth' we translate our sentence, *S,* into 'a suitable part of the English language' and then we simply look and see. Positivist semantics presuppose observation as the place where demonstration ceases. I have shown the incoherence of this conception of knowledge in chapter 4. For positivism 'knowledge', and therefore 'truth', rests on nothing more than a non-rational act of judgement. The observer has only to recognise the given state of affairs or else to fail to recognise it. The latter possibility, as we shall see in the case of Popper, poses a serious problem for any positivist or neo-positivist epistemology.

Finally, what of Carnap's 'rules of ranges' which allow him to formulate a distinction between truths that are analytic and those that are synthetic? An expression is an analytic truth if it holds in every state description. Now, since the 'rules of ranges' define the range of state-descriptions in which a given sentence holds they must determine what analytic truths if any exist in any given object language. For example, from the rules of ranges for the logical connective V ('or') and for atomic sentences it follows:

'that *'Pa'* holds in certain state-descriptions, that '$-Pa$' holds in all the other state-descriptions, and that therefore the disjunction *'PaV$-$Pa'* holds in every state-description.' (Carnap, 1947, p.11)

The existence of analytic truths is established in Carnap's system by stipulation. In particular, the concept of state-description 'which contains for every atomic sentence either this sentence or its negation' ensures that for every sentence, S, 'SV$-$S' holds for all state-descriptions. Now, Carnap maintains that 'state descriptions represent Leibniz' possible worlds or Wittgenstein's possible states of affairs'. The concept of state-description therefore represents a formal constraint on what 'possible worlds' or 'possible states of affairs' can be given in experience.

But no formal constraint of this kind can be justified in terms of the positivist principle of the reducibility of knowledge to the given, for how can it be known that the given must always comply with the principle of contradiction, *viz.,* that for any sentence, *S,* either *S* or not$-S$ is the case? [18] If knowledge is reducible to the given then the notion of any knowledge, even 'the laws of logic', governing the content of all possible givens is plainly absurd.

Thus Carnap's attempt to establish a rigorous distinction between analytic and synthetic, the logical and the factual, cannot be justified in terms of any strict positivist epistemology. It is entirely arbitrary. [19] It follows that Carnap's distinction between formal and factual sciences is equally arbitrary. There can be no strict positivist demonstration that logic and mathematics are formal sciences at all in Carnap's sense. It follows that there can be no rigorous distinction between theoretical and observation languages of the kind that Carnap attempts to establish for that distinction requires precisely that statements in L_T be reducible to statements in L_O by means of purely formal, logical and mathematical, operations. The consequence is clear: if there can be no rigorous distinction between theoretical and observation language then the selection of any one partial language as *the* language of observation must be entirely arbitrary. The positivist concept of a pure a-theoretical observation language stands or falls with the concept of the formal sciences 'which do not have any objects at all; they are systems of auxiliary statements without objects and without content' (Carnap, 1953, p.128). The concept of a pure a-theoretical language of observation cannot be justified within any strict positivist epistemology. The implication of that conclusion has been indicated above, namely, that the positivist notion of the testing of theory against the facts of observation has no rational justification.

Now, we have seen that the vulgar positivism of, say, Mach or Mill, is manifestly inadequate since it does not even attempt to conceptualize the articulation of language and propositions on to the phenomena of experience. This discussion of positivist semantics has shown that positivist epistemology cannot rigorously conceive that articulation. A rigorous positivism requires a strict demarcation between theoretical and observation languages and therefore between formal and factual discourses. Those demarcations are arbitrary and indefensible on positivism's own terms yet the price of rejecting them is to destroy whatever rational coherence there is in the positivist doctrine of the reducibility of science to the phenomena of experience.

5.3 The Epistemology of Model-Building

'Theorising means ordering, structuring; as such it is an isomorphic correlate of material practice, its *'alter-ego'* in the Janus-faced human existence. Exactly like the productive activity, theorising consists in modelling reality. Theories *are* models. Any segment of universe we isolate in order to formulate its regularities presents itself to us as a cybernetic black-box: a processual going concern with only two points – inputs and outputs – open to the investigators' inspection' (Bauman, 1972, p.303)

In these lines we have a concise statement of what might be called the epistemology of model-building. Knowledge of the world is to be obtained through the construction and manipulation of models. Now, if theories *are* models, if theoretical activity consists in the construction of models, then it is the theory that is a model for its domain of interpretation, the empirically given. In this respect the epistemology of model-building inverts the structure of the mathematical theory of models and of positivist semantics. Since theories are models rigour is possible only at the level of the model itself. The relation between the model and the facts it is supposed to represent must be extra-theoretical, a relation between theory, the model, and something exterior to theory, the facts. In this conception science is reduced to the construction of a plausible image and the theoretical activity of the scientist consists solely in the fabrication itself. The act of observation and the selection of some segment of the universe to be modelled are not theoretical activities. The selection of facts to be described, collected and brought together into a model can only be arbitrary with respect to theory since, for this epistemology, theoretical activity comes into play only after the facts have been gathered. If theories are indeed models then fact-gathering cannot be subject to theoretical exigencies. If, as for Bauman, any segment of the universe to be modelled 'presents itself to us as a cybernetic black-box', then any model-builder is free to select his personal black-box as he sees fit. Observation is essentially a-theoretical. Thus, in his paper on 'Social Structure', Lévi-Strauss insists that facts are to be:

'carefully observed and described, without allowing any theoretical preconceptions to decide whether some are more important than others' (Lévi-Strauss, 1968, p.280)

On no account must theory be allowed to govern the selection of facts. Since Lévi-Strauss has not collected all the facts in the world we can only presume that his selection of facts is governed by extra-theoretical considerations.

Once the facts have been collected the scientist may construct models to account for them. Lévi-Strauss cites von Neumann's listing of the requirements of a good model as follows:

'The definition must be precise and exhaustive in order to make a mathematical treatment possible. The construct must not be unduly complicated so that the mathematical treatment can be brought beyond the mere formalism to the point where it yields complete numerical results. *Similarity to reality is needed to make the operation significant. And this similarity must usually be restricted to a few traits deemed 'essential' pro-tempore* – since otherwise the above requirements would conflict with each other' (von Neumann & Morgenstern, 1954, pp.32–3, quoted in Lévi-Strauss, 1968, p.316 – emphasis added)

Theoretical activity consists in the construction of models that are similar in certain 'essential' respects to the empirical domain in question. But how similar is similar and how does one choose among the multiplicity of possible models? The answer is that the facts must be allowed to decide for themselves:

'the best model will always be that which is *true,* that is, the simplest model which, while being derived exclusively from the facts under consideration, also makes it possible to account for all of them' (Lévi-Strauss, 1968, p.281)

In the epistemology of model-building an arbitrariness in the initial selection of facts is compounded by the arbitrary relation of 'similarity' which determines what can plausibly be represented as an image of the facts concerned. Nothing could be further removed from the rigour of mathematical logic or even of positivist semantics. In both cases semantics is a matter of precise and unambiguous rules of correspondence between either one mathematical domain and another or a language and its meta-language. In neither is there room for the arbitrary play of similarity and difference – the 'semantic' rules of the epistemology of model-building. This epistemology shares nothing but the word 'model' with the theory of models in mathematical logic. By no stretch of the imagination can it be said to represent the place and function of models in mathematics or the natural sciences. Where the scientific use of models involves the rigorous articulation of two theoretical domains, the epistemology of model-building effectively proposes an essential arbitrariness in the relation between theory (the model) and its domain of interpretation. There can be no specifically theoretical evaluation of models according to this conception nor can there be any theoretical comparison of competing models. At its best the epistemology of model-building would result in a complex and sophisticated theoretical construct resting on an arbitrary and merely plausible foundation in resemblance.

Now, the inescapable arbitrariness that characterises the epistemology of model-building clearly leaves a nasty hole in its theory of knowledge. This epistemology is often combined with or supplemented by further doctrines which seek to establish the necessity of model-building as a means to knowledge either by maintaining that the world itself is essentially ordered and that knowledge can only reflect its order or by representing models as essentially 'unconscious', as the product of preconceptions or patterns of thought that precede and predetermine the possible forms of knowledge. General Systems Theory[20] maintains that the world is organised into a number of structurally isomorphic levels:

> 'The world is, as Aldous Huxley once put it, like a Neapolitan ice cake where the levels, the physical, the biological, the social and the moral universe, represent the chocolate, strawberry, and vanilla layers. We cannot reduce strawberry to chocolate – the most we can say is that possibly in the last resort, all is vanilla, all mind or spirit. The unifying principle is that we find organization on all levels. The mechanistic world view, taking the play of physical particles for ultimate reality, found its expression in a civilization glorifying physical technology which eventually has led to the catastrophies of our time. Possibly the model of the world as a great organization can help to reinforce the sense of reverence for the living which we have almost lost in the last sanguinary decades of human history' (von Bertalanffy, 1967, p.129)

Apart from its religious overtones the most striking feature of this position concerns its use of certain alleged characteristics of the world to legitimize its conception of the necessary forms of knowledge. It is precisely because the world is a great organization of systems that the construction of theoretical systems gives knowledge of the world. Systems in thought give a knowledge of the real systems to which they correspond. It is precisely because real systems are structurally isomorphic and because, as systems, they share certain general properties that General Systems Theory is capable of integrating the various discrete sciences. Thus knowledge of the world is to be obtained through the construction and manipulation of models, called systems. Knowledge is possible in this way because the world is in fact made up of systems.

An alternative approach to reducing or eliminating the arbitrariness of the epistemology of model-building is to refer to the properties of the knowing subject and, in particular, to the possibilities of biological, psychological or social determination of the categories of thought and therefore of the elements of what will be perceived and the 'unconscious' forms in which what is perceived will be organised. It is these possibilities that are taken up by the so-called genetic epistemology of Piaget and his associates, by Lévi-Strauss, and by the sociology of knowledge. In all cases these developments appear to ensure that what is arbitrary to theory is determined at some other level: it is not really arbitrary at all. In these conceptions any conscious theoretical activity on the part of the subject is founded upon the (biologically, psychologically, socially) pre-given 'unconscious' structure of his thought. [21] Even when certain products of thought appear to tell us nothing about the external world they nevertheless express the structure of the thinking apparatus:

> 'But mathematical thought at any rate reflects the free functioning of the mind, that is, the activity of the cells of the cerebral cortex, relatively emancipated from any external constraint and obeying its own laws. As the mind too is a thing, the functioning of this thing teaches us something about the nature of things: even pure reflection is in the last analysis an internalisation of the cosmos. It illustrates the structure of what lies outside in a symbolic form: "Logic and logistics are empirical sciences belonging to ethnography rather than to psychology" ' [22] (Lévi-Strauss, 1966, p.248 note)

A detailed commentary on this astonishing text cannot be attempted in the present context. What must be emphasised is that the specifically theoretical character of mathematical proof and demonstration is here simply swept aside in the name of the free functioning of the cerebral cortex. In fact, of course, any given mathematician must work upon existing mathematical materials, theories, forms of proof, problems. The place and functioning of these existing materials in mathematical thought is totally ignored in Lévi-Strauss' conception. Furthermore, it is clear that there is nothing in the properties of the 'cells of the cerebral cortex' as such to distinguish those of its mathematical products which are valid from those which are not. The effect of this reference back to the structure of the thinking apparatus (the cerebral cortex) can only be to obscure the significance of the mathematical materials and theoretical constructions necessary to the formulation of a given mathematical result and of the conditions which determine that this result is or is not valid.

In fact there is a more general problem here. If social, psychological or genetic determinations are to be invoked by protagonists of the epistemology of models to account for the 'unconscious' structuring of the human mind then how can it be claimed that the functioning of its 'unconscious' structure does, at least on occasion, result in knowledge? The answer, of course, is to be found in the recourse to the first tendency indicated above: the unconscious functioning of the mind may generate knowledge only because its structures correspond to certain structural features of the world. Consider, for example, Lévi-Strauss' explanation of how 'several thousand years of stagnation' have been able to intervene between the science of the neolithic revolution and modern science:

> 'There is only one solution to the paradox, namely, that there are two distinct modes of scientific thought. These are certainly not a function of different stages of development of the human mind but rather of *two strategic levels at which nature is accessible to scientific enquiry:* one roughly adapted to that of perception and the imagination; the other at a remove from it. It is as if the necessary connections which are the object of all science, neolithic or modern, could be arrived at by two different routes, one very close to, and the other more remote from sensible intuition' (*ibid.*, p.15, emphasis added)

The unconscious functioning of the human mind can produce neolithic and modern science precisely because there are two distinct levels of the world whose organization corresponds to the unconscious structures of human thought. The very possibility of knowledge is the product of a pre-established harmony between the structure of the world, at these levels, and the structure of human thought. Bauman invokes 'the painful process of evolution' to account for a very similar harmony between thought and the world:

> 'One can hardly imagine anything as cruel and stupid as a nature that provided its creatures with logic alone; no living organisms

need to decipher all the secrets of the world they live in – not even those vital to their own survival; *the basic qualities of their world –* and basic means unchangeable in time-spans commensurable with the duration of their life – *are built in to their own structure;* from the painful process of evolution, surviving species emerge with salutory disregard for countless highly improbable states of the world; as a matter of fact, *they manage somehow to make the best of their world only because they have been made to its measure . . .* That is a modern version of Kant's time-honoured conjecture, that the basic structure of perceiving the world is given to cognitive mind *a priori'* (Bauman, *op. cit.,* p.307, emphasis added)

Here Kant is honoured more in the outrageous breach than in the observance.[23] Every biological species is the victim of an evolutionary process which determines the limits and structures of what is 'thinkable' and 'knowable' by members of that species.[24] In Bauman's conception the limits and structures for human animals allow a certain 'play' within which a cultural determination of the categories of thought has its effects. Both the form and the possible contents of our knowledge are determined by our evolutionary development together with additional cultural constraints. A well-meaning Nature, neither cruel nor stupid, guarantees the status of that knowledge by ensuring that 'the basic qualities' of our world are built in to our structure.

Is it necessary to argue that these fantastic doctrines add nothing to the rigour or coherence of the epistemology of models and detract nothing from its absurdity? The notion of a correspondence between the constructions of thought and the world, between the structures of models or theoretical systems and the forms of organization of the world itself, can hardly be subject to proof – for that would involve stepping outside of our knowledge of the world to compare it with the world itself. But if the correspondence theory of knowledge invoked by some versions of the epistemology of model-building is purely dogmatic and incapable of rational defense the pre-established harmony of Lévi-Strauss' or Bauman's conception of knowledge is merely ridiculous. If the alleged *fact* of harmony cannot be demonstrated then the mechanisms invoked to account for it must be entirely speculative. We could just as reasonably invoke some malicious old guy in the sky to account for the 'unconscious' structures of our thought and to plague us with fatuous epistemologies which foster the illusion that these structures do indeed 'correspond' to the structures of the world. Or again, if scientific knowledge is the product of genetic and cultural determination and is said to be guaranteed its status as knowledge merely by 'the painful process of evolution' why not rather invoke a nature both 'cruel and stupid' to produce a scientific knowledge no different in kind from the 'knowledge' that enabled the dinosaurs to survive for millenia?

The epistemology of model-building represents a form of the empiricist conception of knowledge that is so vague and imprecise as to be almost vacuous. Attempts to shore it up with some conception of the world or of thought, or both, as essentially structured merely add a further dogmatic and speculative dimension to what is already completely indefensible.

6. *Popper*

With characteristic modesty Popper opens the first chapter of *Objective Knowledge* with the following assertions:

> 'I think that I have solved a major philosophical problem: the problem of induction. (I must have reached the solution in 1927 or thereabouts.) This solution has been extremely fruitful, and it has enabled me to solve a good number of other philosophical problems. However, few philosophers would support the thesis that I have solved the problem of induction. Few philosophers have taken the trouble to study — or even to criticize — my views on the problem, or have taken notice of the fact that I have done some work on it. Many books have been published quite recently on the subject which do not refer to any of my work, . . .' (*Objective Knowledge,* hereafter *O.K.,* p.1)

If many philosophers find no difficulty in ignoring Popper's work it is unfortunate that so many others, philosophers, social scientists and several eminent physicists, biologists and mathematicians, appear quite unable to do so. Lakatos writes that 'Popper's ideas represent the most important development in the philosophy of the twentieth century.' (Schilpp, 1974, p.241), while Sir Peter Medawar, writing in *Vogue* (Dec. 1973), calls Popper the 'greatest living philosopher'. Eminent natural scientists have testified to the importance of Popper's notion of falsifiability as a concept of the most direct significance to science. Similarly many social scientists have insisted that the notion of the testing of hypotheses against the facts defines the most important distinguishing characteristic of scientific practice. In Popper's conception science is distinguished from metaphysics and from pseudo-sciences such as Marxism and psychoanalysis by the fact that in science, and in science alone, all theories are submitted to the most rigorous and stringent testing.

If, as I argue, the importance so often attributed to Popper's normative conception of scientific practice is completely unjustified, it does necessitate some discussion of his work in this book. But there is a more general and perhaps more significant reason for including an examination of Popper's theory of science. I have argued that a distinction such as Carnap's between theoretical and observation languages cannot be maintained without contradiction in any positivist epistemology. Now Popper has always denied the existence of an a-theoretical observation language and many other philosophers have disputed the possibility of maintaining a rigorous distinction between theoretical and observational languages. Nevertheless, these authors maintain some residual attachment to positivism in the notion that theory is to be tested against the facts of observation. I have suggested that, if the possibility of an a-theoretical observation language is denied – and it cannot be defended – then the doctrine of the testing of theory against the facts has no rational foundation. Now, while he explicitly rejects many of the fundamental tenets of positivist epistemology, Popper has elaborated the most systematic attempt to combine the notions of testing and of the irreducibly theoretical character of all observation into a developed conception of scientific knowledge. Thus the argument that Popper's conception of knowledge is fundamentally incoherent has a more general implication. If it is impossible to establish a rigorous distinction between theoretical and observational languages within positivism and impossible to establish a coherent notion of the testing of theory against the facts without that distinction, then there can be no coherent positivist theory of science.

In this chapter I examine Popper's conceptions of science and of the growth of knowledge. His political and social philosophy will not be considered.[1] If his conception of knowledge is fundamentally incoherent, however, then many, if not all, of his social and political doctrines have no rational foundation. This chapter is divided into three sections. The first outlines Popper's theory of science and the growth of knowledge. In the second I examine the relation between his methodology and the speculative metaphysics on which it depends. While the metaphysics is necessary to the definition of the objective of his methodology, namely, the aim of science, his methodology cannot be shown to have any bearing on the attainment of the objectives defined by his metaphysics. Finally, I consider Popper's concept of testing in relation to his insistence on the irreducibly theoretical character of all observation, and I show that it is possible to combine them only at the cost of theoretical coherence. It follows that his demarcation between science and non-science is vacuous and that his conception of science as characterized by what he calls the 'method of rational criticism' is absurd.

6.1 Popper's Theory of Science

6.1.1 Induction and the demarcation between science and non-science

'A scientist, whether theorist or experimenter, puts forward statements, or systems of statements, and tests them step by step. In the field of the empirical sciences, more particularly, he constructs hypotheses, or systems of theories, and tests them against experience by observation and experiment.' (*The Logic of Scientific Discovery*, hereafter *LSD*, p.27)

The task of the logic of scientific discovery is to give a logical analysis of this procedure. Popper opposes the view that the empirical sciences are characterized by the use of inductive methods, that is, that their theories are established by inferring from singular statements, such as accounts of observations or experiments, to universal statements, such as theories and hypotheses. The problem of induction concerns whether and in what conditions inductive inferences are justified. The problem and Popper's answer to it may be described as follows:

Can the claim that an explanatory universal theory is true be justified by "empirical reasons"; that is, by assuming the truth of certain test statements or observation statements ...? My answer to the problem is the same as Hume's: No, we cannot; no number of true test statements would justify the claim that an explanatory universal theory is true.' (*OK*, p.7) [2]

Popper's answer to the problem of induction depends on his distinction between universal statements on the one hand and singular statements on the other. The sciences are concerned to discover true universal statements and they proceed by testing universal hypotheses or theories against singular statements. The latter refer to what may be observed in particular regions of space and time. Universal statements are not so restricted: they refer to all regions of space and time. Thus the general form of a universal statement is:

'Of all points in space and time (or in all regions of space and time) it is true that . . .' (*LSD*, p.63)

If there are to be any true universal statements then nature has to be characterized by essential uniformities. Thus, as Popper admits, his theory of science presupposes a definite metaphysical conception of nature. Scientific theories consist of universal statements, sometimes called laws of nature. If they are supplemented by statements of particular empirical conditions then it is possible to derive predictions as to what may be observed in particular regions of space and time. For example, the universal statement 'All swans are white' together with the singular statement 'There is a swan in such-and-such a region' entails the prediction 'There is a white swan in such-and-such a region'. Scientific theories are essentially descriptive: they refer to what may be observed in any region of time and space if the appropriate conditions are met. In Popper's conception of science there is no need for 'theoretical terms' in Carnap's sense which refer to 'unobservable' objects or properties.

Now, no finite or denumerable sequence of singular statements can ever cover all points or regions of space and time. It follows that singular statements, no matter how numerous, can never sustain an inference to a universal statement. No amount of observations of white swans can justify the conclusion that all swans are white. But a single black swan is sufficient to falsify that conclusion. Any universal statement can be falsified by finding one point or region at or in which whatever it asserts is not true. Popper therefore maintains that there is an asymmetry in the relation between universal and singular statements. The latter can never justify universal statements, they can only falsify them. Since the sciences aim to discover true universal statements it follows that they cannot proceed by induction. Instead they proceed by deduction and falsification. Theories can be refuted but they can never be proved. The search for true universal statements must therefore proceed through the elimination of those that are false.

Popper's solution to the problem of induction and his conclusion that the sciences proceed through the attempt to falsify universal statements provides him with a simple criterion of demarcation between science and non-science.[3] Science proposes descriptive universal statements that may be falsified by singular descriptive statements and it does attempt to falsify them. Non-science, metaphysics and pseudo-science, do not. Metaphysics advances propositions that cannot be falsified by singular descriptive statements. For example, the proposition that there are true universal statements can never be falsified by any finite sequence of singular descriptive statements. It is therefore metaphysical. Popper is far from hostile to metaphysics. Metaphysics may not be science but that does not mean that it is without meaning. On the contrary, metaphysics may well make a definite contribution to science. For example, in the Preface to the English edition of *The Logic of Scientific Discovery* Popper insists that:

'purely metaphysical ideas — and therefore philosophical ideas — have been of the greatest importance for cosmology. From Thales to Einstein, from ancient atomism to Descartes' speculation about matter, from the speculations of Gilbert and Newton and Leibniz and Boscovic about forces to those of Faraday and Einstein about fields of forces, metaphysical ideas have shown the way.' (*LSD*, p.19)

The pseudo-sciences, for example Marxism and psychoanalysis, are forms of metaphysics which purport to offer universal descriptive statements but they, or rather their proponents, refuse to allow them to be falsified. Consider Popper's comment on the status of psychoanalysis:

' . . . criteria of refutation have to be laid down beforehand: it must be agreed which observable situations, if actually observed, mean that the theory is refuted. But what kind of clinical responses would refute to the satisfaction of the analyst not merely a particular diagnosis but psychoanalysis itself? And have such criteria ever been discussed or agreed upon by analysis?' (*Conjectures and Refutations*, hereafter *CR*, p.38, note 3)

I will return to the significance of Popper's reference to the analyst rather than the propositions of psychoanalytic theory in connection with his doctrine of methodological decisions. What should be noted here is that Popper's dismissal of so many theories as metaphysical pseudo-sciences is crucially dependent on his particular conception of scientific theory. Since Popper rejects even Carnap's distinction between theoretical and observational terms he must interpret every theoretical proposition as essentially descriptive of observable states of affairs. On that interpretation there can be no theoretical proposition, however abstract, that cannot be directly refuted by observation. Popper's criterion of demarcation is an effect of his metaphysical conception of the world as characterized by essential uniformities that may be represented in universal descriptive statements and of science as postulating universal statements and testing them against observable states of affairs. Any theoretical discourse which can be interpreted as proposing universal descriptive statements of the approved kind may therefore be duly accredited as scientific. If a theoretical discourse is represented in some other way then it may be discredited as unscientific. For example, psychoanalysis is unscientific on Popper's reading. Its theories cannot be interpreted as universal descriptive statements since they do not preclude any observable states of affairs. Consider the case of a man who pushes a child into the water with the intention of drowning it and that of a man who sacrifices his life in an attempt to save the child:

> 'according to Freud the first man suffered from repression (say, of some component of his Oedipus complex), while the second man had achieved sublimation.' (*CR*, p.35) [4]

Here the theoretical apparatus of psychoanalysis is interpreted as non-descriptive; it is an empty jargon whose function is to provide an 'explanation' for all possible states of affairs. But, if it precludes no observable state of affairs then psychoanalysis cannot be falsified by observation. It is therefore unscientific.

Thus Popper conceives the relation between theory and observation in the sciences as conforming to the elemental pattern of the asymmetric relation between universal descriptive statements and singular descriptive statements outlined above. Anything which he or his supporters can represent as failing to respect this simplistic scheme must be unscientific.

6.1.2 *Logic of knowledge and psychology of knowledge*

'The question how it happens that a new idea occurs to a man –
whether it is a musical theme, a dramatic conflict, or a scientific
theory – may be of great interest to empirical psychology; but it is
irrelevant to the logical analysis of scientific knowledge. This latter
is concerned not with *questions of fact* (Kant's *quid facti*?) but only
with questions of *justification or validity* (Kant's *quid juris*?).'
(*LSD*, p.31)

The latter are investigated by means of the deductive testing of
theories. This involves analysis of the internal structure of theories and
of their relation to other theories and, especially, of the testing of
theory against observable states of affairs. While Popper appears here
to refer to the logical structure of a theory we shall see below that, in
so far as it is applicable to reality, logic itself becomes a descriptive
theory which may be empirically refutable. Thus logical relations
within a theory or between theories are themselves subject to empirical
refutation. In the last resort, the deductive testing of a theory is always
reducible to a confrontation with the facts. For the logic of knowledge
what matters is not where ideas come from but whether they fit the
facts. The provenance of scientific theories and ideas is relegated to
the realm of empirical psychology. Popper suggests that problems in
existing theory may well have significant effects in determining the
direction of work of scientists but the investigation of such effects
would not be the task of the logic of knowledge.

A related distinction is elaborated in Popper's later work in connection with the notion of world 3, the world of objective knowledge.
There are three ontologically distinct worlds:

'the first is the physical world or the world of physical states; the
second is the mental world or the world of mental states; and the
third is the world of intelligibles, of *ideas in the objective sense*; it is
the world of possible objects of thought ... ' (*OK*, p.154)

There is more than a little ambiguity in Popper's notion of objective
knowledge. For present purposes it is sufficient to say that for Popper
knowledge is 'objective' in that it exists independently of the subjective
state of mind of any individual or individuals. There is an objective
structure of knowledge in books, libraries, newspapers, and so on, and
it has properties which are objective and quite independent of whether

they are recognized by any human subjectivity. 'Knowledge in an objective sense is *knowledge without a knower*; it is *knowledge without a knowing subject.*' (*OK*, p.109)

Now, with regard to this objective structure we can ask two types of question. The first concerns how and by what mechanisms the structure was produced while the second concerns its properties. The logic of knowledge belongs to the second type since it concerns the properties of knowledge rather than its production. It is clear that the distinction involved here need not be restricted to 'knowledge in the objective sense'; it may be applied to any class of objects without exception. For example, in the case of spiders' webs or ants' nests we can investigate their production and we can investigate their properties as objective structures. While the web is produced by the activity of a spider it has properties which are not reducible to that activity. Furthermore, once it has been produced the web will react back on the spider as an external influence on its future activity. Similarly for world 3. Once it exists it reacts back on world 2, the world of mental states of human animals, and thereby may affect the structure of world 1, the world of physical states, through our application of the knowledge it contains.

The analogy between the objective structure of knowledge on the one hand and the equally objective structures of spiders' webs and ants' nests, or, for that matter, those resulting from human sewerage disposal, on the other hand, may seem far fetched but Popper intends it in all seriousness:

'the third world is a natural product of the human animal, comparable to a spider's web.' (*OK*, p.112)

Just as the spider interacts with his web so we interact with our world 3. Indeed:

'it is through this interaction between ourselves and the third world that objective knowledge grows, and . . . there is a close analogy between the growth of knowledge and biological growth; that is, the evolution of plants and animals.' (*ibid.*)

6.1.3 Popper's anti-subjectivism

Science is objective in the sense that its theories cannot be reduced to the content of any individual consciousness. Once a theory has been propounded it may be subjected to testing against observable states of affairs. For any given test the theory will either survive or not survive it. The process of testing scientific theories does not involve or depend on the subjective beliefs of any individual human subject, since a test performed by one person may be repeated by someone else. Both the theory and the singular observation statements against which it is tested are objective, i.e. irreducible to the content of any individual consciousness. In this respect, at least, Popper is no positivist. There can be no question of reducing the content of scientific theory to any supposedly basic and irreducible elements of what is given to consciousness. In fact there is no place in Popper's conception of knowledge for irreducible elements of knowledge at all. So, whereas Carnap must always suppose the possibility of an a-theoretical observation language Popper can happily insist that all observation without exception is made in the light of theory. There are no extra-theoretical primitive observation statements on the basis of which scientific theory may be constructed.

Popper repudiates all positivist conceptions of the relation between theory and observation. Thus there can be no question of conceiving the testing of theory in terms of any positivist recourse to the elements of experience. On the contrary:

> 'scientific statements must be objective, then those statements which belong to the empirical basis of science must also be objective. i.e. intersubjectively testable.' (*LSD*, p.47)

Objectively, in this sense, requires intersubjective testability. The testing of a theory therefore involves comparing the predictions of that theory with basic statements, that is, with singular descriptive statements which are themselves objective. Basic statements must be intersubjectively testable.

> 'We thus arrive at the following view. Systems of theories are tested by deducing from them statements of a lesser level of universality. These statements in their turn, since they are to be inter-subjectively testable, must be testable in like manner — and so *ad infinitum*.' (*ibid.*)

Popper insists that there is no danger of an infinite regress. Popper does not require that every statement in science be tested, merely that it be testable. There are no statements which simply have to be accepted. Thus, in Popper's system, there is no point at which demonstration has to stop. There are always points at which it does stop but there are no logical reasons why it should ever do so.

6.1.4 *Methodological decisions*

Theories are to be tested against descriptions of observed states of affairs and either rejected or provisionally accepted and then subjected to further tests. Unfortunately things are not so simple. One complication has been indicated in the previous section. The deductive testing of any theory must involve reference to basic statements which are also testable. Now universal statements and basic statements are both descriptive. It follows that if a given universal statement contradicts a given basic statement then at least one must be false. In the event of a test resulting in such a contradiction it seems that we must reject either the theory or the basic statement and we may reject both. Thus the decision to reject a theory on the basis of any test requires a prior decision to accept certain basic statements. Only the acceptance of basic statements can provide the logical grounds which Popper's theory requires for rejecting theories which appear to contradict them.

In practice, we are told, the situation is usually even more complex. The derivation of predictions from universal statements often requires some specification of the empirical conditions in a particular region of space and time, the use of other theories and some application of logic or of pure mathematics. In such cases what is tested is not so much any one universal statement as a complex system of theories, singular descriptive statements and elements of logic and mathematics. If that system fails its test as a result of our decision to accept some basic statements then which part of the system should we reject? We have seen that all theories and all singular descriptive statements are testable but the same is true of logic and mathematics:

> 'Insofar as a calculus is applied to reality, it loses the character of a *logical* calculus and becomes a descriptive theory *which may be empirically refutable*; and in so far as it is treated as irrefutable, i.e. as a system of *logically true* formulae, rather than a descriptive scientific theory, it is not applied to reality.' (*CR,* p.210)

But if logic, other theories, and singular descriptive statements are all refutable in principle then no test can ever provide a logically conclusive refutation of any one universal statement. The observation of a black swan by be interpreted as disposing of the theory that all swans are white or as a refutation of elementary formal logic.

How, then, is the scientist to proceed? He decides to test a certain universal statement and he therefore makes the appropriate observations. Having provisionally decided to accept the resulting basic statements he compares them with his more or less complex system of theories, singular descriptive statements, logic and mathematics. If he finds a contradiction then he has a problem. He must decide which part or parts of the system to reject. Logic cannot help him here. Instead he must provisionally decide that the result of the test entails the rejection of such-and-such a part of his system of theory. That decision may be mistaken and it is always open to further testing. *Refutation is always a matter of decision.*

Now, the fact that no test is ever logically conclusive for any theory means that we can effectively immunize any given theory against empirical refutation by the simple expedient of interpreting test results as refuting auxiliary hypotheses, singular descriptions or, if all else fails, logic itself. Thus it is not the structure of a theory as such which determines whether it is testable and falsifiable but rather the methods we apply to it.

'The question whether a given *system* should as such be regarded as a conventionalist or an empirical one is therefore misconceived. *Only with reference to the methods applied* to a theoretical system is it possible to ask whether we are dealing with a conventionalist or an empirical theory.' (*LSD*, p.82)

The implication is clear. The difference between science and metaphysics is not a function of their concepts and relations between concepts. It is a function of how we decide to treat them. It is the behaviour of the analyst rather than the structure of psychoanalytic theory as such which determines whether or not it is scientific. Similarly for Marxism or theology. It is the behaviour of Marxists and theologians that counts, not the character of their concepts.

Thus Popper's demarcation criterion between science and nonscience, while it appears to refer to the character of theories, actually involves a normative conception of scientific and unscientific forms of behaviour. To be scientific is to accept a behavioural norm [5] which Popper describes in terms of methodological decisions:

'We decide that if our system is threatened we will never attempt to save it by any kind of conventionalist stratagem.' (*ibid.*)

This norm is methodological: it cannot be justified in our based upon any empirical science. In effect, it is based on metaphysics, and Popper has frequently insisted that what is and what is not an acceptable scientific explanation changes over time. These 'big changes' he describes in terms of 'metaphysical research programmes' for science.[6] Thus the content of scientific knowledge at any time is a function of intersubjective decisions based on methodological norms derived from 'metaphysical research programmes'. The demarcation between science and non-science is an effect of the prevailing metaphysics.

As a final complication we should note that the making of observations in science is conceived by Popper as a function of training:

> 'Any empirical scientific statement can be presented (by describing experimental arrangements, etc.) in such a way that anyone who has learned the relevant technique can test it.' (*LSD*, p.99)

And again:

> 'I have no intention of *defining* the term "observable" or "observable event" . . . I think that it should be introduced as an undefined term which becomes sufficiently precise in use: as a primitive concept whose use the epistemologist has to learn, much as he has to learn the term "symbol", or as the physicist has to learn the use of the term "mass-point".' (*ibid.*, p.103)

Thus the result of any test, and therefore the content of scientific knowledge, must depend on the forms of training which prevail within the scientific community at the time. Now, we have seen that the rejection of a theory on the basis of a test requires *inter alia* the prior decision to accept the relevant basic statements. If the basic statements are not accepted then no methodological decisions in the world can enable us to reject any theory through deductive testing. In the last resort basic statements must be accepted or rejected on the basis of prevailing experimental technique. The function of training therefore provides a means for obtaining acceptance of basic statements at least from other members of the scientific community. In Popper's system, as Lakatos has noted, unanimity on basic statements 'can be reached by expelling the minority as pseudoscientists or cranks.' (Schilpp, 1974, p.243) When all else fails the danger of an infinite regression in the testing and retesting of basic statements by the scientific community may be averted by the elementary rule that might is right.[7]

6.2 Rational Criticism and the Growth of Knowledge

Popper's theory of science depends on a definite metaphysical conception of nature as characterized by certain essential uniformities. Because nature is so organized there will be universal statements which are *true*, that is, which correspond to the facts of nature. However, the very fact of their universality ensures that universal statements can never be shown to be true. Thus, while we know from Popper's metaphysics that there are true universal statements we can never hope to establish that any scientific theory actually is true. But we can certainly hope to eliminate those theories which are false. In Popper's theory the aim of science is to get nearer to the truth and it does so by fulfilling the method of rational criticism. This method involves the clear formulation of problems and the rigorous testing of proposed solutions according to the methodological rubrics indicated above. The growth of knowledge proceeds through the elimination of error. Popper often represents this process in the following schema:

$$P_1 - TT - EE - P_2$$

We start from a problem and we formulate a tentative solution or tentative theory which we then subject to the severest possible tests in a process of error-elimination. The elimination of error leads us to the formulation of new problems which 'arise from our own creative activity'. (*OK*, p.119) Not only is this process supposed to lead to the growth of knowledge but it also serves Popper as an epistemological analogue to natural selection. In his paper 'Evolution and the Tree of Knowledge' Popper writes of the natural selection of hypotheses that it is 'a competitive struggle which eliminates those hypotheses which are unfit'. (*OK*, p.261) The difference between scientific knowledge and pre-scientific or animal knowledge is that the former is subjected to systematic and conscious criticism. This has the advantage that:

> 'while animal knowledge and pre-scientific knowledge grow mainly through the elimination of those holding the unfit hypothesis, scientific criticism often makes our theories perish in our stead, eliminating our mistaken beliefs before such beliefs lead to our own elimination.' (*ibid.*)

Popper insists that this statement is not meant metaphorically. There is an evolutionary tree of knowledge and it is governed by the regulative idea of *truth as correspondence with the facts*.

'Together with the fact that our curiosity, our passion to explain by means of unified theory, is universal and unlimited, our aim of getting nearer to the truth explains the integrative growth of the tree of knowledge.' (*OK*, p.264)

The method of rational criticism is the mechanism of a teleological growth of knowledge in the direction of increasing verisimilitude.

Unfortunately, even if we were to refrain from questioning the status of Popper's metaphysical conception of the world, it would be impossible to establish either that the method of 'rational criticism' leads to the growth of scientific knowledge in the sense of increasing verisimilitude or that it has any coherent foundation in his metaphysics and theory of knowledge. I am not concerned at this stage with the question of whether deductive testing, in Popper's sense, can be said to represent the method of science, that is, whether the relation between theory and observation can be reduced to the elemental pattern of the asymmetric relation between universal descriptive statements and singular descriptive statements. I return to the question of theory and observation in the concluding section of this chapter. The present argument is concerned with the relation between Popper's specification of the aim of science and his account of its method, in particular with the question of whether there is any rational basis for the claim that the latter has a bearing on the attainment of the former. We shall see that there is not.

Consider first the question of the aim of science, namely, getting nearer to the truth. Popper uses the concept of truth in the sense of the classical theory that truth is correspondence to the facts. He regards Tarski's theory of truth as 'a rehabilitation and an elaboration of the classical theory'. (*OK*, p.323) Because of Tarski it is legitimate to talk of 'truth' and 'correspondence to the facts'. Now, as I have shown in the previous chapter, Tarski's concept of truth concerns a relation between two languages: an object language in which statements are formulated and a metalanguage which contains names of statements in the object language and sentences having the same meaning as statements in the object language. If *P* represents a name and *p* represents a metalinguistic 'translation' of the statement *P* then, following Tarski's definition, we can make metalinguistic assertions such as:

$$P \text{ is true if and only if } p.$$

Thus Tarski's theory of truth establishes a clear and rigorous concept of truth by means of precisely determined relations between an object language and a metalanguage. But Popper's theory of science is not concerned primarily with relating the language of science to some metalanguage of the language of science. It is concerned with relating scientific statements to the world, to the essential uniformities of nature. Tarski's theory tells us nothing about the relation of language to the world and it certainly cannot legitimize any conception of truth as correspondence with some extra-linguistic reality. It is this latter correspondence that is required for Popper's theory of science. If, in order to talk of the truth or falsity of scientific statements, he has recourse to some metalanguage then he merely transposes the question of correspondence to the world from one language to another. In one of his examples Popper uses German as an object language and English as the metalanguage. Consider the statement 'Der Mond besteht aus grünem Käse'. This statement is false but testable. It is therefore scientific. Now, we can formulate the conditions of the truth of our statement as follows:

> 'The German statement "Der Mond besteht aus grünem Käse" is true if and only if the moon consists of green cheese.' (Cf. *OK*, p.326)

Fine. But the facts have still to be established and, in Popper's theory of science, that would lead us away from relations between English and German to the relation between an English statement and the world. His use of Tarski's definition of truth resolves none of the problems of his correspondence theory of knowledge. Popper's metaphysics assures us that there are true universal statements; it remains to be shown that what he describes as 'rational criticism' is able to lead us in their direction.

Now, it is clear that any systematic application of the method of rational criticism must involve a change in the content of what passes for knowledge at any given time in 'the game of science'. (*LSD* p.53) But why should we suppose, as Popper does, that it also leads to a growth of knowledge in the sense of increasing verisimilitude? The importance of that question should be clear. Unless it can be shown that the application of Popper's method does indeed entail a *growth* of scientific knowledge then it is impossible to justify that method in terms of Popper's metaphysics and his specification of the aim of science. If the method of rational criticism cannot be shown to lead to the growth of knowledge then Popper's insistence on the necessity of testing and falsifiability can rest on nothing but blind faith.

But, if it is impossible to establish that any theory is true then it must also be impossible to establish that one theory is nearer to the truth than any other. Indeed, Popper frequently appears to recognize this point. For example, in his paper 'Truth, Rationality, and the Growth of Scientific Knowledge' Popper tells us that the question 'How do you know that the theory t_2 has a higher degree of verisimilitude than the theory t_1?' must be answered as follows:

> 'I do not know – I only guess. But I can examine my guess critical-ly, and if it withstands severe criticism, then this fact may be taken as a good critical reason in favour of it.' (*CR*, p.234)

And again:

> 'even after t_2 has been refuted in its turn we can still say that it is better than t_1, for although both have been shown to be false, the fact that t_2 has withstood tests which t_1 did not pass may be a good indication that the falsity-content of t_1 exceeds that of t_2 while its truth content does not.' (*CR*, p.235) [8]

The circularity of Popper's position here is evident. If it is possible to establish that one theory is nearer to the truth than another theory then it may be possible to argue that what Popper describes as the method of rational criticism does indeed lead to the growth of knowledge. Popper merely offers a guess and suggests that the guess be subjected to rational criticism. 'Rational criticism' is to be used to provide 'a good critical reason in favour' of the guess that one theory really is closer to the truth than a competing theory. Thus the only argument that Popper can offer to support the assertion that 'rational criticism' does lead to the growth of knowledge is itself dependent on the method of 'rational criticism'. In effect we are asked to accept that rational criticism leads to the growth of knowledge because rational criticism gives a good reason for accepting that it does.

Popper's conception of scientific theory as consisting of universal statements ensures that no theory can be shown to be nearer the truth than any other. While it may be possible to maintain that one theory is better than another in the sense of surviving more severe tests it can-not be shown that the 'better' theory is any closer to the metaphysical utopia of true universal statements. There is nothing but blind faith and empty dogmatism to support the view that 'rational criticism' leads to the growth of knowledge. In the absence of such a faith it must seem that the game of science is entirely destructive: it can show that theories are false but it has nothing positive to offer. But can it even show that theories are false? Popper's doctrine of methodological decisions and his remarks on the function of the training of scientists suggests that the procedure of deductive testing can provide no rational grounds for rejecting any theory which fails its test. We have seen that no test can ever be logically conclusive so that the 'refutation' of a theory is a matter of decisions, conventions and forms of training. A theory which fails its test is one that falls foul of the forms of training current within the community of scientists in question and of their methodological decisions to accept certain basic statements, not to question various other theories or the empirical applicability of formal logic, etc. The test itself provides no more grounds for the conclusion that a theory which fails is false than it does for the conclusion that one which does not fail is true. While Popper constantly alludes to 'good reasons' for accepting or rejecting basic statements, for accepting or rejecting hypotheses and theories, and so on, the reasons cited are never commensurate with the conclusion we are asked to draw. Reasons are 'good' in so far as they conform to Popper's specification of the rules of the game of science; in effect they must satisfy the conditions of 'rational criticism'. But reasons that are 'good' in that sense cannot entail the conclusion that such-and-such a hypothesis is false or that such-and-such a theory is nearer to the truth than some competing theory.

Consider, for example, the status of basic statements in Popper's theory. Popper has been criticized by positivists for the consequences of his refusal to allow that any statement can find its justification in experience.

'Experience can motivate a decision, and hence an acceptance or rejection of a statement, but a basic statement cannot be justified by them — no more than by thumping the table.' (*LSD,* p.105)

Why, then, should Popper insist that basic statements should refer to states of affairs that can be observed, that is, *experienced*? It is our *decision* which is decisive in Popper's theory of science, not our observaton. In effect, as Ayer points out, Popper has a very simple way of assessing the truth or falsity of basic statements:

'True basic statements are those that we decide to accept; false basic statements are those that we decide to reject.' (Schilpp, 1974, p.687)

In reply, Popper first admits that the acceptance or rejection of a given basic statement is arbitrary 'from a purely logical point of view' and then argues that, like the verdict of a jury, it is far from being 'completely arbitrary'.

> 'The jury decides about a fact – say, whether or not Mr. A killed Mr. B. Its decision is the result of prolonged deliberation; much time is needed for coming to a common decision (which is the meaning of "convention" intended here). But who would say that a jury which has long and seriously debated the issue decided "completely arbitrarily"? Its decision is the result of a common effort to *find the truth.*' (Schilpp, 1974, p.1111)

This reply is entirely beside the point. The problem at issue concerns the logical capacity of accepted basic statements to support conclusions based on them. Popper offers a 'good reason' in the shape of the seriousness of the scientific jury and the effort it devotes to its task. Unfortunately the problem concerns not the existence of effort and seriousness on the part of the jury but whether they are put to any useful purpose. Popper's 'good reason' has no bearing at all on this latter question. The inadequacy of Popper's position may be seen if we consider the case of a hypothetical scientific jury which accepts basic statements on the results of a long and careful examination of chicken entrails. Suppose now that some hypothetical sceptic were to question the logical status of basic statements derived in this fashion. An equally hypothetical 'Popper' might well reply that of course the acceptance of basic statements was logically arbitrary but that nevertheless a jury of carefully trained inspectors of chicken entrails had long and seriously debated the issue and that, therefore, far from being completely arbitrary its decision was the result of a common effort to find the truth.

If the aim of science is to get nearer to the truth in the sense of Popper's metaphysical conception of the world then not one of the 'good reasons' to which he alludes is commensurate with the conclusion that the method of rational criticism has any bearing on the attainment of that aim. Popper's defence of his methodology and his criterion of demarcation is this:

> 'My only reason for proposing my criterion of demarcation is that it is fruitful.' (*LSD*, p.55)

This defence is on a par with the 'good reasons' he invokes at other points in his argument and is vulnerable to the same criticism.

6.3 Theory, Observation and Testing

Popper rejects the positivist notion of the reducibility of knowledge to the phenomena of experience. Nevertheless, there are at least two significant respects in which his methodological doctrine bears comparison with that of the most elaborate and compendious of positivist methodologies outlined in Mill's *A System of Logic*. In both, the aim of science is defined with reference to a definite metaphysical conception of the world as populated by essential uniformities. Those uniformities exist and it is the job of science to discover them or, at least, to produce better and better approximations to them. I have shown that Mill's conception of the world is such that no methodological rules can ever be shown to be effective. Thus Mill's methodology has no rational foundation in the metaphysics on which it nevertheless depends for the definition of its objectives. We have now seen that Popper's methodology is similarly related, or rather unrelated, to his metaphysics. While his metaphysics is necessary to define the objective of his methodology, his methodology cannot be shown to have any bearing on the attainment of that objective. There is a sense in which Popper, unlike Mill, recognizes the glaring discrepancy between his methodology and its objective since he admits that the degree of verisimilitude of any theory cannot be known. His 'solution' to the problem posed by that discrepancy is disarmingly simple. He explicitly recognizes that the discrepancy exists and then proceeds almost as if nothing had happened, invoking a plethora of 'good reasons', 'critical discussions' and even, as his jury analogy effectively requires, 'good intentions', none of which are capable of supporting the weight of argument that Popper's theory places on them. Where Mill disposes of the problem by the sleight of hand of his circular justification of induction by induction Popper tries to smother it with a mass of irrelevant, and therefore empty, verbiage.

A second area of comparison concerns the articulation of scientific propositions on to the realm of phenomena to which they allegedly refer. Mill treats that articulation as unproblematic and fails to develop an elaborated conception of language. We have seen that twentieth century logical positivism and associated positions have posed the problem of the articulation of scientific propositions and the real and that they have attempted to resolve it by means of the concept of a primitive observation language in which propositions 'point to' the content of the given and 'represent' its structure. In the two previous chapters I have described some of the internal problems which have led to the breakdown of the theory of an a-theoretical observation language. Briefly, the positivist distinction between theoretical and observation languages requires that elementary logic be non-empirical; logic must represent the structure of all possible experience. Thus any rigorous distinction between the languages of theory and of observation must lead to a contradiction within positivist epistemology: on the one hand all knowledge is reducible to the phenomena of experience; on the other hand elementary logic determines in advance the structure of all possible experience and it therefore represents a 'knowledge' that is independent of any experience. For this and other reasons many authors have denied the possibility of a rigorous distinction between the languages of theory and of observation while retaining a residual allegiance to the positivist doctrine of the reducibility of knowledge to the phenomena of experience.

Popper, too, rejects the logical positivist distinction between theoretical and observational languages and, like Mill, he appears to treat the articulation of scientific propositions on the realm of phenomena as essentially unproblematic. Consequently, while he has a great deal to say on the functions and significance of language, he fails to develop an elaborated conception of the articulation of language on to the world. In the remainder of this chapter I argue that the rejection of the concept of an a-theoretical observation language must remove any possible rational foundation for the notion of the 'testing' of hypotheses against the facts of observation. Popper's own conception of the nature of scientific language therefore entails the absurdity of his methodological prescriptions and of his criterion of demarcation between science and non-science. Similarly the notion of testing can have no rational foundation in a residual positivist epistemology which fails to recognize a rigorous distinction between the languages of theory and of observation. Since, as I have shown, that distinction itself entails a contradiction within positivist epistemology it follows that there can be no rational positivist or neo-positivist defence of the doctrine that science proceeds through the testing of hypotheses against the fact of observation.

In Popper's work the disjunction between the propositions of science and the objects to which they refer is enshrined in the thesis of *realism,* the thesis of the reality of the world. The scientific tradition defined by the regulative ideal of versimilitude, is a realist tradition:

> 'This regulative ideal of finding theories which correspond to the facts is what makes the scientific tradition a realist tradition: it distinguishes between the world of our theories and the world of facts to which these theories belong.' (*OK,* p.290)

Now, to propose such a distinction is to pose a problem of the status of the concepts and theoretical structure of the propositions of science in relation to the objects to which they are supposed to refer. I am not concerned here with the question of whether some particular proposition can be said to correspond to the facts but with the more general issue of the relations between the realm of scientific discourse on the one hand and the realm of real objects on the other. If the two realms are conceived as distinct then it cannot be presumed that the concepts and relations between concepts of the one are adequate to represent the structure of the other. For example, if the structure of the real is distinct from that of scientific discourse then distinctions made in the one may well not represent any difference in the other and, conversely, different objects may well be subsumed under the same concept. If the structures are indeed distinct then it is possible that there are no true propositions. If Popper is to speak of truth as correspondence with the facts then he must show that the structure of scientific discourse is such as to make such correspondences possible. Tarski's theory of truth cannot help him here since it remains within the sphere of relations between two languages.

It should be noted that the problem of discrepancy between scientific discourse and the objects to which it refers is not peculiar to Popper. Analogous difficulties must arise within any positivist epistemology which attempts to reduce knowledge to the phenomena of experience. If experiences are distinct from statements about them, then only a doctrine of the pre-established harmony between language and the order of experience can avoid the problem of discrepancy. Once knowledge is conceived in terms of a correspondence between two distinct realms, between propositions on the one hand and real objects, experiences, or what have you, on the other, once it is a matter of both a *distinction* and a *correspondence* which bridges what has been distinguished, then the fact of the former must make problematic the possibility of the latter. But, in positivist epistemology or in Popper's epistemological realism, if the possibility of correspondence is problematic then it can never be shown 'to exist. Any attempt to investigate or to establish some proposed correspondence must have recourse to further propositions whose status is no less problematic than those of the propositions under investigation.

It is for this reason that a doctrine of the pre-established harmony between language and the world is required to overcome the possibility of a discrepancy between them. This, in effect, is the thesis of Wittgenstein's *Tractatus* and of the logical positivist postulate of an a-theoretical observation language. There is a language of elementary propositions whose distinct constants 'point to' different elements of the world and whose logical grammar reproduces the structure of the world. The possibility of a correspondence is established by the simple expedient of effacing the problematic distinction. I have shown that the notion of an a-theoretical observation language must conflict with the fundamental theses of positivist epistemology since it postulates, in logic, a knowledge that is independent of experience. In addition, since it cannot hope to be established it is clear that the thesis of pre-established harmony can rest on nothing but an act of faith – with an open or surreptitious vote of thanks to the old guy in the sky who made it all possible.

Now, to reject the postulate of an a-theoretical observation language is to preclude the notion of the pre-established harmony between the language of scientific observation and the world. Popper and all those residual positivists who dispute the possibility of a rigorous distinction between the languages of theory and observation are condemned to the thesis of a discrepancy between the language of scientific observation and the objects or experiences which it is supposed to describe. Thus Popper insists that statements of observation are always interpretations, 'that they are interpretations in the light of theory'. (*LSD,* p.107n) If observation or description is always theoretical, theory is always descriptive. We have seen, for example, that, in Popper's view, logic and mathematics, insofar as these are applied to reality, are empirical and therefore falsifiable. It follows that every proposition, however abstract, can be interpreted as a description of some real or postulated state of affairs. There are no terms or propositions which refer to unobservable objects or unobservable properties of objects. In addition, we have seen that, in Popper's theory, the recording of observations is not only made 'in the light of theory' but that it is a function of the training of scientists in the use of scientific instruments. Theory is therefore implicated in observation in the interpretation of results and, at least for Popper, in the construction of the instruments which make those results possible.

What are the implications of this rejection of the postulate of an a-theoretical observation language for the notion of the testing of hypotheses against the facts? In the positivist epistemology of Carnap the status of the concept of testing is clear and unambiguous: because there are protocol sentences which directly represent the structure of the given it follows that hypotheses which contradict the relevant protocol sentences must be false; they cannot correspond to the given. Here the concept of testing is a consequence of the postulate of pre-established harmony. Popper rejects that postulate. I have just quoted his assertion that observations are made in the light of theory. He continues:

> 'That is one of the main reasons why it is always deceptively easy to find *verifications* of a theory, and why we have to adopt a *highly critical* attitude towards our theories if we do not wish to argue in circles: the attitude of trying to *refute* them.' (*ibid.*)

Theories must be severely tested against the facts, they must be measured against basic statements, accepted statements of observation. Now, if conflict between basic statement and hypothesis is to entail the *falsification* of the latter then the former must stand in as a surrogate for the facts. But that possibility is specifically precluded once the postulate of an a-theoretical observation language is denied. The comparison of hypothesis and basic statement cannot then be interpreted as equivalent to the comparison of hypothesis with reality. The notion that testing, as Popper describes it, involves the falsification and refutation of theories or hypotheses is simply fatuous. If theory is inescapably implicated in observation then testing cannot be a rational procedure. If testing is a rational procedure then there must be an a-theoretical mode of observation governed by a pre-established harmony between language and the real. To maintain, as Popper does, both the rationality of testing and the thesis that observation is an interpretation in the light of theory is to collapse into a manifest and absurd contradiction. Popper's theory of science is therefore strictly incoherent.

It is necessary to insist on the significance of this conclusion. If there is no positivist observation language then the experimental practice of the sciences cannot be conceived as a matter of working on a given nature. On the contrary, and even in terms of Popper's own conception of scientific theory, the sciences work on constructs which are produced through the operation of its theory and instruments, (and these latter in their turn depend on theory). It follows that the relation between theory, instrument, and observation must be conceived as internal to the practice of the science concerned.[9] When observation statements are hypostatized and are represented in opposition to the theoretical conditions of their production the result is a more or less speculative conception of the relation between theory on the one hand and 'the facts of observation' on the other. For example, Popper's own speculative metaphysics is required to close the gap opened up by his hypostatizing of the status of basic statements in relation to the theories and instruments implicated in their production.

If there is no positivist observation language then experiment and observation in the sciences cannot be reduced to the Popperian notion of testing. Whatever Popper, neo-positivist philosophers of science, and many practising scientists may believe, the sciences cannot proceed by any process resembling Popper's account of deductive testing. It is only the internal incoherence of his own theory that allows Popper to represent what he regards as science as being characterized by testing. Strictly speaking his criterion of demarcation between science and non-science is vacuous and rational criticism, as he defines it, is an irrational absurdity. In particular, then, his ideological polemic against Marxism and psychoanalysis as metaphysical pseudo-sciences is made possible only by the incoherence of his own conception of science: it has no rational foundation.

7. *The Critique of Empiricism and the Analysis of Theoretical Discourse*

There have been many critiques of the empiricism of the academic social sciences and it has even been claimed that the critique of empiricism is now fashionable in sociology. [1] In this chapter I begin by examining two of the more serious forms of this 'fashionable' critique in order to establish both its theoretical force and its limitations. I consider first the trenchant and in many respects extremely successful critique of sociological methodology advanced by David and Judith Willer in *Systematic Empiricism: critique of a pseudo-science* and secondly that based on Althusser's critique of 'the empiricist conception of knowledge'. Several of my own publications and much of the argument of the preceding chapters falls into this latter category. Within the general area of the critique of empiricism it is necessary to distinguish between, on the one hand, the analysis and critique of a methodology or an epistemology in the sense of a theoretical doctrine within which a definite body of procedural rules for scientific practice may be elaborated and, on the other hand, a critique directed at the alleged results of the application of such rules, for example, a critique of survey-type sociology as 'empiricist' and therefore not scientific but ideological. In the Willers' book and in a great deal of 'Althusserian' work we find both a critique of empiricism understood as an epistemological doctrine and an extension of that critique to what are held to be the products of empiricist methods. I propose to examine the validity of that extension and to argue that, however effective the critique of epistemology may be, its extension leads to an invalid and logically ineffective mode of critique.

The Willers' concept of empiricism is limited to what is often described as the British Empiricist Tradition in philosophy (Hume, Mill, Russell, etc.) and related positions. Althusser's definition of 'the empiricist conception of knowledge' as outlined in *Reading Capital* is pitched at a level of generality which, at least in intention, subsumes the whole field of classical epistemology. The force of these authors' critique of empiricist epistemology and methodology is indisputable but, as we shall see, serious difficulties arise as soon as these authors extend their critique, or others extend it for them, to what they represent as a real empiricist process of knowlege. If there is a real process which conforms to the concept of empiricism developed by the Willers' or by Althusser then what they describe as the essential elements of that process must also exist. For the Willers there is indeed a realm of observational knowledge, of 'given' facts, and empiricism is simply a non-scientific, non-theoretical mode of relationship to that realm. For Althusser the situation is more complex but his conception of ideology implies that there are 'givens' which human subjects appropriate in the formation of ideological discourse. In this sense there is a real empiricist process of knowledge and it takes place in ideology. I argue that, in both cases, their conceptions of empiricism as a real process of production of knowledge and of science as a different real process generate inescapable problems and result in logically impossible theories of the process of production of knowledge. The critique of empiricist epistemology and methodology cannot be extended to a critique of what might seem to be products of the realization of empiricist protocols.

Now, these arguments raise a more general problem which concerns not so much the demarcation between science and non-science as forms of production of knowledge but rather the manner in which the process of production of discourse is conceived, namely, as the realization of an extra-discursive conceptual totality. What is at stake here is what I shall call the rationalist conception of the production of discourse in which whether what is to be realized is conceived as a methodology, an author's presuppositions or even, as with Althusser, a (vertical) system of concepts which underlies, but does not appear in, the order of concepts in discourse, the relation between what appears in the discourse and its extra-discursive conditions is conceived as one of coherence and logical consistency. This conception will be shown to be a particular case of the more general rationalist conception of action outlined in the Introduction in which human action, variously conceived, provides a mechanism for the realization of ideas. Weber's concept of action is rationalist in this sense: 'meanings' are realized through the mechanisms of consciousness and will. I argue that the rationalist conception of action can be maintained only at the price of theoretical incoherence and, in particular, that therefore no rationalist conception of the production of discourse can be tenable.

It follows from this critique that a rigorous separation should be maintained between problems concerned with the logical properties of the order of concepts of a discourse and those concerned with its process of production. Rationalism, in the above sense, conflates these two types of problem. I conclude this chapter by considering some of the implications of the preceding arguments and of that separation for the analysis of theoretical discourse.

7.1 Systematic Empiricism: Critique of a Pseudo-science

The Willers conceive of empiricism as an epistemological and methodological doctrine which advocates the production of knowledge by means of the application of various sorting and generalising procedures to given facts. Empiricism maintains that all knowledge is based on and reducible to what the Willers call 'empirical knowledge'. This type of knowledge:

'is gained by experience or sensation alone, and is clearly shared by men with the higher animals. Like all animals with well-developed sensory organs and a nervous system, man learns from his environment, developing expectations useful for survival ... Man, however, has an advantage over other animals in his extensive ability to communicate empirical knowledge to his fellows. It is this simplest and most fundamental type of knowledge that man shares with some other members of the animal kingdom' (*Systematic Empiricism,* p.7)

The distinctive feature of empiricism is that it regards this fundamental type of knowledge as the sole basis of thought so that man gains knowledge only through sensory experience.

The Willers' examination of various empiricist methodological positions involves first the argument, to which I shall return, that empiricism is not science and secondly a form of internal critique to show that empiricist methodology has no rational or logical basis, that is, that its arguments do not support its conclusions and that the methodological rules which it advocates are therefore without foundation. The best example of this latter is probably their critique of Mill's conception of knowledge by induction and of his canons of argument. The attempt to establish the universality and effectivity of induction by means of induction is simply absurd. Furthermore, if phenomena are indeed governed by 'laws of nature' of the kind Mill proposes, if there are regular and recurrent sequential relations between the appearances of different phenomena, then Mill's canons of agreement and difference, and so on, can never hope to establish those 'laws'. Thus methodological doctrines based on Mill's epistemology are logically absurd and impracticable.

In their internal critique of Mill's *A System of Logic* and of other 'empiricist' methodological positions the Willers have provided extremely effective analyses of many of the positivist methodological doctrines which appear to dominate the contemporary social sciences. However, as I have suggested in chapter 4, there is an aspect of their critique of empiricism which leads to very serious problems. In particular, they maintain that empiricism represents a real form of knowledge so that the fundamental error of empiricist epistemology lies, in effect, in its failure to acknowledge the existence of other forms of knowledge. In fact, we are told, there are three distinct types of thought which may be schematically represented in the following diagram:

	Empirical	Rational	Abstractive
Theoretical		o———→o	o ↑ o
Observational	o———→o		↓ o o ↑

Three types of thought (Systematic Empiricism, p.15)[2]

These types of thought and their combinations constitute the forms of knowledge that are possible. Empirical knowledge remains at the level of observation; it attempts to relate observables to other observables in a more or less systematic fashion. Science, on the other hand, involves all three kinds of thought. Rational thought is concerned with concepts and relations between concepts. It therefore uses theoretical forms of argument and theoretical demonstration. Concepts are not defined in terms of observationals 'but by their relationship to each other' (p.24). A scientific theory 'is a constructed relational statement consisting of non-observable concepts connected to other non-observable concepts' (*ibid.*) Thus, while empiricism and science are both concerned with observables the latter also involves concepts and rational connections between concepts. Since concepts and observables are the concern of different types of thought science must also involve a type of thought which is capable of relating the two levels. Concepts and observables are brought together by means of relations of abstraction. Thus, the Willers' conception of science involves the postulation of a distinction between concepts and observables on the one hand and of a correspondence between them on the other. There is indeed a realm of given facts and of observational knowledge and empiricism is simply a non-scientific, non-theoretical mode of relationship to that realm. Where science involves relations between concepts and observables the empiricist conception of science merely involves relations between empirical categories of different levels of generality; it confuses general empirical categories with concepts. The difference between empiricist and scientific conceptions of science is represented in the Willers' figure (figure 1).

Now, if the Willers' distinction between science and empiricism is to be sustained it is essential that they establish a clear demarcation between the relations of abstraction, characteristic of the sciences, and the relations between more and less general empirical categories characteristic of empiricism. We shall see that no such rigorous demarcation is possible within their conception of knowledge. In fact they have some difficulty in specifying precisely what an abstractive relation is:

> 'While empiricism and rationalism have dominated Western philosophy, the type of knowledge sought by some philosophers of the East rests on a different kind of thinking. Eastern knowledge has been gained through abstraction from the empirical to the pure idea, such as *nirvana*. Such thinking which bridges the empirical and the rational will be termed *abstractive*; ... A more modern example of abstractive thought may be found in the work of Max Weber, who proposed the use of ideal types as a crucial part of his sociological methodology' (pp.12–13)

But examples are no substitute for the concept they are alleged to ex-

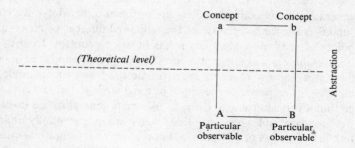

Scientific Conception of Science   Empiricist Conception of Science

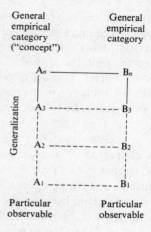

(Observational level)

FIGURE 1. Comparison of the structure of science from empiricist and scientific points of view

emplify. Abstractive thought is supposed to relate concepts and observables. What we require, then, is not to be told *that* it relates them, that in its conceptual purity Weber's ideal type 'cannot be found anywhere in reality' (*The Methodology of the Social Sciences,* p.90), but rather some specification of how precisely concepts and observables are brought together in abstraction. The nearest approach to such a specification is given in the following comparison between abstraction and the empiricist process of generalisation which relates observable to observable.

'Abstraction is a matter of establishing an isomorphism between theoretical non-observables and empirical observables. Whereas generalization is confounded by the problem of figuring out "How similar is similar?" because of the unlimited number of observable points of similarity, abstraction has no such problem. In abstraction, empirical circumstances may either be manipulated in the laboratory or elsewhere to approximate the [theoretical] model in all relevant respects, or they may be fixed while the model is varied so that it is isomorphic to them . . . Whereas generalization involves the unanswerable problem that there are a potentially infinite number of points of comparison between any two empirical events, this is not true when empirical cases are abstractively related to theory . . . The model has a denumerable set of characteristics (limited by the theory) and consequently the number of points of comparison with any empirical event is limited to that number. Abstraction, therefore, does not have the problem of determining the point at which one has exhausted a sufficient number of points of comparison to claim that two events are similar. Abstraction, indeed, is not a process of comparing empirical events at all.' (p.26)

Here the relation of abstraction is conceived in terms of the epistemology of models examined in chapter 5. Theory, with its rational connections and rational proof, is conceived as a conceptual model which has to be related to observables and their empirical connections. And there is a point by point comparison between the one and the other, at least in the sense that elements of the model have to correspond to determinate observationals. But, if there has to be a correspondence between concepts and observationals, how does the abstractive relation between the two differ from the types of relations between observables postulated by empiricism?

Consider, for example, the relatively sophisticated empiricist conception of science elaborated in the works of Rudolph Carnap examined in Chapter 4. In his later work we find a rigorous distinction between a theoretical language on the one hand and an observational language on the other. Both are necessary to science. The theoretical language consists of a set of terms that are related by means of the fundamental postulates of scientific theory and by the calculi of logic and pure mathematics. The observational language on the other hand consists of terms which designate observable objects, observable properties of objects and observable relations between them. Elements of the theoretical language are therefore related in the mode of 'rational thought' while the observation language defines the field of 'empirical thought'. Since both are necessary to science they are connected by definite correspondence rules which define particular theoretical terms in relation to, and by means of, observational terms. For Carnap, in effect, theory becomes a complicated symbolic formalism for expressing complex regularities at the observational level, a sophisticated empiricism.

Now, Carnap's sophisticated empiricist conception of science can be readily interpreted as postulating a realm of rational and a realm of empirical thought and specifying the nature of the relation between them. How, then, does it differ from that of the Willers? The answer is that Carnap tells us precisely what the relation between theoretical and observational terms is supposed to be. Every theoretical term is related to observationals through a definite system of concepts *and* correspondence rules. The Willers on the other hand do not and cannot tell us what their abstractive relation is. But their concept of theoretical models requires that there be determinate, i.e. definable, relations between concepts and observables; otherwise the notion of a rigorous point by point comparison between model and empirical event is simply absurd. In effect correspondence rules are necessary to the Willers' position. Yet, if they tell us what the rules are, then their position reduces to a complex and sophisticated empiricism – an improvement on much of sociology no doubt but still an empiricism. Thus the contradiction: science requires rational knowledge in which concepts are defined not by reference to observables but only in relation to other concepts, but the connection of rational and empirical knowledge in science requires that concepts are defined by reference to observables through correspondence rules. Only their failure to conceptualize the character of the abstractive relation prevents that contradiction from appearing directly in the text. If there are observables and if *concepts* are connected to them by correspondence rules then the relations between these concepts are governed both by their theoretical relations as concepts and by what may be empirically observed. The Willers' conception of science, like that of Carnap requires a pre-established harmony between conceptual relations and the world. Their concept of science is just a complicated empiricism.

7.2 The 'Althusserian' Critique of Empiricism

In *Reading Capital* and in several of the papers in *For Marx* Althusser elaborates a concept of the general structure of classical epistemology, 'the empiricist conception of knowledge', and concepts of science and ideology as distinct forms of knowledge. These concepts have provided the foundation of two quite distinct 'Althusserian' critiques of empiricism. One is the critique of epistemology and, by extension, of the associated methodological doctrines of the kind that I have developed in the preceding chapters. The other is the critique of particular substantive discourses as 'empiricist' and therefore as ideological. Thus, it is argued, Political Economy, Sociology, History, etc., are forms of theoretical ideology, that is, they are theoretical but unscientific. Examples of this mode of critique are given below. I shall argue that this second mode of critique is based on a concept of ideology as a real empiricist process of knowledge and on a logically incoherent theory of the difference between science and ideology as forms of knowledge. Thus, however effective the critique of epistemology may be, the 'Althusserian' critique of what it calls 'theoretical ideology' is invalid and logically ineffective.

7.2.1 The empiricist conception of knowledge

'The empiricist conception of knowledge presents a process that takes place between a given object and a given subject. At this level, the status of the subject (psychological, historical, or otherwise) and of this object (discontinuous or continuous, mobile or fixed) is not very important. This status only affects the precise definition of the variants of the basic problematic, while the basic problematic itself is all that concerns us here. The subject and object, which are given and hence pre-date the process of knowledge, already define a certain fundamental theoretical field, but one which cannot yet in this state be pronounced *empiricist*. What defines it as such is the nature of the process of knowledge, in other words a certain relationship that defines knowledge as such, as a function of the *real object* of which it is said to be the knowledge. The whole empiricist process of knowledge lies in fact in an operation of the subject called *abstraction*. To know is to abstract from the real object its essence, the possession of which by the subject is then called knowledge.' (*Reading Capital*, pp.35–6)

Here Althusser offers a concept of empiricism which, unlike that of the Willers, is intended to encompass the whole field of classical epistemology.[3] The concept of 'the empiricist conception of knowledge' designates a conception which counterposes subject to object, knowledge to being, theory to fact, and so on, and which represents knowledge as a function of an operation of 'abstraction' on the part of the subject, whether this subject is conceived as empirical or transcendental, as an individual or a community (e.g. of scientists). Knowledge is therefore a function of the conditions in which that operation is thought to take place. Empiricism involves a definite conception of the subject, the object and the relation between them and it derives protocols for the evaluation of knowledge claims from its 'knowledge' of that relation. 'Empiricism' in this sense is not restricted to anything like the Willers' conception, that is, to the British empiricist tradition and their associates. It subsumes the classical rationalist epistemologies as well as, for example, the epistemologies of Kant and Weber since, although they do not conceive the subject as merely a passive recipient of knowledge, they nevertheless retain the fundamental structure of the counterposition and correlation of subject and object.[4]

Althusser argues that the empiricist conception of knowledge is logically impossible, that it involves an inescapable play on words resulting, in his example, in the conflation of real object with object in knowledge, that is, of an object outside of knowledge with an object that is constituted or represented in knowledge in the form of determinate propositions.[5] The most general form of the fundamental problem of empiricism concerns the following feature: that any empiricist theory of knowledge requires a knowledge of the fundamental conditions of the knowledge process, that is, of the fundamental features of the subject, object, and relation between them. Many instances of this general structure and of the inescapable difficulties to which it gives rise have been examined in the preceding chapters. For example, the derivation of Mill's four methods of experimental inquiry requires that the world does indeed consist of an infinite multiplicity of phenomena and that their appearance is governed by regular and recurrent sequential relations called 'laws of nature'. Fine: induction and the canons of inquiry provide a real knowledge of the world because the world is *really* structured by laws. And how do we know that? By induction. The inescapable circularity and ultimate dogmatism of this position is evident.

An immediate consequence of this critique of empiricism is that there can be no epistemological protocols of scientific practice, no extra-scientific guarantees that what the sciences produce is indeed knowledge. Thus, in the first part of *Reading Capital* and in 'On the Materialist Dialectic' in *For Marx* Althusser follows Bachelard in maintaining that, in so far as there are protocols for scientific practice, these are essentially internal to the science in question. Forms of proof and canons of scientific practice are always specific to the science in question; they cannot be derived from any extra-scientific, or rather supra-scientific, epistemology.[6] Similarly scientific experimentation can no longer be conceived as a process of comparison or testing of theory against the real. On the contrary, experimentation and scientific practice in general must be conceived as specifically theoretical processes, that is, as interiorised within knowledge, and scientific instruments, for example, as 'materialised theory'.[7]

Finally, Althusser's critique of epistemology requires that knowledge can no longer be conceived as involving a relation of abstraction between knowledge on the one hand and the real on the other. There is no longer any question of maintaining both a *distinction* and a *correlation* between real object located firmly without knowledge and object of knowledge constituted within knowledge. Thus the classical epistemological problems concerning, say, the conditions in which valid knowledge is possible, can no longer arise:

> 'Unlike the "theory of knowledge" of ideological philosophy, I am not trying to pronounce some *de jure* (or *de facto*) *guarantee* which will assure us that we really do know what we know, and that we can relate this harmony to a certain connexion between Subject and Object, Consciousness and the World' (*ibid.*, pp.68–9)

Instead Althusser attempts to pose a different problem, that of the 'knowledge effect', which concerns the mechanism whereby a particular discourse functions as a knowledge and not as something else, not as 'a hammer, a symphony, a sermon, a political slogan, etc.' (*ibid.*) What is at stake here is not an epistemological question such as 'How do we know that knowledge really does correspond to its real object?' or 'How do we know that it really is a knowledge "and not a poached baby elephant" (*ibid.*, p.57)?' Rather it concerns the question of what, in the forms of order of the discourse, constitutes scientific discourse as a specific form of discourse as distinct from theoretical ideology or from a sermon, poetry, fiction, etc. How does the order of appearance of concepts in, say, the discourse of *Capital* function to constitute an object in knowledge? In *Reading Capital* the problem of the knowledge effect is explicitly conceived as concerning the order of appearance of concepts in determinate discourses and as a function of the system of concepts, or problematic, which is held to govern their order of appearance in discourse:

> 'The knowledge effect acts, then, in the duality or duplicity of the *existence of the system,* which is said to 'develop' in the scientific discourse, on the one hand, and on the other of the *existence of the forms* of order of the discourse, precisely in the 'play' (in the mechanical sense of the term) which constitutes the *unity of dislocation* of the system and of the discourse. The knowledge effect is produced as an effect of the scientific discourse, which exists only as discourse of the system, i.e., of the object grasped in the structure of its complex constitution' *(ibid.,* p.18)

I will return to the problems involved in this conception of theoretical discourse as generated by a problematic which is absent from the discourse itself but nevertheless governs the order of exposition of its concepts. For the present it is necessary only to note that Althusser recognises at least two distinct types of knowledge effect: the *ideological* knowledge effect and the *scientific* knowledge effect. Both are a function of specific forms of order of appearance of concepts and, therefore, of the problematic that governs those forms of order. In addition, we are told, the ideological knowledge effect 'depends on other social functions which are dominant in it'. *(ibid.,* p.67) Thus theoretical ideology is defined both in terms of the specificity of its order of concepts, which produces its particular knowledge effect, and by the dominance of 'other social functions' which are necessarily extraneous to theory. We shall see that the insistence on both conceptual and extra-conceptual determinations in the case of theoretical ideology generates inescapable problems for Althusser's theory of science and ideology as distinct forms of knowledge.

7.2.2 *Science and ideology as distinct forms of knowledge*

A traditional way of making the distinction between science and non-science is by reference to epistemological protocols: knowledge conforms to the protocols and non-knowledge fails to conform to them, it is either ideological rubbish or else a special kind of knowledge, say, metaphysics or theology. For example, Popper's criterion of demarcation between science and metaphysics is made by means of the notion of 'testability' which provides an extra-scientific protocol for scientific practice. Now, since he rejects the claims of epistemology to legislate for the sciences, Althusser can hardly base his distinctions between science and theoretical ideology on any epistemologically derived protocols. If a demarcation between science and theoretical ideology is nevertheless to be maintained then it must be established in a different fashion. In this section I outline Althusser's definitions of, and distinctions between, science, ideology and theoretical ideology. Science refers to a determinate form of production of knowledge that is governed by a determinate problematic, that is, by a determinate system of concepts and relations between concepts.[8] Scientific knowledge is produced within and by the operations of the concepts of scientific problematics. Since protocols are internal to the problematics of the sciences, since they are constituted by their own specific systems of concepts, it follows that there can be no such thing as *the* scientific-method-in-general, only scientific methods. The sciences are not defined by *the* scientific method but by their own specific problematics; they are sciences (in the plural) not merely separate aspects of science in general.

Neither ideology nor theoretical ideology are governed by problematics in the same way as the sciences. For purposes of a brief exposition it is sufficient to introduce these concepts by means of the Glossary provided by the translator and vetted by Althusser for the English edition of *Reading Capital*

> 'Ideology is the "lived" relation between men and their word, or a reflected form of this unconscious relation, for instance a 'philosophy', etc. It is distinguished from a science not by its falsity, for it can be coherent and logical (for instance, theology), but by the fact that the practico-social predominates in it over the theoretical, over knowledge. Historically, it precedes the science that is produced by making an epistemological break with it, but it survives alongside science as an essential element of every social formation, including a socialist and even a communist society.' (*Reading Capital*, p.314)

There are several elements to be noted here: ideology is defined by reference to a 'lived' relation between men and their world – elsewhere Althusser refers to images, myths, experiences, etc.; theoretical ideology appears here in the shape of a 'reflected form' of this 'lived' relation; in ideology in contrast to the sciences 'the practico-social predominates over the theoretical'; finally, ideology is an essential element of every social formation. This last is straightforward: if ideology is defined with respect to human consciousness, [9] that is, in terms of the 'lived' relation between men and their social conditions of existence, then so long as there are men there will be ideology. [10]

Now, since ideology is conceived in terms of the consciousnesses of human subjects, the demarcation between science and ideology may be represented as a distinction between their respective modes of production of knowledge. In the sciences the production of knowledge is governed by its problematic and by the protocols, canons of argument and forms of demonstration which it defines. The non-sciences represent those modes of production of knowledge that are governed, directly or indirectly, by the structure of the consciousness of human subjects and therefore by whatever governs that structure. The historical emergence of a science therefore requires a shift from one mode of production of knowledge to another; from a form of theorising or of rumination governed by the consciousness of the subject to a form of theorising governed by a determinate order of concepts. The concept of 'epistemological break' refers to this shift from the dominance of one mode of production of knowledge to that of another. [11]

The location of theoretical ideology in relation to science and ideology imposes the double restraint which I have noted above: on the one hand it is governed by its problematic, by a determinate system of concepts; on the other it is dominated by the 'practico-social' through the medium of the 'lived' relation which it reflects. It is like science in that it produces its knowledge effect through the operation of concepts in the production of discourse. But it is unlike science in that its concepts are themselves dominated by extra-conceptual interests, by the practico-social. This conception of ideology and theoretical ideology in terms of the consciousness of human subjects allows Althusser to bring together his conception of the demarcation between science and ideology on the one hand and the traditional Marxist conception of the social formation as consisting of economic, political and ideological levels on the other. Because theoretical ideology is dominated by ideology which is itself located at a definite structural level in the social formation it follows that theoretical ideology provides, *inter alia,* a mechanism for the representation of class interests in the realm of theory.[12] Ideology and theoretical ideology belong to the social formation and therefore, so long as there are classes within it, they provide an arena of the class struggle. The sciences on the other hand, since they are not dominated by the 'practico-social' through the medium of 'lived' relations must be conceived as autonomous. They are governed by their problematics and not by the consciousnesses of human subjects, not by 'lived' relations between men and their social conditions of existence and the class interests which these relations represent.

Finally, it should be noted that the conception of ideology in terms of consciousness and of theoretical ideology as its reflected form implies that there is a real empiricist process of knowledge and that it takes place in ideology and also, therefore, in theoretical ideology. The human subject appropriates a knowledge of objects that are given in the content of his consciousness, i.e. in his 'lived' relation to his conditions of existence. The 'object' in this case is not, of course, a *real* object but rather one that is constituted in and given by ideology. Ideology and theoretical ideology are therefore empiricist; they produce 'empiricist' knowledges.

7.2.3 *The critique of theoretical ideologies*

The conception of ideology as the location of a real empiricist process of knowledge provides the foundation of a critique of particular substantive discourses, Political Economy, Sociology, History, as empiricist, and therefore ideological, because they operate with given objects. Theoretical ideology, a form of theory dominated by ideology, works with what is given to the knowledge process by ideology. A good example of this mode of critique appears in chapter 7 of *Reading Capital,* part II, 'The Object of Political Economy'. Political Economy is represented as a form of theoretical discourse that is constituted in part by the intervention of 'given', i.e. extra-discursive, extra-theoretical, elements, of a 'given' realm of economic facts. Thus:

> 'Political Economy's pretensions to existence are a function of the nature and hence of *the definition of its object*. Political Economy gives itself as an object the domain of 'economic facts' which it regards as having the obviousness of *facts*: absolute givens which it takes as they 'give' themselves, without asking them for any explanations. Marx's revocation of the pretensions of Political

Economy is identical with his revocation of the obviousness of this 'given', which in fact it *'gives itself'* arbitrarily as an object, pretending that this object *was given it*' (*Reading Capital,* pp.158–9)

Here it seems that discourse is constituted by a 'given' which is not really a given at all: in effect it is given *to* theory *by* ideology. It is precisely this supposed effectivity of ideology in the realm of theory which constitutes theoretical ideology as such. Political Economy cannot be scientific because it is governed by ideology, because it must operate with elements that are given to theory.

It is easy to see how this mode of critique could be extended to provide a general critique of the academic social sciences and of history. They are empiricist because they define themselves in relation to particular given objects, the 'past', the 'facts' of social life, and so on. In our Introduction to *Pre-Capitalist Modes of Production* Paul Hirst and I have argued:

'The empiricism of the academic social sciences and of much Marxist scholarship has serious theoretical effects. In so far as certain facts are represented as 'given' in the real or as 'given' by history they must fall below the level of theoretical determination: they cannot be the product of an explicit theoretical practice. The empiricism of these disciplines therefore ensures that these 'facts' are ideological constructs and that their 'theories' are, at best, sophisticated theoretical ideology' (p.3)

Similarly the sociology of a Durkheim or a Weber cannot be scientific because it pretends to operate with 'givens', with given 'social facts' or with a mass of empirically given material that must be sorted and ordered by means of ideal types.

The general structure of this form of critique of 'empiricist' discourses may be outlined as follows. First, it is a consequence of the critique of the empiricist conception of knowledge that knowledge never operates with direct apperceptions of the real. Therefore, all elements of knowledge must be conceived as constructed elements; they are never given directly by the real as such. Now, the conceptions of science and ideology as distinct modes of production of knowledge implies that the construction of elements may take place in the realm of theory, through the operation of concepts governed by a determinate problematic, or else it may take place in ideology. Elements constituted in ideology are, in effect, *given* to theory prior to the operation of the theoretical knowledge process. In the sciences the elements of knowledge are constituted within theory through the operation of concepts — hence the attraction for Althusserian theory of the Bachelardian notion of scientific instruments as theory incarnate, as the materialisation of theory. In theoretical ideologies the operation of concepts is restricted to the manipulation of ideological givens. Finally, if a theoretical discourse is constrained by its very definition to work on givens then ideology must intervene at the most fundamental level of that discourse. Hence the conclusion: Sociology, History, Political Economy, or whatever, cannot be scientific.

The final steps of this argument deserve further comment. The argument begins with a conception of two distinct modes of production of theoretical discourse: one governed by the operation of concepts and the other governed by an operation of concepts that is itself dominated by ideology through the agency of human subjectivity. The basic contradictions of this conception will be considered below. For the moment it is important to note that the next step in the above argument depends on an answer to the question: 'How can this conception of the *production* of discourse sustain a critique of particular products, say, of Ricardo's *Principles of Political Economy and Taxation* or of Parsons' *The Structure of Social Action?*'. It is clear what the answer must be. The critique of discourse as empiricist and therefore as ideological must require that the process of production of the discourse leaves its mark on the product. Thus, in the work of Althusser, we find that the demarcation between science and ideology functions not only at the level of the process of production of discourse but also at the level of the product of that process. There are scientific and ideological modes of production of theoretical discourse and there are scientific and ideological knowledge effects. The latter refer to features of the discourse itself which may serve as an index of how that discourse was produced.

I will return to the consequences of this conflation of the process of production of discourse with the conceptual structure of the discourse itself. But first I want to indicate a certain practical difficulty. Theoretical ideology is to be identified by discovering the little droppings or tell-tale marks which show the trained eye that ideology has been at work here. For example, in *Reading Capital* (p.160f.) Althusser establishes the ideological character of Political Economy in this way. He takes as his text an extract from Lalande's *Dictionary* but he could equally well have taken the Preface to Ricardo's *Prin-*

ciples. It is the work of a few lines to discover that the secret of Political Economy's basic definition lies in a supposedly *given* sphere of human wants. Political Economy is therefore theoretical ideology. Or again, we could take a work such as Durkheim's *The Rules of Sociological Method* and discover the secret of his definition of sociology in an alleged realm of 'given' social facts. [13] But, because of the critique of the empiricist conception of knowledge we know that these 'givens' are not given by the real at all. They must be given by ideology. Thus Durkheim's 'science' must be placed in the trash-can along with Political Economy, History, etc., etc.

Now the practical difficulty that arises in this mode of critique is that the tell-tale indices of ideology which one finds in Political Economy or Sociology can also be found in what are normally held to be scientific texts. It is easy to establish, for example, that several rather crude positivist and Machist conceptions play a crucial role in the exposition of Einstein's 1905 paper 'On the Electrodynamics of Moving Bodies' – the paper which first introduced his 'principle of relativity'. A more serious difficulty, from the point of view of Althusser's defence of the scientific status of Marxism, is posed by the evident presence of numerous empiricist formulations in the work of Marx and even in *Capital* itself: the references to real and apparent motions, inner essence and outer appearance, or the reference to England as the classical ground where capitalist relations 'occur in their most typical form, and most free from disturbing influences',

> 'That is the reason why England is used as the chief illustration in the development of my theoretical ideas' (*Capital*, I, p.19) [14]

If Marx poses a problem in this respect then how much worse is the case of Lenin in whose works we find numerous references to the *facts,* frequently conceived in a positivist form, the use of 'given' statistical tables, and so on.

In the later chapters and Appendix of *Reading Capital,* part II, Althusser is clearly much concerned by the presence of these 'empiricist' and therefore ideological elements in Marx's text. In this case, however, they do not serve as an excuse to put him in the trash-can of ideology alongside Ricardo, Durkheim, and numerous others who tried hard to get to science but never quite made it. Instead Althusser adopts a different mode of treatment of Marx's text. For example, referring to the ambiguous positions outlined in volume 3 of *Capital* he writes of Marx's confusion between the thought-concrete and the real-concrete, between the object in knowledge and the real object, and adds:

> 'whereas in reality, the concrete of volume 3, i.e. the *knowledge* of ground-rent, profit and interest, is like all knowledge, *not the empirical concrete but the concept,* and therefore still always an abstraction' (*Reading Capital,* p.189)

Marx only *appears* to be dealing with empirical givens. In fact it is all in the realm of theory. Similarly:

> 'when Lenin describes the peculiar *'circumstances'* of Russia in 1917; when Marx (and the whole Marxist tradition) explains, with the aid of a thousand examples, that such and such a contradiction will dominate according to the case, etc., they are appealing to a *concept that might appear to be empirical*: the 'conditions' ... *On the contrary, it is a theoretical concept'* (*For Marx,* pp. 206–7 – emphasis added)

In the sciences the order of discourse is governed by its problematic, by the operation of concepts, even when the formulations in the text suggest otherwise. In *Reading Capital* (p.182f) Althusser attributes many of the empiricist formulations in *Capital* to the fact that Marx is operating in practice with a concept, namely 'structural causality', that he is unable to develop explicitly.

I have examined this notion of 'structural causality' elsewhere. [15] What must be noted here is that the sciences and the theoretical ideologies appear to call for quite different modes of analysis of their texts. In the case of the sciences we look for concepts and relations between concepts, logical dependence, consistency, compatibility and incompatibility, and so on. The status of particular concepts and arguments may therefore be examined in terms of their consistency with the system of concepts and positions developed in the discourse in question. For example, in *Reading Capital,* part II, chapter 8, Althusser examines the concepts of 'production' and 'labour process' developed in *Capital* and is able to establish that:

> '*the social relations of production are on no account reducible to mere relations between men, to relations which only involve men, and therefore to variations in a universal matrix, to inter-subjectivity* (recognition, prestige, struggle, master-slave relationship, etc.). For Marx, the social relations of production do not bring *men*

alone onto the stage, but the *agents* of the production process and the *material conditions* of the production process, in specific "combinations" ' (*ibid.*, p.174)

The conception of social relations of production as intersubjective relations is incompatible with the basic concepts of *Capital*. That conclusion is established by means of an examination of the concepts and positions developed in *Capital*; it can be defended even against certain of Marx's own expressions where, for example, 'in a terminology still inspired by his early anthropological philosophy, it is tempting to oppose, literally, relations between men and relations between things' (*ibid.*). The important points in the present context concern not so much whether, as I would argue, Althusser's conclusion on this point is correct but rather the terms in which the problem is posed. First, the status of the conception of 'intersubjective relations' in the discourse of *Capital* is to be determined not by reference to any philosophical or epistemological protocols, for example, those of a philosophical anthropology, nor even in terms of manifest statements by Marx himself. It is to be determined solely by means of an analysis of the concepts and relations between concepts required for the positions developed in the discourse of *Capital* itself. The status of 'intersubjective relations' *as a concept* is a function of its relations with the concepts of *Capital* and not of any explicit statements by Marx concerning that status. [16]

But while the sciences are to be analysed in terms of their concepts and relations between concepts, the theoretical ideologies are treated in an entirely different fashion. In the analysis of theoretical ideology we must look for the tell-tale marks, the droppings of ideological contamination. In theoretical ideology empiricist formulations are to be taken at their word and read as an index of the ideological character of the process of production of the discourse. In the sciences all formulations which appear in the text are to be examined in relation to the concepts of the discourse. Now, it is clear that this difference in the mode of treatment of theoretical discourses can be defended only if the difference of science and theoretical ideology is known in advance. Accordingly the outcome of the analysis of Political Economy is never in doubt: it merely confirms what we already knew, namely, that Political Economy is theoretical ideology and Marxism is a science. The same point applies to the critiques of Sociology, History, etc., sketched above. The conclusion that they are not scientific is the product of a teleological mode of analysis [17] in which the known conclusion determines how the discourse is to be approached in the first place. Thus the 'practical difficulty' I have indicated may be overcome provided that we already know which is science and which is ideology.

Secondly, it is clear that to pose the question of the status of particular concepts in relation to the basic concepts of a discourse requires that those basic concepts be identified. This point raises a general problem for the analysis of discourse to which I shall return briefly in my conclusion. It is sufficient to note here that Althusser's own practice in this respect is far from satisfactory: it involves not only a general *a priori* demarcation of discourses into sciences and ideologies but also a specific conception of the basic concepts of Marxist theory. At this level Althusser's position is far from being derived from an analysis of the concepts and relations between concepts developed in the discourse of *Capital* itself since it also involves general epistemological positions concerning, in particular, distinct concepts of causality which, in his view, underlie the discourses of the sciences and ideologies. For example, he argues that the concept of 'structural causality' underlies but does not appear in the discourse of *Capital*. I argue in the following section that this notion of concepts 'underlying' the order of appearance of concepts in discourse is untenable. The idealist and teleological character of the concept of 'structural causality' has been demonstrated by Paul Hirst and me in *Pre-Capitalist Modes of Production*.

We can now return to the question I have posed above in respect of the final steps in the general argument leading to the critique of theoretical ideology, namely, 'how can a conception of the *production* of discourse sustain a critique of its product?'. I have shown that the answer, namely, that the process of production leaves its mark in the product, leads to a 'practical difficulty' which can be overcome only if the difference between scientific and ideological theoretical products is presumed to be known independently of the application of the critique. It follows that the application of what I have called the 'Althusserian' mode of critique to what are thought to be theoretical ideologies and of a quite different mode of analysis to what are thought to be sciences is entirely without rational justification. To treat features of discourse as an index of its mode of production in the one case and not in the other is to fall into an indefensible dogmatism in which pre-determined conclusions govern our treatment of theoretical discourses. If the sciences are to be analysed in terms of their concepts and relations between concepts then all theoretical discourse must be analysed in the same fashion.

Finally, it may be noted that Althusser's demarcation between science and ideology as distinct modes of production of knowledge depends on a curious and extremely problematic counterposition of 'the practico-social' on the one hand and 'the theoretical' on the other. If the practico-social is to predominate over the theoretical in the case of theoretical ideology and not to predominate in the case of science then 'the practico-social' and 'the theoretical' must be comparable and, at some level, they must be equivalent: theoretical discourse may be dominated by one or by the other. Two points should be made here. First, since theoretical ideology is conceived as specifically theoretical, the predominance of the practico-social can be effective only in so far as it is represented in the concepts of the discourse and the character of the relations between them. Thus, as far as the analysis of discourse is concerned, the decisive questions are always a matter of the concepts and the relations between them. The coherence or incoherence, consistency or inconsistency, of the discourse can be settled *at the level of its concepts alone* without reference to the further questions of whether and in what respects those concepts can be said to represent extra-discursive practico-social interests and forces. Similarly, for example, the incompatibility of the conception of social relations of production as *intersubjective* relations with the basic concepts of *Capital* can be established in terms of its character as a concept and in relation to other concepts without reference to the question of its allegedly ideological character. In the analysis of its concepts the question of the domination of the discourse by a system of concepts *or* by the practico-social cannot arise.

Secondly, in Althusser's demarcation between science and ideology, the predominance of the system of concepts or of the practico-social is supposed to be effective in the process of production of theoretical discourses. The conception of the logical effectivity of concepts in the process of production of discourse poses problems which I shall discuss in a later section. For the present I want to argue only that 'the practico-social' and 'the theoretical' can no more be treated as equivalents at the level of the process of production than they are at the level of the structure of the discourse itself. The conception of science and theoretical ideology as distinct modes of production of theoretical discourses poses a problem with regard to the articulation of the theoretical practice of a science on to other levels or forms of social practice. Theoretical ideology, as we have seen, is dominated by the practico-social through the mechanism of ideology; it is characterized precisely by the fact that it is implicated in the structure of the social formation. In any class society, therefore, theoretical ideology provides, *inter alia,* a mechanism for the representation of class interests in the realm of theory. It follows from the nature of the proposed demarcation between modes of production of theoretical discourse that the sciences cannot be implicated in the structure of the social formation in this way. Thus, in his critique of Gramsci's conception of science, Althusser insists that science is not part of the social formation. To include science within the superstructure would be:

> 'to attribute to the concept "superstructure" a breadth Marx never allowed, for he only ranged within it: (1) the politico-legal superstructure, and (2) the ideological superstructure (the corresponding "forms of social consciousness"); except in his Early Works (especially the 1844 Manuscripts), Marx *never included scientific knowledge in it.* Science can no more be ranged within the category "superstructure" than can language, which as Stalin showed escapes it.' (*Reading Capital,* p.133) [18]

On the contrary, the birth of a science:

> 'inaugurates a new form of historical existence and temporality which together save science (*at least in certain historical conditions that ensure the real continuity of its own history – conditions that have not always existed*) from the common fate of a single history: that of the "historical bloc" unifying structure and superstructure.' (*ibid.* – emphasis added)

Here science is conceived as autonomous from the social formation, yet, short of the most flagrant idealism, it can hardly be conceived as essentially 'opposed to the material world, the faculty of a "pure" transcendental subject or "absolute consciousness"' (*ibid.,* p.42) Althusser therefore insists that the system of theoretical production has a determinate objective reality and that it involves relations with nature and with other levels of social practice. Thus, the 'autonomy' of scientific practice, the internality of its protocols:

> 'is not at all exclusive of organic relations with *other practices*

which ... *occasionally go so far as to induce more or less profound re-organizations in their theoretical structure* ... Taking Marx as an example, we know that his most personally significant practical experiences ... *intervened in his theoretical practice, and in the upheaval which led him from ideological theoretical practice to scientific theoretical practice.' (ibid.* – emphasis added) [19]

At this point the attempted demarcation between science and theoretical ideology is reduced to an impossibility. Theoretical ideology is distinguished from science precisely by the fact that it is implicated in the structure of the social formation through the mechanisms of ideology which constitute the consciousness of human subjects. Yet, in the case of Marx, the shift from theoretical ideology to science is conceived as a function of *experiences,* that is, of changes in the consciousness of the subject, Marx. Thus, Marx's scientific practice is, like his ideological theoretical practice, a function of determinate ideological conditions. More generally we find that whilst theoretical ideology is implicated in the social formation science, since it can hardly be conceived of as entirely independent of all social conditions, has its own determinate social conditions of existence. Yet, in so far as it does have determinate social conditions of existence, science cannot but be implicated in the effects of the struggles and developments which affect the maintenance or non-maintenance of those conditions; it cannot but he implicated in the conditions of the class struggle and their outcome. There can be no question of theoretical ideology being implicated in the effects and conditions of the class struggle and science not being implicated in them. Thus the demarcation between science and theoretical ideology cannot be sustained in the form that Althusser makes it. It is not a matter of *either* 'the theoretical' *or* 'the practico-social' but of both. The latter may belong to the conditions of production of theoretical discourse but the question of the dominance of the one by the other can hardly arise. In particular, then, Althusser's demarcation cannot be used to justify a difference in the modes of analysis of what are thought to be the discourses of science and of theoretical ideology.

7.3 The Production of Theoretical Discourse

This chapter began with a distinction between two forms of critique of empiricism. One operates at the level of the concepts and relations between concepts within a specific discourse and attempts to establish a conceptual inadequacy at that level. The Willers' critique of Mill, Althusser's critique of the empiricist conception on knowledge, and many of the examinations of particular epistemological positions in the previous chapters provide examples of this mode of critique. The other critique of empiricism is aimed at what is thought to be an empiricist practice or at those discourses which are held to be products of such a practice. Thus the authors of *Systematic Empiricism* advance a critique of certain epistemological and methodological doctrines which they extend to a critique of the practical realization of these doctrines: 'Systematic Empiricism' is a real process of production of knowledge but it does not produce science. Or again, the 'Althusserian' critique of Political Economy, Sociology, History, etc., depends on a mode of reading which identifies those substantive discourses as the product of an empiricist practice. For example, Political Economy is ideological because it is condemned by its very definition to work on what is *given* to theory by ideology.

Althusser's treatment of the discourse of the sciences, of Marxism in particular, is in marked contrast to his treatment of what he regards as theoretical ideology. Scientific discourse is to be analyzed in terms of the concepts and relations between concepts which are entailed in the positions developed in the discourse in question. Particular concepts and arguments may then be examined in terms of their consistency with the system of concepts and positions developed in that discourse. In this way, as Althusser's treatment of the concept of 'intersubjective relations' has shown, it may be possible to establish that positions which are manifestly present in the text are nevertheless incompatible with the basic concepts of the discourse. I have argued that if the sciences are to be analyzed in this way, in terms of their concepts and relations between concepts, then all theoretical discourses must be analyzed in the same fashion.[20] Indeed, Althusser's own critique of epistemology is the product of precisely such an analysis: the empiricist conception of knowledge is inadequate *as a conception* not because it is ideological but because it is logically incoherent, because it involves a dogmatism, a circularity, an inescapable 'play on words'. I shall return briefly to the concepts involved in this mode of analysis of discourse in my conclusion.

Now, the attempt to extend the critique of empiricist epistemological positions to a critique of empiricist practice must move away from a strict analysis of the concepts and relations between concepts of determinate discourses towards an analysis based on the conception of the *realization* of certain concepts or doctrines in the process of production of theoretical discourses. This conception depends on a theoretical conflation of questions concerning the conceptual structure of discourse with the question of the production or generation of discourse. For example, in the Willers' critique of Systematic Empiricism and again in the 'Althusserian' critiques of Political Economy, Sociology, etc., we find an identification of certain empiricist conceptions of the production of knowledge with the real processes of production of non-scientific knowledge: the empiricist conception of knowledge is realized in empiricist practice. Similarly, at least in Althusser, a distinction defined at the level of the process of production of knowledge reappears at the level of the order of concepts in discourse in a distinction between scientific and ideological knowledge effects: the process of production must leave its mark on the product. I have argued that the attempts, in the works of Althusser and of the Willers, to establish a demarcation between the processes of production of scientific and non-scientific knowledge are rationally indefensible.

But there is a more general problem here. It concerns not so much the question of demarcation as the manner in which the process of production of knowledge is itself conceived, namely, as the realization of an extra-discursive conceptual totality. I shall attempt to formulate the point at issue here in its most general form but it may be helpful to begin with a few examples. Consider, first, Althusser's conception of the process of production of knowledge. We have seen that he conceives of theoretical discourse as being, in a certain sense, the product of its problematic. The problematic is a system of concepts which 'determines the definition of each concept, as a function of its place and function in the system.' (*Reading Capital,* p.68) and it also determines the order of appearance of concepts in the discourse itself. The problematic *underlies* the forms of order of the discourse but:

> 'these forms only show themselves as forms of the order of appearance of concepts in scientific discourse as a function of other forms which, *without themselves being forms of order, are nevertheless the absent principle of the latter.' (ibid.* p.67, emphasis added)

By partial analogy with structural linguistics the (vertical) system of concepts develops in the discourse by means of the (horizontal) forms of order of appearance of concepts which it underlies. [21] Here the problematic is conceived as an extra-discursive totality, a system of concepts and relations between concepts which is held to be responsible for the production of the discourse itself. Relations between concepts constitute the real conditions of the production of the theoretical discourse in which they are realized. The discourse must therefore be read as the expression of an extra-discursive conceptual totality. [22]

As a second example we might consider the widespread notion of 'methodology', conceived as a definite body of procedural rules for scientific practice derived from some more or less explicit epistemology. Methodology proposes a set of rules which are intended to be followed and which, it is claimed, can be relied on to produce a genuine knowledge. 'Systematic Empiricism' represents a definite methodology in this sense. In their critique the Willers argue that Systematic Empiricism can be realized in practice but that it only results in empiricist knowledge, not in scientific knowledge. Here an extra-discursive body of rules is held to be responsible for the production of determinate substantive discourses, for example, the research reports of investigators who appear to be using the methods of systematic empiricism. In social science methodology, and in the Willers' critique of its dominant forms, substantive discourses are conceived as products of the application of a methodology. Similarly, in Popper's theory of science, scientific progress is conceived as resulting from the application of his methodological rules. 'Science' is the realization of Popper's methodology.

Finally, we might refer to all those cases in the sociology or the history of science, in the sociology of knowledge or the history of ideas in which particular discourses are conceived as the product of an author's presuppositions or as the expression of a particular world-view. This tendency, which accounts for what appears in discourse by means of extra-discursive presuppositions, world-views, or what have you, is so widespread that it is hardly worth citing examples; the work of Lukacs; Sartre's insistence that the great philosophies, of Locke, Kant-Hegel, Marx, are 'unsurpassable until *the historical moment whose expression they are* has been surpassed' (*The Problem of Method*, p.7, emphasis added); Kuhn's notion of the paradigm as governing the practice of 'normal science'; and so on. In all these cases an extra-discursive order of concepts is conceived as being responsible for and as realised in the discourse whose production it governs.

Now, I have claimed that there is a general problem here which may be posed with respect to each of the range of positions indicated in these examples. That problem concerns the conflation of what might be called the logical or conceptual conditions of existence of the formulations of a discourse with what are thought to be the real conditions of its production. In order to see what is at stake in this conflation and for ease of exposition it will be convenient to consider the case of presuppositions. There is one very precise sense in which discourse may be said to involve 'presuppositions', namely, that any proposition stated in the discourse must be dependent on definite concepts and relations between concepts. Let us call these concepts and relations *the logical or conceptual conditions of existence* of the proposition in question. In this sense every proposition formulated in a discourse has its own conceptual conditions of existence − although those conditions may not be explicitly formulated and they may well be contradicted by other positions that are formulated in the discourse. For example, Popper's insistence that the method of deductive testing leads to the growth of knowledge in the sense of increasing verisimilitude requires that singular descriptive statements function as a surrogate of the real. In short, certain of Popper's propositions concerning the growth of knowledge require, as their conceptual conditions of existence, that singular descriptive statements be formulated in an a-theoretical observation language in the strict positivist sense. We have seen that those conceptual conditions of existence are flagrantly contradicted by numerous other propositions in Popper's discourse. In that respect Popper's discourse may be said to be logically incoherent. Presuppositions, understood in this sense as the logical or conceptual conditions of existence of propositions, entail no reference to any putative process of production or generation of the discourse. There is no suggestion that *logical* conditions of existence have any 'real' effectivity in the generation of discourse.

So far so good. But the term 'presupposition' is sometimes used to refer, *in addition,* to extra-discursive conditions that are held to be responsible for the production of discourse. [23] Presuppositions in this sense tend to be located in the consciousness of authors: they are exterior to, and precede the production of, the discourses in which they are realized. These presuppositions belong to the general category of extra-discursive mechanisms that may be proposed to account for the appearance of determinate discourses or of determinate propositions within them. Since the relation between extra-discursive presuppositions and the propositions of the discourse is conceived on the model of the conceptual relations between propositions and their logical conditions of existence, if presuppositions are to function as a mechanism of the generation of discourse then the logical or conceptual conditions of existence of its propositions must be conflated with the real mechanisms of their production. Thus discourse is conceived as the real effect of its logical conditions of existence and therefore as having a definite real logical coherence, at least in respect of relations between propositions of the discourse and their presuppositions. It is clear that Althusser's concept of problematic and the notion of the real effectivity of methodological protocols involve similar conflations of conceptual relations on the one hand and the relations between propositions and the extra-discursive conditions of their generation on the other.

What is at stake in these conceptions, then, from the relative simplicity of the notion of presuppositions or of the realization of methodological protocols to the sophistication of Althusser's conception of problematic as the determinant element in the process of production of theoretical discourse, is what might be called the rationalist conception of the production of discourse. It is rationalist not necessarily in the sense of entailing a rationalist epistemology but rather in that it represents the relations between the propositions of a discourse and the real conditions of their production on the model of internal relations between concepts. I argue that no rationalist conception of the production of discourse is tenable. Before proceeding to that argument, however, it may be noted that this conception is itself only a special case of the rationalist conception of action in which the act or its product is conceived as the *realization* of a conceptual totality. Rationalist epistemology conceives of the world as a rational order in the sense that is parts and the relations between them conform, whether by chance or by design, to concepts and the relation between them, the concept giving the essence of the real; the rationalist conception of action proposes a mechanism of the realization of the idea either in the will and consciousness of a human subject or else at some supra-individual level of determination. The theological affinities of this conception are evident. Weber's concept of action, as opposed to behaviour, as 'consciously guided' or as 'oriented in its course' by *meanings* is rationalist in this sense. The relation between action and its meaning is one of coherence and logical consistency; the action realizes logical consequences of its meaning. Where theology postulates God as the mechanism *par excellence* of the realization of the idea Weber conceives of man as a lesser but essentially similar creature. Two other examples are worth nothing. The first is Peter Winch who, in *The Idea of a Social Science,* argues:

> 'that social relations really exist only in and through the ideas which are current in society; or alternatively, *that social relations fall into the same logical category as do relations between ideas.'*
> (p.133, emphasis added)

Social relations are therefore a species of internal relations between concepts. Winch conceives of human conduct as a matter of following a rule. The relation between conduct and rule is once again supposed to be one of coherence and logical consistency. For a different and rather more sophisticated example we might refer to the later works of Talcott Parsons where the distinct sub-systems of action are conceived as organized into a 'cybernetic hierarchy of control'. [24] Lower level systems function as conditions in relation to the higher levels while these higher levels function as controls over those below them in the hierarchy. In so far as the conditioning factors leave the situation indeterminate then the higher level controls come into play. The cultural system, which consists in systems of ideas or beliefs, systems of expressive symbols, and systems of value orientation, is supposed to be at a higher level than the social and personality systems and these in turn are above the biological organism in the hierarchy of control. The hierarchical organization of systems implies that social and personality systems appear as the realizations of cultural patterns subject only to the exigencies of conditioning factors defined at these or lower levels. Thus Parsons' theory of the sub-systems of action attempts to combine a rationalist conception of action with a conception of the real effectivity of conditioning factors. [25]

I have given these examples merely to indicate the level of generality of what is at stake in the following argument. The rationalist conception of action may be represented as a theoretical humanism, where the primary mechanism of the realization of conceptual relations is located in the will and the consciousness of individual human subjects, or as a theoretical anti-humanism where, as in Althusser's conception of the production of knowledge, as, to some extent, in Parsons' theory of action systems, and as in Husserl's theory of the history of the sciences and of philosophy, the primary mechanism of realization is located at another level and it subordinates the human individual to its functioning. [26] In all cases, whether humanist or not, the point at issue concerns the conception of action as the realization of internal relations between ideas so that the relation between action and idea is one of coherence and logical consistency. For ease of exposition I shall confine my argument to the case in which presuppositions are supposed to function in the production of discourse, but, as I shall indicate, it may readily be generalized to cover other cases.

Let us suppose, then, that the generation of discourse is governed by a system of one or more presuppositions in the sense that the relation between all propositions and their extra-discursive presuppositions is one of coherence and consistency. This is not to say that all logical consequences of the presuppositions must appear but rather that the presuppositions rigorously determine what may appear by rigorously excluding propositions that are contrary to them. Whatever mechanism may be responsible for producing the propositions which do appear must conform to the rigorous determination of the presuppositions themselves. It is in this sense that we must understand the notion that a problematic underlies the forms of order of concepts in a discourse or that methodological protocols are responsible for the production of determinate substantive discourses. The rationalist conception of the production of discourse postulates first an extra-discursive conceptual totality, a system of concepts and relations between concepts, problematics, methodological protocols, presuppositions, or whatever, and secondly processes of production of determinate discourses which are somehow constrained (the mechanism is rarely specified) to conform to the prior determination of that extra-discursive sysem of concepts.

I argue that the rationalist conception of the production of discourse cannot be sustained without denying the very possibility of contradiction in discourse. For, in the event of contradiction in discourse, neither of the contradictory propositions could be accounted for by reference to the extra-discursive system of concepts. Their appearance could be accounted for only by conceiving the process of production as *overriding* the postulated extra-discursive constraints. Where discourse is supposed to be governed by a system of presuppositions the appearance of logical contradiction in the discourse or among the postulated presuppositions ensures that the content of discourse cannot be rigorously determined by its presuppositions. If contradiction is possible then discourse cannot be the product of *rationalist* mechanisms.

This argument can be elaborated as follows. We have supposed, for the sake of argument, that presuppositions govern the production of discourse. Now, it is easy to show that this assumption implies that the presuppositions must be logically coherent among themselves and that therefore all possible discourse must be logically coherent. This can be done by considering a hypothetical discourse which is governed by a system of presuppositions that is *not* internally coherent. In that case, there will be some contradictory presuppositions. Let A and B be two contradictory presuppositions. Then among the propositions 'generated' by A there must be at least one whose contrary may be 'generated' by B. But, if there are such contradictory presuppositions then the presuppositions cannot govern which propositions appear in the discourse. If rigorous consequences of A do appear at any point in the discourse why are they not rigorously excluded by B? Where, as in this case, the presuppositions are in conflict, their effects must cancel out. But then what does appear cannot be accounted for by reference to the presuppositions alone. The conclusion is clear: if extra-discursive presuppositions do govern the generation of discourse then the presuppositions of any discourse together with the totality of their logical consequences must form a logically coherent system. If they do not then the discourse is indeterminate. Conversely, if a logically incoherent discourse such as Popper's is possible then presuppositions cannot rigorously determine the content of discourse.

Now this argument turns on the point that if presuppositions in a given system do conflict then what appears in the discourse cannot be accounted for as a logical consequence of the presuppositions themselves. In the event of inconsistency no real effectivity can be attributed to logical relations; the process of production of discourse cannot be constrained to conform to the requirements of mutually conflicting presuppositions. It might seem that the situation could be saved for the rationalist conception of the effectivity. of presuppositions by introducing some conception of a hierarchy of presuppositions such that, in cases of conflict, the hierarchical structure determines which is to be effective in the discourse. But such a hierarchy could not be structured around logical relations alone since it would have to regulate the effectivity of logically contradictory presuppositions; the determination of priority in such a case can hardly be a function of logical relations between the presuppositions concerned. It follows that what appears in discourse would not be the rigorous effect of presuppositions alone but only such effects as are allowed by the extra-conceptual hierarchy. That determination can hardly be conceived in terms of rigour and coherence. Thus, to invoke such a hierarchy is to admit that the content of discourse is not generated as a rigorous effect of its presuppositions.

It follows that the assumption that presuppositions do govern the generation of discourse implies that all discourse without exception must be logically coherent. We can hardly invoke one mechanism of generation for the case where a discourse turns out to be consistent and a quite different mechanism where it does not. The conflation of 'presupposition' in the sense of the logical conditions of existence of the propositions of a discourse with what are thought to be the 'real' mechanisms of its production must be rejected as untenable. Discourse cannot be conceived as a function of logical relations with extra-discursive presuppositions. Precisely similar conclusions apply to the notion of problematic as both providing the logical conditions of existence of propositions and governing the production of a discourse and also to all conceptions of discourse as the application of a determinate system of methodological rules. In the event of inconsistency in the problematic or the rules the outcome must be indeterminate so that what does appear in the discourse can only be a function not only of extra-discursive but also of extra-conceptual determinants. Rationalist conceptions of the production of discourse can cope with inconsistency only by invoking quite different determinations to account for what appears in discourse. Thus, short of the relativist position which appears to deny the existence of logical contradiction,[27] rationalist mechanisms can be conceived as functioning only by courtesy of extra-conceptual forms of determination. The assumption of a rationalist conception of the production of discourse together with the recognition of the possibility of inconsistency must entail the primacy of non-rationalist determinations. But, to admit the primacy of non-rationalist determinations is to reject the rationalist conception itself.[28] The rationalist conception of the production of discourse must therefore be rejected as untenable.

Is it necessary to add that these arguments may be extended to the rationalist conception of action in all its forms? Weber has been examined at length in chapter 1 but consider the other two examples cited above. In these cases the problem is somewhat complicated but not essentially altered by the introduction of extra-conceptual pertinences; these provide the conditions of the realization of internal relations between ideas. Winch tells us that human conduct is a matter of the following of rules and also that 'the notion of following a rule is logically inseparable from the notion of *making a mistake*' (*The Idea of a Social Science,* p.32). Is it possible to follow inconsistent rules in one's conduct, for example, in the course of writing a book? It is clear that inconsistency must introduce an element of indeterminacy of the kind I have indicated above: conduct is a function of rules when they do not conflict and of something else when they do. Perhaps Winch could avoid indeterminacy by invoking a super-rule which regulates the application of particular rules by reference to features of the situation of action in such a way as to prevent conflict between rules from arising.[29] There are two cases here. First, if the conduct is that of writing a theoretical text, then it is clear that any such super-rule can avoid indeterminacy only by reference to extra-conceptual exigencies. Where two rules come into conflict my super-rule may tell me, for example, to follow one in the morning and the other in the afternoon: in the morning I affirm that there is no a-theoretical observation language and in the afternoon I affirm that deductive testing leads to the growth of knowledge. Thus to invoke a super-rule in this case is to reject the rationalist conception of the production of discourse. In all other cases a super-rule might appear to avoid the problems arising out of inconsistency by specifying extra-conceptual conditions in which one rule or the other has priority. The effect of that manoeuvre is simply that theoretical indeterminacy enters Winch's system at a different level. Winch states: 'the notion of following a rule is logically inseparable from the notion of *making a mistake*'. If a person's conduct never deviates from the rules then there is

> 'no *sense* in describing his behaviour in that way, since everything he does is as good as anything else he might do, whereas the point of the concept of a rule is that it should enable us to *evaluate* what is being done' (*ibid.*)

If conduct *never* deviates from the rule then to specify the rule is merely to describe whatever conduct takes place. The concept of rule-governed conduct would then be entirely vacuous. But if mistakes with respect to our super-rule are even conceivable then the situation is once again indeterminate: the super-rule is followed in all cases except those in which it is not followed. Thus for Winch to insist that conduct is a matter of following a rule is either to maintain that all conduct is theoretically indeterminate or else surreptitiously to invoke non-conceptual mechanism which determine when rules will be followed and when they will not.

Parsons' theory is, of course, altogether more sophisticated. And it is further complicated by the fact that the 'cybernetic hierarchy of control' includes not only the cultural, social and personality systems together with the behavioural organism and its physical-organic environment in that order, but also, at the very top of the hierarchy, 'ultimate reality'.[30] This last is explicitly conceived as being inaccessible to scientific forms of cognition. Now, although the cultural system is located immediately below 'ultimate reality' in the hierarchy of control it is by no means always internally consistent. We are told, for example, that:

> 'Very close approximations to complete consistency in the patterns of culture are practically never to be found in large complex social systems. The nature and sources of mal-integration of cultural patterns are as important to the theory of action as the integration itself.' (Parsons *et al.,* 1962, p.22)

But, if inconsistency at this level is possible, how is the functioning of culture in the hierarchy of control to be conceived? Since higher level controls are effective in precisely the cases where lower-level conditions leave the situation indeterminate, it follows that theoretical indeterminacy at the cultural level itself cannot be resolved by reference to the lower-level systems. Indeterminacy at this level implies that cultural 'controls' are effective only by courtesy of some higher-level mechanism. The realization of culture patterns at lower levels, for example, in the norms and collectivities of the social system, can only be a function of a level of control above that of culture. Thus, inconsistency at the cultural level entails a necessary theoretical indeterminacy in Parsons' theory of action systems which can hardly be resolved by reference to the mechanisms of 'ultimate reality' since these are not accessible to theoretical determination. On the other hand, to invoke a mechanism other than 'ultimate reality' to counteract theoretical indeterminacy would be to reject the rationalist conception of action which is the foundation of Parsonian theory.

Further consequences of my arguments here are not investigated in the present text [31] but I have said enough to show that the theoretical indeterminacy identified above in the rationalist conception of the production of discourse must also appear in other forms of the rationalist conception of action. Since that indeterminacy is a necessary effect of the basic concepts of the rationalist conception of action it can be overcome only at the cost of theoretical incoherence.

7.4 Conclusion

I conclude this chapter by commenting briefly on the implications of the preceding arguments for the analysis of discourse. It follows from my critique of the rationalist conception of the production of discourse that a rigorous separation should be maintained between:
(a) the logical conditions of existence of the propositions of discourse and the logical character of the relations between the concepts entailed in these conditions – in short, the logical character of the order of concepts of discourse;
and (b) the process of production or generation of discourse.
To insist on such a separation is not to preclude the development of forms of theorization of discourse independent of the analysis of its logical character, for example, analyses of style, grammar, etc. But it is to insist that internal relations between concepts cannot be conceived as governing the mechanisms involved. The consequences for Althusser's or any other rationalist theory of the production of discourse must be quite devastating. In particular it is impossible to maintain that methodological or other protocols can be effectively realized in particular theoretical discourses. It follows that no critique of methodological doctrines can be carried over to a critique of those substantive discourses which have been represented as if they were the products of determinate methodological protocols. Thus, if we do maintain a rigorous separation between the order of concepts of a discourse and the process of production of a discourse then there is at least one unfortunate consequence, namely, that all the easy critiques of Political Economy, Sociology, History, and so on, of the kind indicated above, in short the easy anti-empiricist critiques of theoretical discourses other than epistemology and methodology, must be invalid and logically ineffective. If theoretical discourses are to be criticized it can no longer be because they are alleged to be derived from some empiricist process or from epistemology but only because of an inadequacy at the level of their concepts and the relations between those concepts. To claim that the sociology of a Durkheim or of a Weber is empiricist and therefore ideological is to suppose that it is the product of a rationalist mechanism governed by an empiricist knowledge

process which takes place in ideology. A critique based on its ideological character or on its alleged empiricism must therefore be logically ineffective.

The analysis of the logical character of the order of concepts of a discourse cannot proceed by reference to any alleged process of production of that discourse. I have argued that discourse must be analysed in terms of the concepts and relations between concepts which are entailed in the positions developed in the discourse in question, and I have suggested that, in contrast to his treatment of what he regards as theoretical ideology, Althusser's analysis of the discourse of *Capital* does have this general character, albeit to a very limited extent. I have tried to give some further indication of what is involved in this mode of analysis in the previous section by means of the concept of the logical conditions of existence of the propositions of a discourse. Very schematically, we can say that every proposition in a discourse 'presupposes' certain concepts and relations between concepts. But, since there can be no question of conceiving logical conditions of existence as having any real effectivity in the generation of discourse, there can be no *presumption* of the coherence of a discourse nor of rigour in the development of its positions. Popper's theory of the growth of knowledge, for example, is manifestly not coherent. The logical conditions of existence of one proposition may well conflict with those of another. The analysis of discourse is concerned with the logical properties of the system of concepts and relations that are logically presupposed by the propositions of the discourse in question.

At this point it is necessary to introduce a further concept, namely, that of a 'hierarchy of concepts'. The necessity of this concept can be shown as follows. In the case of any reasonably complex or lengthy theoretical text it is usually easy to discover instances in which one proposition appears to contradict another. For example, I have referred to Althusser's investigation of the status of the concept of 'intersubjective relations' in relation to the system of concepts in *Capital* and to the problem this raises with respect to the identification of the basic concepts of a discourse. Althusser's conclusion, that the concept of 'intersubjective relations' is incompatible with the system of concepts of *Capital* might be interpreted as implying either that the concept of 'intersubjective relations' has no place in the science of Marxism or that the concepts of *Capital* are mutually incoherent. Similar points may be made with respect to the minor inconsistencies that may be found in most theoretical texts.

The concept of 'hierarchy of concepts' provides a means for determining the significance for its overall coherence of the inconsistencies that may be established within a discourse. There is a hierarchy of concepts to the extent that the formation of certain concepts of a discourse depends on, or 'presupposes', certain other concepts. For example, in our paper 'Talcott Parsons and the Three Systems of Action' Stephen Savage and I have shown that the concepts of the functional prerequisites in Parsons' theory depend both on the concepts of the action frame of reference and on the concepts of system and of the differentiated systems of action, i.e., the social, cultural and personality systems. The concepts of the functional prerequisities therefore belong to a level of discourse below that of the fundamental concepts of action and of action systems. It should be emphasised that the hierarchy of concepts is a matter of the relations which obtain between the concepts entailed in the propositions of the discourse. It does not depend on any explicit claims and assertions an author may make concerning those relations. The relations of hierarchy, coherence, and so on, hold or fail to hold in the concepts of a discourse irrespective of any beliefs or intentions which may be invoked on the part of the author.

In Parsons' case it is not difficult to show that his discourse is based on two separate orders of concepts – those of the action frame of reference and those of system and the differentiated systems of action – and that the bulk of his substantive theory may be derived as lower level effects resulting from the fusion of these two orders of concepts. We argue that the bringing together of these two orders of concepts at a fundamental level of Parsons' discourse results in a crucial logical incoherence. It is a crucial incoherence precisely because it is located at the most fundamental level of Parsons' discourse since this ensures that the effects of this incoherence must be felt throughout his work. They cannot, in other words, be restricted to any relatively discrete area as would be the case, for example, with respect to logical problems located at the level of his concepts of education, the family, etc. It follows that, quite apart from the theoretical indeterminacy involved in his rationalist conception of action, the major substantive positions advanced in Parsons' discourse within the sphere of sociology or more generally in his proposed 'sciences of action' have no coherent theoretical basis.

It should be clear from this short outline that the analysis of the logical character of the order of concepts of discourse is itself a

theoretical exercise involving *inter alia* concepts of the logical
character of the order of discourse, hierarchy of concepts, coherence,
derivation, and so on. Further elaboration of the theory of discourse
involved in this mode of analysis must await future publications but it
is necessary here to distinguish the mode of critique which it makes
possible from those modes of critique that merely counterpose one
theoretical position to another or which are based on particular
epistemological or methodological positions. Where the former merely
establish differences between one position and another, the latter
operate through the application of a definite set of epistemological or
methodological protocols whose function is both to reconstruct the
'content' of the discourse in question and to register any discrepancies
between that content and the requirements of the protocols – for example, Popper's polemics against Freud or Marx [32] and many
sociological critiques of Parsons. [33] Quite apart from the internal
problems of the theories from which they derive, all these critiques are
merely *dogmatic*; at their best they can only hope to establish that
propositions of one discourse fail to conform to conceptual relations
established in other discourses. Yet, as I have argued in preceding
chapters, there is no possibility of an extra-theoretical court of appeal
which can 'validate' the claims of one position against those of
another.

As against these dogmatic modes of critique the mode of analysis
suggested here may be described as strictly 'internal'. It is concerned
to investigate the concepts and relations presupposed in the formulation of the propositions of the discourse in question, their logical conditions of existence, and to investigate the logical properties of the
relations between these concepts. These properties concern the
coherence or incoherence, consistency or inconsistency of the discourse and their location at determinate levels in its hierarchy of concepts. A given discourse may, of course, be totally incoherent but if it
is at all theoretical, if, that is to say, it exhibits any level of rigour and
logical coherence, hierarchical relations will obtain between at least
some of its concepts. In theoretical discourses, where hierarchical
relations between concepts can be identified, it may be that certain
concepts or sets of concepts are relatively independent of the major
substantive concepts of the discourse. For example, the
epistemological, stylistic and grammatical protocols that sometimes
appear in substantive social scientific discourses often bear no relation
to the substantive concepts involved. I have argued that protocols can-

not be conceived as governing the production of discourse. If incoherence can be demonstrated at the highest level in the substantive concepts of a discourse, then we must conclude that the discourse is fundamentally incoherent and that the substantive positions which it develops have no coherent theoretical foundation. In this way it can be shown, for example, that in spite of its extremely high level of rigour in comparison with the bulk of sociological literature Parsons' discourse is primarily and fundamentally incoherent.

To the second of the two areas demarcated above, namely, that of the production or generation of discourse there is little I can add by way of positive indications at this stage. The negative effects of my arguments in this chapter should be clear enough and it is hardly necessary to add that the concepts of the logical character of the order of concepts, hierarchy, logical conditions of existence, and so on, are in no way intended to refer to putative mechanisms of the generation of discourse. I am not proposing a theory of discourse as the realization of a *logos*. On the contrary, I have argued that the rationalist conception of the production of theoretical discourse is but a particular case of a more general rationalist conception of action in which the world, or some particular part of it, is conceived as the realization of the idea. These rationalist conceptions may be humanist or anti-humanist in character; they may locate the principal mechanism of the realization of ideas in the attributes of the individual human subject, in particular in its will and consciousness, or they may locate it at a supra-individual level of determination. This last may be conceived in various forms: Parsons' 'cybernetic hierarchy of control'; Husserl's 'universal subjectivity' which realizes itself, *inter alia,* 'as human subjectivity, as an element of the world' (Husserl, 1970a, p.113); the consciousness and will of a class-subject as in many idealist versions of Marxism;[34] and, as we have seen, Althusser's conception of problematic as an extra-discursive system of concepts governing the order of appearance of concepts in discourse. Althusser completely rejects all humanist conceptions of the production of discourse and his own position has the very great merit of insisting on the importance of concepts and relations between concepts, on argument and demonstration, and on the question of the relative coherence of a system of concepts. Indeed, as I have suggested, his analyses of the status of particular concepts in relation to Marxist theory are sometimes exemplary. Unfortunately he locates the pertinence of concepts and the relations between concepts as much in the process of production of discourse as in the conceptual relations of the discourse itself. He therefore lapses into a rationalist conception of the production of discourse.

This collapse of one of the most sophisticated contemporary interpreters of Marxism and the most rigorous critic of classical epistemology into a rationalist, and therefore idealist, conception of the production of theoretical discourse may serve as an index of the dangers which confront us in this area. If the dominance of rationalist conceptions of human action has been successfully challenged by Marx in his theory of modes of production and, at another level, by Freud in the theory of the unconscious, no such theoretical emancipation has yet been achieved with respect to the problems of the production of discourse.[35] There, in theories ranging from the creativity of the individual scientist or scientific community to that of the scientific problematic itself, the rationalist conception of action reigns supreme.

Notes to the Text

Introduction

1. The rationalist conception of action is examined at length in my forthcoming paper 'Humanism and Teleology in Sociological Theory'.
2. It is clear that this conception of social facts conflicts with Durkheim's fundamental rule. cf. Hirst, 1975.
3. Lukacs attempts to overcome these problems in *History and Class Consciousness* with the postulate of the working class as both subject and object of history.
4. The relativist tendency is taken to an extreme in Winch, 1970.
5. Neo-Kantianism is conventionally divided into the Marburg and the Heidelberg schools. Where the former is primarily concerned with questions of logic and epistemology and with the conditions of knowledge in the natural sciences the latter attempts to theorize the conditions of knowledge in the cultural or historical sciences. The Heidelberg school conceives of culture as a realm of the realization of values in human existence. The philosophy of history is conceived as interpreting the products of the cultural sciences in the light of universal values. Dilthey differs from the Heidelberg school in rejecting the conception of universal values and in denying the division of the human subject into an empirical and a transcendental part. I have not attempted to examine these differences in this book. References to English language works or translations on the Heidelberg school and on Dilthey are given in the bibliography. See especially works by Dilthey, Rickert, Hodges, Mandelbaum and Antoni. An extremely elementary survey of doctrines of 'understanding' is given in Outhwaite, 1975.
6. In so far as history is, for Kant, the realization of an idea the mechanism

of realization is not conceived at the level of the consciousness and will of the human individual but at the level of nature as a whole. 'The history of mankind can be seen, in the large, as the realization of Nature's secret plan ...' (Kant, 1963, p.21)

7. But see note 5 for the position of the Marburg school.

8. cf. Outhwaite's comment: 'the question why social life or the behaviour of other people is in some sense intelligible to us need not be discussed in terms of an *a priori* 'social' form of apperception; *it is enough to say that we live in the same world as our fellow men and have a certain amount in common with them'* (Outhwaite, 1975, p.61, emphasis added) Outhwaite's comment manifestly begs the question: everything turns on his being able to establish that what men do have in common is sufficient to sustain the postulated forms of understanding.

9. There are many forms of this type of argument. Perhaps the most rigorous is that given in Strawson, 1959, see especially chapter 3.

Chapter 1

1. There is considerable debate within sociology concerning the precise significance of the differences between these texts from different periods and on the nature of Weber's transition from historian to sociologist. (For references to the more recent literature see Torrance, 1974.) Needless to say these questions are of no concern in this text.

2. The theoretical individualism apparent in Weber's definition of relationships and collectivities is a logical consequence of his definition of action in terms of the individual actor who is a free, transcendent being. Thus 'action ... exists only as the behaviour of one or more individual human beings' (*Theory*, p.101). This individualistic *definition* of relations and collectivities does not prevent Weber outlining conceptions of collective action, for example with reference to *shared* values (cf. Jones, 1975).

3. cf. the discussion of Schutz's distinction between 'objective' and 'subjective' meanings in chapter 2.

4. Meanings, as conceived here, are essentially extra-linguistic. They may be *expressed* in speech but they are not constituted there. Action in general, and speech in particular, is the free creative act of a transcendent rational being. The meaning of action or discourse must always be *postulated* by the observer. Thus 'subjective interpretation' is essentially speculative. For an excellent discussion of the absurdity of such extra-linguistic conceptions of meaning and consciousness see Volosinov, 1973.

5. This concept of 'instrumental rationality' opens up the possibility of a sphere of action not governed by *values* in any strict sense, a merely formal rationality. That possibility is most clearly realized in Weber's concept of capitalism, in which the market functions as a sphere of instrumental rationality abstracted from values, and also in the formal rationality of bureaucracy. Modern capitalism, which requires both a market economy and a developed bureaucratic organisation, leads to the meaninglessness of the world. It becomes an iron cage of formal, instrumental rationality entirely abstracted from values:

'For the last stage of this cultural development, it might well be truly said: "specialists without spirit, sensualists without heart; this nullity imagines that it has attained a level of civilization never before achieved" ' (*Protestant Ethic*, p.182)

6. See the Introduction for the neo-Kantian character of this conception of the essence of man as *rational*. It should be clear that Weber's classification of types of action is not a necessary logical consequence of this metaphysical concept of the essence of man. Whilst the exigencies of the expression of meanings in the medium of the behaviour of human animals may well require *some* conception of borderline types of action the specific concepts of affectual and traditional action cannot be established in this way.

7. It is for this reason that Weber treats primitive men as closer to the animals than us civilized creatures of the West. For example, he notes that domestic animals react to human commands in ways that are 'by no means purely instinctive and mechanical' and adds: 'there is no *a priori* reason to suppose that our ability to share the feelings of primitive men is very much greater' (*Theory*, p.104)

8. Nevertheless it would be an error to interpret Weber as merely reproducing the Hegelian philosophy of history. Where Hegel represents History as a process of auto-development Weber's explicit conception of history is very different. For example, in his Introduction written in 1920 to his works on the World Religions Weber poses the problem of the development of the West in terms of a 'combination of circumstances'. Thus the different histories of the West and the East are to be accounted for in terms of different 'combinations of circumstances'. In fact, of course, Weber's textual assemblage of 'combinations of circumstances' has the character of special pleading for a conclusion known in advance. The speculative empiricism of Weber's methodology should not be allowed to obscure the teleological character of his fundamental concepts. cf. my 'Humanism and Teleology in Sociological Theory'.

9. cf. Kant's 'Idea for a Universal History' where the conception of history as leading to the full development of human capacities is explicitly advanced. For example, the eighth thesis begins: 'The history of mankind can be seen, in the large, as the realization of *Nature's secret plan* to bring forth a perfectly constituted state as the only condition in which the capacities of mankind can be fully developed . . .' (Kant, 1963, p.21, emphasis added). Nature has chosen men's antagonism in society to achieve this end. This conception of Nature's secret plan is a Kantian *Idea*; it regulates empirical investigation but it cannot be established by it.

10. cf. Parsons' concurrence in Parsons, 1971, p.139.

11. cf. Parsons' comment in his Introduction to *Theory*, p.12.

12. The transcendent status of the human essence is central to Weber's treatment of the significance of possible racial differences as 'non-understandable uniformities underlying what has appeared to be specifically meaningful action' If such differences were to be established 'they would have to be treated by sociology as given data in the same way as the physiological facts of the need for nutrition or the effect of senescence on action' (*Theory*, p.94). Merely biological differences do not affect the human essence, since that is

extra-phenomenal, but they may affect the forms and conditions in which it realizes its intentions.

13. Weber's anti-psychologism is a necessary consequence of this conception of action. The means-end relation is a rational relation based on technical considerations; it is not a function of psychological, i.e. natural, mechanisms. Thus Weber remarks 'how erroneous it is to regard any kind of psychology as the ultimate foundation of the sociological interpretation of action' (*Theory*, p.108).

14. See, e.g., the editors' Introduction to *From Max Weber*. Even in *The Protestant Ethic*, frequently cited in this connection, the religious and idealist character of Weber's position is quite clear. Weber's Introduction describes the text as concerned with 'the influence of certain religious ideas on the development of an economic spirit, or the *ethos* of an economic system. In this case we are dealing with the connection of the spirit of modern economic life with the rational ethics of ascetic Protestantism. Thus we treat here only one side of the causal chain' (p.27) Weber's problem concerns the connection between one set of ideas and another. The 'causal' relations involved are essentially spiritual. The other 'side of the causal chain' therefore concerns the influence of an economic *ethos* on the development of religious ideas.

15. cf. the discussion of Schutz's very similar position in chapter 2.

16. See the analysis of Weber's concepts of meaning and behaviour in section 1. It is clear that 'chinese ossification' entails a significant reversion to the borderline state between action and merely animal behaviour, to a state that, in a very real sense, is less than fully human.

17. For examination of the effects of the latter see Hindess, 1973c.

18. Contrast the very different 'Hegelian' position of Lukacs. Lukacs conceives of knowledge as the consciousness of classes with the bourgeoisie and the proletariat (in successive periods) as the dominant subjects (the agents) of history. In this conception an identity of essence between the class subject as actor and class subject as knower is a real possibility. Such a condition of adequation, of true knowledge of the extra-phenomenal meaning of history, is precluded by Weber's neo-Kantian epistemology.

19. For the absurd consequences of such a position see the discussion in Hindess, 1973c. A similar position on the relations between meaning and overt behaviour was advanced in some of my own earlier work, e.g., Hindess, 1971a.

20. In *Methodology*, Weber uses the term 'ideal type' more generally so that it refers, *inter alia*, to these 'historical individuals' constituted by considerations of value-relevance. (e.g. p.91).

21. Lukacs attributes Weber's irrationalism to an effect of his class position as a result of which Weber is forced into 'the irrationalism of the imperialist epoch which is engendered by false replies to correct questions (correct because posed by reality itself)' (*op. cit.*, p.395). Lukacs' explanation is based on his expressive and teleological conception of knowledge and its relation to class positions. Nevertheless he correctly identifies the relativist and irrationalist consequences of Weber's epistemological concepts.

22. cf. Schutz's closely related criterion of adequacy with respect to 'common-sense interpretations'.

23. See also the excellent discussion of Mill in Willer & Willer, 1973.
24. The problem of the discursive status of positions which are represented as the products of empiricist protocols is considered in chapter 7.
25. It is surprising, therefore, to find Parsons, normally the most rigorous of sociological theorists, remarking: 'It is by means of this concept that Weber, in a highly ingenious way, has bridged the gap between the interpretation of meaning and the inevitably more complex facts of overt action' (*Theory*, p.100, note 21). The concept may well be ingenious but it is certainly not logically coherent.

Chapter 2

1. cf. Garfinkel's interpretation of Schutz in 'The rational properties of scientific and common-sense activities' in Garfinkel 1967.
2. These other writers are not examined in this chapter, nor is there any discussion of the development of Schutz's thought, in particular, his ruminations on 'the problem of relevance' and his increasing interest in American pragmatism after his move to New York. In spite of these and other minor changes there is a remarkable consistency, not to say repetition, in his published work. Indeed much of the argument in his American papers is devoted to summarising and paraphrasing his earlier work; this is particularly apparent in his discussions of the 'foundations' of the social sciences. See Hindess, 1973c, for a critique of the epistemological doctrines of the ethnomethodologists, Douglas and Cicourel.
3. An Act is not an act or an action. It refers to the constituting activity of consciousness, not to the external indications or manifestations of that activity: 'If we simply live immersed in the flow of duration, we encounter only undifferentiated experiences that melt into one another in a flowing continuum ... |It| is only by an Act of reflective attention that I catch sight of the retentional modification and therewith of the earlier phase' (*PSW*, p.51).
4. Thus Schutz describes the social scientist's ideal typical constructs as 'theoretical systems embodying testable general hypotheses in the sense of Professor Hempel's definition' (*CP1*, p.63). In fact Schutz's conception of theoretical systems is quite different from that of logical empiricism; in particular, the status of 'unobservables' in Schutzian or Weberian constructs is quite different from their status according to logical empiricist philosophy of science. cf. the discussion of Carnap in chapter 4.
5. Duhem (1969) appropriates this slogan for his conventionalist history of physical and astronomical theory up to the seventeenth century. According to the conventionalist account, scientific theories are a product of arbitrary conventions among scientists. The conventions are governed by considerations of utility and simplicity: they are designed to promote a convenient, useful and exact description of the corresponding, observational or experimental phenomena. Hence the slogan: 'to save the phenomena'. Physics and metaphysics are completely autonomous: neither has any bearing on the other. Thus Duhem can be a Catholic in his metaphysical beliefs and a positivist with respect to science. Nevertheless, while it is possible for believers and non-believers to work together in science, Duhem insists that

'the belief in an order transcending physics is the sole justification for physical theory' (Duhem, 1954, p.335).

6. In empiricist philosophies of science the theory of a science appears as the formal representation of features of its given real object, for example, of regularities in the appearance of phenomena, in relations between experiences, etc. Most contemporary variants distinguish between terms of a theory which are said to have a direct empirical referent and terms which are not, between observation terms (and observation language) and theoretical terms (and theoretical language). The most rigorous and systematic elaboration of this distinction is provided by the work of Carnap which I discuss in chapter 4. Theoretical terms are related to observation terms by means of the deductive structure of the theory. Both Schutz and Lazarsfeld use terms which are theoretical in this sense. They differ of course over the precise status which they assign to observation (and therefore to non-observables) and over the precise character of the deductive articulation of their theories.

7. Thus Van Breda (in the preface to *CP1*) quotes a letter of Husserl's: 'I am anxious to meet such a serious and thorough phenomenologist, one of the few who have penetrated to the core of the meaning of my life's work, access to which is unfortunately so difficult, and who promises to continue it as representative of the genuine *Philosophia perennis* which alone can be the future of philosophy' (p.X).

8. Schutz's 'phenomenological' sociology is little more than a development of Weber's methodological views and of the individualist idealism of the German *Geisteswissenschaften* tradition. Schutz's philosophical borrowings (from Husserl, Bergson, and later from pragmatism) are different from those of Weber (Heidelberg neo-Kantianism), but they serve precisely the same function. Schutz's work combines the irrationalism and personalism of the German idealist with the conventionalist positivism of speculative empiricists such as Duhem and Lazarsfeld. Weber, of course, is the classic point of union of these two traditions.

9. See Bachelard, 1968, for an excellent commentary on this text of Husserl.

10. This leads Husserl to the project of universal self-knowledge. Thus:
'The path leading to a knowledge absolutely grounded in the highest sense, or (this being the same thing) a philosophical knowledge, is necessarily the path of universal self-knowledge — first of all monadic, and then intermonadic . . . The Delphic motto, 'know thyself' has gained a new signification. Positive science is a science lost in the world. I must lose the world by *epoché*, in order to regain it by a universal self-examination.' (Husserl, 1970c, pp.56–7).

11. Otherwise there is not one transcendental Ego but a series of constituting-constituted Ego's extending to infinity. See also note 18.

12. It is this psychologism which allows him to take up the work of James, Dewey, Mead, without too much trouble. For other consequences see the papers in *CPIII*, especially 'Type and Eidos in Husserl's Late Philosophy'.

13. See, for example, the Fifth Meditation, Husserl, 1970c, pp.89–151.

14. cf. Husserl's comments on contemporary positivism: 'In like fashion, every return to "pure experience", and above all the current reflections of positivism in this regard, remains content with nature as already idealized,

which is equally true of the logician when he enquires about the empirical foundations of knowledge' (Husserl, 1973, p.45).

15. In the *Crisis* Husserl argues that Galileo performed:
   'the surreptitious substitution of the mathematically substructed world of idealities for the only real world, the one that is actually given through perception, that is ever experienced and experienceable – our everyday life-world. This substitution was promptly passed on to his successors, the physicists of all the succeeding centuries.'
   'Mathematics and mathematical science, as a garb of ideas ... encompasses everything which, for scientists and the educated generally, *represents* the life-world, *dresses it up* as "objectively actual and true" nature. It is through the garb of ideas that we take for *true being* what is actually a method' (Husserl, 1970a, pp.48–9, 51)

16. See Merleau-Ponty's attempt to reduce Husserl to a philosopher of existence in, for example, 'Phenomenology and the Sciences of Man', Merleau-Ponty, 1964a, 'the Philosopher and Sociology', Merleau-Ponty, 1964b, and in Merleau-Ponty, 1962.

17. See the discussions of logic (Husserl, 1973) and of geometry (Husserl, 1970a, appendix VI). I argue in chapter 3 that the problem of the reduction of knowledge to original experience is not resolved by this procedure. If experience is now always impregnated with logical and other idealizations then the invocation of a history *within* knowledge leads to the postulation of a mythical first idealization, the original sin of knowledge. cf. Althusser, 1970, pp.60–3.

18. This need for a transcendental logic leads into the danger of an infinite regress. If transcendental subjectivity is subject to norms:
   'a new transcendental investigation is necessary in order to relate its norms to a higher-subjectivity, since no content but, rather, only consciousness has the authority to be posited in itself.If transcendental logic truly grounds logic, there is no absolute logic (i.e. logic subjecting the absolute subjective activity to its norms). If there is an absolute logic, it can draw its authority only from itself; it is not transcendental.' (Cavaillès, 1947, p.65).

19. e.g. Lazarsfeld, 1954; Lazarsfeld & Oberschall, 1965; Kuhn & McPartland, 1954.

20. 'After he had acquired his degree he joined a banking firm in which he came to hold a most responsible position and with which he remained in association throughout his life. In New York, he became affiliated with the New School for Social Research and, for many years, combined his work in the banking firm with his academic duties.' (Gurwitsch, 1959, p.141).

21. Since 'the stream of history *can* be reduced to the genuine experiences of other men, experiences which occur within the immediacy of individual streams of consciousness' (*PSW*, p.213) it is clear that each moment of objective time is nothing but the immediate presence of all individual streams of consciousness to each other in this moment. Each consciousness, then, expresses the (same) essence of the present moment. The true subject of history is therefore the 'continuous We-relationship' (*ibid.*, p.214) that exists in the pre-predicative world of directly experienced social reality. The 'world of objective mind' is the world of this (lobotomised) World Spirit; it is not a world

of individual subjects. If there is an objective time then the social world is not reducible to the behaviour of individuals. If the world is so reducible there is no objective time. Schutz's objective time leaves no room for his 'freedom'.
22. So also must the philosopher's: 'Schutz's familiarity with the social sciences and with social reality proved highly fruitful for his work in philosophy proper.' (Gurwitsch, 1959, p.142).

Chapter 3

1. The English language edition (Husserl, 1970a) includes a number of additional papers and fragments published as appendices. These include the text 'The Origins of Geometry' and the Vienna lecture 'Philosophy and the Crisis of European Humanity'. All references to this book give the page number only.
2. Particularly the Vienna lecture, 'The Origins of Geometry', and Husserl, 1973.
3. See, for example, the works of Merleau-Ponty and Schutz. The latter's interpretation has been discussed in chapter 2. For the former see Merleau-Ponty, 1962, and 'The Philosopher and Sociology' in Merleau-Ponty, 1964b.
4. These two positions are well represented in the different functions assigned to the criterion of testability in Popper and in logical empiricism. In both cases testability distinguishes between science and metaphysics. For the latter metaphysics is meaningless, for the former it is not scientific but may be meaningful.
5. But see Kant's proposal for a naturalistic science of history in his 'Idea for a Universal History' in Kant, 1963.
6. Positions of this kind have been elaborated in recent English philosophy, e.g. in Winch, 1958. For an account of the similarities between analytic philosophy and the Geisteswissenschaften tradition see Apel, 1967.
7. Perhaps it is necessary here to comment on those readings which would distinguish the earlier anti-psychologistic Husserl from his later transcendentalism. For a recent example šee Pivcevic's review of the *Logical Investigations* (Husserl, 1970b) in which he argues both that Husserl's phenomenological analysis of logic 'makes good sense' and that there 'is no reason why this analysis should force us into adopting a radically transcendental position in Husserl's sense, i.e., the position of a "Transcendental-phenomenological idealism"' (Pivcevic, 1971, p.471). This distinction between Husserl's anti-psychologism and his transcendentalism cannot be seriously maintained. In a review published as early as 1903 the descriptions of phenomenology are said 'to deal neither with lived experiences nor classes of lived experiences of empirical persons ... Phenomenology knows nothing of persons, of my experiences or those of others, and surmises nothing regarding them: it raises no questions in regard to such matters, attempts no determinations, constructs no hypotheses' (Husserl, 1970b, p.48 – quoted in the 1913 Foreword to the second German edition). It is true that Husserl does not develop all the consequences of this position for some years

but this radical anti-psychologistic empiricism is already a transcendental empiricism in all but name.

8. Thus Ricoeur in what is nevertheless a useful commentary on the *Crisis* examines this text for 'Husserl's views on the crisis of philosophy and contemporary science. These views constitute the core of the second part of the *Crisis*.) (Ricoeur, 1967, p.161.)

9. I return to this question in chapter 7.

10. For examples see the texts of Ricoeur and Pivcevic referred to above and the extremely selective readings of Husserl practiced by Schutz and Merleau-Ponty.

11. Compare, for example, the position of Popper: 'it was during the summer of 1919 that I began to feel more and more dissatisfied with these three theories — the Marxist theory of history, psychoanalysis and individual psychology; and I began to feel dubious about their claims to scientific status. My problem perhaps first took the simple form, "What is wrong with Marxism, psychoanalysis and individual psychology? Why are they so different from physical theories, from Newton's theory, and especially from the theory of relativity?" ' (Popper, 1963, p.34). Popper's problem is to find a criterion of scientificity which includes physics but excludes Marxism and psychoanalysis. It should be clear that what is or is not duly accredited by philosophy is that philosophy's reading of the science in question. Such an empiricist reading, whether it 'recognises' the science or not, always a distortion of the science. Popper's vulgarisation of Marxism is well known. For an analysis of recent Popperian distortions of psychoanalysis see Cosin, Freeman and Freeman, 1972.

12. See Husserl, 1969, chapter 6 and especially §96, 'The transcendental problems of intersubjectivity and of the intersubjective world', and the Fifth Meditation in Husserl, 1970c.

13. Ricoeur *op. cit.*, Gurwitsch, 1966, and Carr's translator's Introduction to the *Crisis*, pp.xxxi–xxxviii.

14. For the concept of a definite manifold see Husserl, 1962 §72 and Husserl, 1969 chapter 3.

15. For an excellent short analysis of Bachelardian concepts see 'Gaston Bachelard's Historical Epistemology' in Lecourt, 1975.

16. This is essentially the position adopted by Koyré with regard to the scientific advances of Newtonian mechanics. See especially 'Newton and Descartes' in Koyré, 1965.

17. See note 11 and Fichant 'L'idée d'un histoire des sciences' in Fichant & Pecheux, 1969. A large part of this last text is translated in *Theoretical Practice* no. 3/4, 1971.

18. The adequacy of Husserl's account of Descartes, Hume and Kant is not in question here. In fact his analyses are not concerned to elicit the views of these individuals but rather to determine the meaning of the teleology that is expressed and represented in their intentions and activities. It is this theoretical objective that governs his mode of analysis of their positions.

19. I refer here to the Liebnizian conception of the form of unity of the totality of the world in which, in the formulation of the 'Discourse on Metaphysics', §ix, every individual substance, i.e. each part of the whole, 'ex-

presses the whole universe in its own manner'. It is 'like an entire world and like a mirror of God, or indeed of the whole world which it portrays, each one in its own fashion; almost as the same city is variously represented according to the various situations of him who is regarding it' (Leibniz, 1902, pp. 14–15). This mode of expressive causality which governs the relations of part and whole is reproduced in Hegel's conception of the totality and also in Husserl's world-constituting subjectivity.

20. cf. Hegel's elaboration of the concept of the World-Historical individual in the Introduction to Hegel, 1956.

21. This difficulty is most acute in the case of logic which is thought to provide *norms* for subjectivity. If logic is an accomplishment of subjectivity there is no absolute logic, if there is an absolute logic it cannot be a subjective accomplishment. See especially Husserl, 1969, and the discussions of that work in Bachelard, 1968 and Cavaillès, 1947.

22. See note 19.

23. See note 18. It should be clear that Husserl's rejection of an author-centric mode of analysis is not based on the concept of the logical conditions of existence of the propositions of a discourse briefly outlined in chapter 7. Husserl's search for underlying meanings implies a quite different mode of analysis.

24. Althusser (1972, pp.161–186) introduces this concept to designate a property which he believes to be common to the structure of the conceptions of history of both Hegel and Marx. For a critique of the concept of 'structural causality', which he attributes to the work of Marx, see Hindess & Hirst, 1975, chapter 6.

25. Essentially the same argument applies to the relation between other positive sciences and transcendental inquiry. Hence Fink's outline proposal for the continuation of the *Crisis* (published as appendix x) suggests 'the idea of all the sciences being taken back into the unity of transcendental philosophy' (p.400).

Chapter 4

1. See Kolakowski, 1972, for a good general survey of positivism and Ajdukiewicz, 1973, for an outline of the relations between positivism and other epistemologies.

2. Although they develop this answer into a position that is strictly precluded in Kant's theory. Compare, for example, Rickert, 1962, and Kant's 'Idea for a Universal History' in Kant 1963.

3. Wittgenstein appears to make a similar point with regard to his own arguments:

'My propositions serve as elucidations in the following way: anyone who understands me eventually recognises them as nonsensical, when he has used them − as steps − to climb up beyond them. (He must, so to speak, throw away the ladder after he has climbed up it). He must transcend these propositions, and then he will see the world aright.' *Tractatus*, 6, 54.

4. cf. the excellent demolition of Mill's methodology in D. & J. Willer, 1973.

5. The implication that there may be phenomena with no beginning is a

curious one in view of Mill's subsequent identification of phenomena with 'distinguishable sensations or other feelings'.

6. This last 'law' appears to be Mill's attempt to formulate one of Newton's 'laws of motion'. It is incorrectly stated by Mill. The effect of 'pressure' is to disturb a state of rest or of uniform motion by producing acceleration. When 'pressure' is removed acceleration ceases but motion does not.

7. See Kolakowski, 1972, chapter 5, for a good short account of Mach and Avenarius. The epistemology of these authors and of their Russian followers is savagely criticised by Lenin in *Materialism and Empirio-Criticism* and by Plekhanov in *Materialismus Militans*.

8. There is a brief outline in Feigl & Blumberg, 1931.

9. In his Preface to the second (1961) edition Carnap expresses a preference 'for use as basic elements, not elementary experiences, but something similar to Mach's elements.' (p.vii).

10. The 'picture theory' of language is rigorously developed in Wittgenstein's *Tractatus*.

11. See 'Psychology in Physical Language' (1932) – English translation in Ayer, 1959.

12. Logical positivism treats all ontology, and therefore its own phenomenalism, as strictly meaningless. Ontological doctrines are to be replaced by 'the practical decision' to use, say, a phenomenalistic or a physicalistic language. See, e.g. Carnap's 'Replies and Expositions' in Schilpp, 1963, p.868f.

13. For examples of the conventionalist position see Duhem, 1963, 1969, and Poincaré, 1963, n.d.

14. See 'Physics of a Believer' in Duhem, 1963.

15. For an excellent example see the discussion of the 'data matrix' in Galtung, 1967.

16. See Carnap's 'Autobiography' in Schilpp, 1963, p.56f.

17. It need hardly be said that positivist methodology in sociology barely recognises the existence of theory in even this limited sense. For example, while Stinchcombe admits the existence of other concepts his book deals 'only with observational concepts' (Stinchcombe, 1968, p.38). See also the discussion of dispositional and theoretical terms in Rudner, 1966.

18. See, for example, Hempel's contribution to Schilpp, 1963, and 'Empiricist Criteria of Cognitive Significance' in Hempel, 1965, and also the first two papers in Quine, 1963. cf. the discussion of positivist semantics in chapter 5.

19. cf. Popper's outline and discussion of a physicalistic interpretation of 'There exists an omnipotent, omnipresent, and omniscient personal spirit' and Carnap's reply in Schilpp, 1963, p.207f. and 880f.

20. cf. 'Positivist Semantics and the Semantic Concept of Truth' in chapter 5.

21. This conclusion is strongly argued by Koyré in 'An Experiment in Measurement' in Koyré, 1968. In my pamphlet on statistics (Hindess, 1973c) I have shown that the production of social statistics must be analysed without reference either to positivist conceptions of the given or to subjectivist conceptions of the state of consciousness of the observer.

Chapter 5

1. See Heisenberg 1949 and 1959.
2. The philosophical writings of Mach and Duhem are classical examples of this tendency. Several contributors to the Shanin volume attempt to use contemporary biology in this fashion.
3. For the whole of this section see also Badiou, 1969, Canguilhem, 1963 and Hindess, 1971b. Some of the errors of my earlier text are corrected in the present chapter.
4. It is impossible to avoid vulgarisation in the following elementary exposition. On the whole logic texts written by or for philosophers cannot be relied upon. Those available in English are generally by logical positivists or empiricists or else by those 'ordinary language' philosophers who do philosophical logic. Positivist semantics tends to assimilate the mathematical concept of interpretation of a formal system (which involves rigorously defined relations between mathematical domains) with the epistemological notion of designation. I present here only what is required to establish the distinction between mathematical semantics and the positivist notion. Martin, 1964, is generally reliable as a commentary on logical formalisation. The following mathematical texts require perseverance in abstraction but little mathematical training: Cohen, 1966; Davis, 1958; Kleene, 1966; Mendelson, 1966; Smullyan, 1961.
5. With the conventions introduced in the text the following axioms define a first-order calculus for unitary predicates:
   1. $A \rightarrow (B \rightarrow A)$
   2. $(-A \rightarrow -B) \rightarrow (B \rightarrow A)$
   3. $[A \rightarrow (B \rightarrow C)] \rightarrow [(A \rightarrow B) \rightarrow (A \rightarrow C)]$

Axiom 2. is required if $-A$ is to be derived from $A \rightarrow -B$ and $-B$ by means of the derivation rules.

6. For example, if the correspondence function assigns the same element, u, to each constant of the formal system then the following expression cannot be valid: $(Ex) \, (Ey) \, [(P(x) \rightarrow -P(y) \rightarrow (-(-P(y) \rightarrow P(x))]$.
7. The term 'first-order' is used to distinguish formal systems with predicates having constants and variables as arguments from those in which there are predicates having other predicates as arguments or in which there are predicate quantifiers.
8. What then, is the status of formal systems in which an axiom or theorem of this calculus is denied? Suppose, for example, that $-(-(-A) \rightarrow A)$ is a theorem of a formal system (informally it states that the negation of not$-A$ does not imply A). If such a system contains the axioms of the first-order predicate calculus then it is incoherent. Otherwise, since that calculus is valid for all models, the system has no model. More precisely it has no model in the domain of a set theory which contains the axiom of choice. Very schematically that axiom asserts that for any set whose members are sets there is a set containing exactly one element from each of the member sets. A version of this axiom plays a crucial roles in many of the constructions and proofs of Russell's and Whitehead's *Principia Mathematica*. But there are other set theories in which, for example, the negation of the axiom of choice may be an

axiom. The first-order predicate calculus would not be valid for an interpretation in such a theory. A formal system containing the above theorem has no model in a set theory with the axiom of choice but it may still be coherent. Set theory without the axiom of choice provides models of formal systems in which the principle of contradiction does not hold. For the history of set theory see Bourbaki, 1960, and 'Remarques sur la formation de la Théorie Abstraite des Ensembles' in Cavaillès, 1962.

9. English translation in Gödel, 1962. There are many expositions. The account given in Martin, *op.cit.*, is excellent and not too technical for the non-mathematician. See also Rosser, 1939.

10. In Husserl's case this norm would represent the whole of mathematics as a number of discrete, isolable, and strictly analytic formal systems which can be 'grasped' or 'mastered' by the intuition of a knowing subject. (cf. Cavaillès, 1947, pp.44–78). Wittgenstein's doctrine on mathematics is very similar in this respect.

11. This reading has been used, for example, to show the superiority of man over any possible computing machine (machines are formal systems governed by axioms, man creates axioms) (Nagel & Newman, 1959) and to support a metaphysical conception of free-will. (Lucas, 1970).

12. cf. Canguilhem, 1963.

13. e.g. von Bertalanffy, 1952.

14. A rather different position is taken by Popper in his paper 'Why are the calculuses of logic and arithmetic applicable to reality?' (in Popper, 1963). Part of his answer contains the assertion: 'Insofar as a calculus is applied to reality, it loses the character of a *logical* calculus and becomes a descriptive theory *which may be empirically refutable,* and insofar as it is treated as irrefutable, i.e. as a system of *logically true* formulae, rather than a descriptive scientific theory, it is not applied to reality' (p.210). For Popper there is no necessary correspondence between the logical structure of language and reality: 'We are all most intimately acquainted with a world that cannot be properly described by our language, which has been developed mainly as an instrument for describing and dealing with our physical environment – more precisely, with physical bodies of medium size in moderately slow motion. The indescribable world I have in mind is, of course, the world I have "in my mind" . . .' (p.213).

15. Hempel, 'Empiricist Criteria of Cognitive Significance' in Hempel, 1965, and Quine, 'Two Dogmas of Empiricism' in Quine, 1953.

16. cf. the discussion of 'truth' in Ajdukiewicz, 1973, pp.9–21.

17. Notice that the semantic definition of truth applies only to formalized languages for which an appropriate metalanguage may be constructed. The distinction between the language in which propositions are formulated and the metalanguage which contains names of propositions is required to escape logical paradoxes such as the following. Let p designate the fourth sentence in this note. p is not a true sentence. It is easy to show that p is a true sentence if and only if p is not a true sentence.

18. The parallel with mathematical logic is instructive here. There are coherent first-order formal systems in which the negation of the principle of contradiction (i.e. $-(-(-A) \succ A)$) is a theorem. Such systems may have models

in a set theory without the axiom of choice (cf. note 8). Carnap's 'rules of ranges' require that 'possible states of affairs' be governed by some equivalent of the axiom of choice.

19. Tarski and Quine have both argued that no rigorous demarcation between analytic and synthetic is possible. See 'On the Concept of Logical Consequence', Tarski, 1956, p.409f., and Quine, *op.cit.*

20. For a brief exposition see von Bertalanffy, 1967. See also the references given in note 8, p.119, of that text and von Bertalanffy, 1974.

21. The peculiar significance for such a conception of the study of the model-builder himself should now be clear. Once we can construct a model of the model-building activity of the human mind than the circle of knowledge will be finally closed; everything that can be known will be contained in this, the ultimate model. It only remains for the content to be unpacked. 'The aim is to arrive at a kind of "generative grammar" of culture as a semiotic system' (Bauman, *op.cit.,* p.319). This 'generative grammar' would be generative of all culture and therefore of all possible knowledge.

22. The quotation is from E. W. Beth, *The Foundations of Mathematics,* p.151.

23. Kant's transcendental philosophy specifically precludes all determination of the categories of thought by natural causes, in particular, by the naturalistic psychology of Locke and Hume. The *a priori* categories are conditions of existence of phenomena; they cannot be phenomena to be explained by particular sciences. The attempt to 'modernise' Kant by reference to biological evolution as the origin of *a priori* categories is by no means peculiar to Bauman.

24. Another paper in Shanin's collection suggests 'that we regard living organisms as systems which generate and test hypotheses about their environment'. In the case of the bacterium 'it is probably evident to the reader that the obvious candidates for such hypotheses are the genes, or more generally the hereditary material of the bacterium' (Goodwin, 1972, p.371). Popper's evolutionary epistemology involves a similar conception. For other references see Campbell, 1974, especially appendix iv, 'Biological Evolution as the origin of the *A Priori* Categories of Thought and Perception in Man.' All such positions require an outrageous play on words such as 'knowledge', 'hypothesis', etc.

Chapter 6

1. There is an effective demolition of Popper's ignorant and misleading critique of Hegel in W. Kaufmann, 'The Hegel Myth and its Methods' in Kaufmann, 1960. For discussion of Popper's interpretation of Plato see the papers in Bambrough, 1967.

2. Popper also refers to Hume's 'psychological' problem of induction, namely, why all reasonable people nevertheless expect and believe that instances of which they have no experience conform to those of which they do have experience. Where Hume refers to custom and habit, to repitition and the association of ideas, Popper maintains that there is no such thing as induction by repitition. Hume's 'psychological problem' does not arise.

3. Popper frequently suggests that this criterion provides the solution to an earlier problem: 'My problem perhaps first took the simple form, "What is wrong with Marxism, psychoanalysis and individual psychology? Why are they so different from physical theories, from Newton's theory, and especially from the theory of relativity?" (*CR* p.34). For an excellent critique of Popperian interpretations of psychoanalysis see Cosin *et al.,* 1972. Popper's attack on the scientific status of Marxism is examined in Williams 1975.

4. See Cosin *et al., op. cit.,* p.132f for discussion of this and other examples.

5. Lakatos takes this conception to its conclusion: 'a good rationality theory must anticipate further basic value judgments, unexpected in the light of their predecessors or even lead to the revision of previously held value judgments' (Schilpp, 1974, p.250).

6. cf. Schilpp, 1974, p.1070 and *O.K.* chapter 5 and appendix.

7. In spite of the crucial significance of training, intersubjective agreement, and the like in his theory of science Popper remains implacably opposed to any sociology of science, e.g., to Kuhn's 'sociological' conception of science as a 'community of workers held together by a routine' (cf. Schilpp, 1974, p.1144f). The difference is far from clear but it seems that for Popper the norm establishes what is or is not scientific while he interprets Kuhn as representing the community of scientists as the primary determinant of what passes for science.

8. Popper quotes these passages in his reply to Lakatos in Schilpp. 1974, pp. 1011-2. He adds: 'What we demand of a theory t_2 in order that it should be better (or nearer to the truth) than t_1 ...' (p.1012). But what is at issue is precisely the connection between being 'better' and being 'nearer to the truth'.

9. The implications of this conception of the relation between theory, instrument and observation has been most fully elaborated in the work of Bachelard. For an excellent account of the basic concepts of Bachelard's theory of science see 'The Historical Epistemology of Gaston Bachelard' in Lecourt, 1975.

Chapter 7

1. For example, in the publicity material issued by the organisers of the 1975 British Sociological Association Summer School for Graduates.

2. cf. Judith Willer, 1972, especially chapter 3.

3. But see note 15, p.35 where Althusser acknowledges that the generality of his critique goes beyond what can be sustained by the concept outlined in the text.

4. It is necessary to insist on this point since the generality of Althusser's concept is often misunderstood. See, for example, Pickvance, 1973, for his comments on Hindess 1973a and my reply 1973b.

5. cf. *Reading Capital,* part 1, section 10, p.34f.

6. Bachelard maintains, further, that, far from philosophy governing the practice of the sciences, the latter must develop or generate epistemologies appropriate to their own practices. Philosophy follows on from, and is subordinate to, the sciences. See especially the Preface to Bachelard, 1968. Althusser, similarly, maintains that revolutions in philosophy follow and are

induced by transformations in the sciences: Plato after the birth of Greek mathematics, Descartes after Galileo, Kant after Newton, etc. See especially 'Lenin and Philosophy' in Althusser, 1971.

7. 'On the Materialistic Dialectic' in *For Marx*. For an outline of Bachelard's position see Lecourt, 1975.

8. In 'On the Materialist Dialectic' Althusser represents the process of knowledge as a process of production involving three 'generalities': Generality I represents raw material, Generality II the means of production and Generality III the knowledge produced. In the production of theory Generality II, that is, the theories, concepts and instruments, in short, the problematic, is the determinant element. The sciences and theoretical ideologies are distinguished by reference to their Generality II.

9. See especially 'Ideology and Ideological State Apparatuses' in Althusser, 1971 for an elaboration of this position.

10. cf. 'Marxism and Humanism' in Althusser 1969.

11. Bachelard discusses several examples of this 'epistemological break' in Bachelard, 1964. In Althusser's work the 'mode of production' analogy is decisive. In the production of knowledge Generality II is the determinant element, not the raw material, Generality I, nor the product of the knowledge process, Generality III. Thus the 'break' refers not so much to the emergence of a full-blown and elaborated scientific theory, a new Generality III, but to the emergence of a mode of production of knowledge governed by the operation of concepts which leads to the progressive reorganisation and reconstruction of the previous ideological problematic. Althusser maintains, for example, that, in spite of the epistemological break constituting the emergence of scientific Marxism, Marx's writings, his Generality III's, do not completely escape from theoretical ideology.

12. cf. 'Lenin and Philosophy' in Althusser, 1971, for the argument that philosophy represents the class struggle in theory.

13. cf. Hirst, 1975.

14. cf. Althusser's commentary, *Reading Capital*, p.194ff.

15. Hindess & Hirst, 1975, p.271f.

16. To rely on explicit statements by an author is to suppose that the author is correct in his assessment of his work. cf. Hirst, 1972.

17. The teleological character of Althusserian analyses of theoretical discourse was first demonstrated in an unpublished paper by Stephen Savage.

18. In fact the notions of base and superstructure have little value in Marxist theory. See the Introduction to Hindess & Hirst, 1975, pp.16–17.

19. cf. 'On the Young Marx' in *For Marx* and the Foreword to Althusser, 1971.

20. See Hindess and Savage, 1977, for an analysis of the work of Parsons in these terms.

21. The analogy is to the two axes of linguistics: speech (horizontal) and syntax (the absent 'vertical' system present in the forms of speech). See Badiou, 1967, for a systematic elaboration of this analogy, cf. the useful discussion of theories of reading (Althusser, Structuralism, and History of Ideas) in Williams, 1974.

22. cf. Althusser's argument for the necessity of a 'symptomatic' reading in

Reading Capital, especially, p.24f.

23. This conception is explicitly developed in Collingwood, 1939 and 1940.

24. See the outline in Parsons, 1966, chapter 2.

25. See Hindess & Savage 1977 for the argument that Parsons' combination of the action frame of reference with his conception of autonomous sub-systems of action is logically incoherent.

26. cf. *Reading Capital* pp.41–2. 'This definite system of theoretical practice is what assigns to any given thinking subject (individual) its place and function in the production of knowledges.' For Parsons see the reference in note 24 and for Husserl see chapter 3.

27. cf. Winch's argument in 'Understanding a Primitive Society' which takes this relativist tendency to an extreme: 'the forms in which rationality expresses itself in the culture of a human society cannot be elucidated *simply* in terms of the logical coherence of the rules according to which activities are carried out in that society. For . . . *there comes a point where we are not even in a position to determine what is and what is not coherent in such a context of rules,* without raising questions about the point which following those rules has in that society' (pp.93–4, emphasis added).

28. cf. 'We cannot understand the irrational and to suppose that we can is to run into vicious circles; but we can understand the rational in more than one way' (Hollis, 1970, p.220)

29. For example in Winch, 1970, he refers to the fact 'that many contradictions we might expect to appear in fact do not in the context of Zande thought, *where provision is made for avoiding them.'* (p.91, emphasis added)

30. cf. Parsons, 1966, pp.28–9.

31. The properties of the rationalist conception of action are examined in a forthcoming paper, 'Humanism and Teleology in Sociological Theory'.

32. See Cosin *et. al.,* 1972, and Williams, 1975.

33. See Hindess & Savage, 1977, for a brief discussion.

34. These positions are castigated by Althusser in *Reading Capital,* part 2, especially chapters 4 and 5. Unfortunately, as Paul Hirst and I have shown, his own interpretation of Marxism is equally problematic in some respects. cf. Hindess & Hirst, 1975, chapter 6 and conclusion.

35. Foucault has consistently opposed humanist conceptions of the production of discourse but the precise status of his own proposals is far from clear. The rules of formation of objects proposed in *The Archeology of Knowledge* certainly suggest a rationalist conception of discursive practice but the references to 'institutions', 'economic and social processes', 'systems of norms' and the astonishing project of a 'pure description of discursive events' (p.27) suggest a crucial eclecticism. Indeed, in his extremely perceptive review of *The Archeology* Williams argues that the decisive terms of Foucault's theory 'are thought using a mish-mash of the left-overs of a variety of ancient and modern discourses' (Williams, 1974, p.63).

Bibliography

Ajdukiewicz, K., 1973, *Problems and Theories of Philosophy,* London, Cambridge University Press

Althusser, L., 1969, *For Marx,* London, Allen Lane; The Penguin Press

Althusser, L., 1971, *Lenin and Philosophy and other Essays,* London, NLB

Althusser, L., & Balibar, E., 1970, *Reading Capital,* London, NLB

Antoni, C., 1962, *From History to Sociology: The Transition in German Historical Thinking,* London, Merlin Press

Apel, K-O., 1967, *Analytic Philosophy of Language and the Geisteswissenschaften,* Dordrecht, D. Reidel

Ayer, A. J., (ed.), 1959, *Logical Positivism,* London, George Allen & Unwin

Ayer, A. J., 1974, 'Truth, Verification and Verisimilitude' in Schilpp, 1974

Bachelard, G., 1964, *The Psychoanalysis of Fire,* Boston, Beacon Press

Bachelard, G., 1968, *The Philosophy of No,* New York, The Orion Press

Bachelard, S., 1968, *A Study of Husserl's Formal and Transcendental Logic,* Evanston, Northwestern University Press

Badiou, A., 1967, 'Le (re)commencement du matérialisme dialectique', *Critique,* tome xxiii, no.240

Badiou, A., 1969, *Le concept de modèle,* Paris, Maspero

Bambrough, R., (ed.), 1967, *Plato, Popper and Politics,* Cambridge, Heffer

Baumann, Z., 1972, 'Praxis: the controversial culture-society paradigm' in Shanin (ed.), 1972

Bertalanffy, L. von, 1952, *Problems of Life,* London, Watts

Bertalanffy, L. von, 1967, 'General Systems Theory' in N. J. Demerath III & R. A. Peterson (eds.), *System, Change & Conflict,* London, Collier-Macmillan, New York, The Free Press

Bertalanffy, L. von, 1974, *General Systems Theory,* Harmondsworth, Penguin

Blumberg, A. E., & Feigl, H., 1931, 'Logical Positivism: a new movement in European philosophy', *The Journal of Philosophy,* vol. xxviii

Blumer, H., 1967, 'Society as Symbolic Interaction' in J. G. Manis & B. N. Meltzer (eds.), *Symbolic Interaction,* Boston, Allyn & Bacon

Bourbaki, N., 1960, *Eléments d'Histoire des Mathématiques,* Paris, Hermann

Campbell, P. T., 1974, 'Evolutionary Epistemology' in Schilpp, 1974

Canguilhem, G., 1963, 'The Role of Analogies and Models in Biological Discovery' in A. C. Crombie (ed.), *Scientific Change,* London, Heinemann

Carnap, R., 1936, 'Testability and Meaning', *Philosophy of Science,* vol. 3 & 4

Carnap, R., 1947, *Meaning and Necessity,* Chicago, The University of Chicago Press

Carnap, R., 1953, 'Factual and Formal Science' in H. Feigl & M. Brodbeck (eds.), *Readings in the Philosophy of Science,* New York, Appleton Century-Crofts

Carnap, R., 1956, 'The Methodological Character of Theoretical Concepts', *Minnesota Studies in the Philosophy of Science,* vol. 1

Carnap, R., 1958, *Introduction to Symbolic Logic,* New York, Dover Publications

Carnap, R., 1959, 'Psychology in Physical Language' in Ayer, 1959

Carnap, R., 1963, 'Autobiography' & 'Replies & Expositions' in Schilpp, 1963

Carnap, R., 1968, *The Logical Structure of the World,* London, Routlege & Kegan Paul

Cavaillès, J., 1960, *Sur la logique et la thèorie de la science,* Paris, P.U.F.

Cavaillès, J., 1962, *Philosophie Mathematique,* Paris, Hermann

Cohen, P. J., 1966, *Set Theory and the Continuum Hypothesis,* New York, Benjamin

Collingwood, R. G., 1939, *An Autobiography,* Oxford, The Clarendon Press

Collingwood, R. G., 1940, *Essay on Metaphysics,* Oxford, The Clarendon Press

Cosin, B. R., Freeman, C. F., & Freeman, N. H., 1972, 'Critical Empiricism Criticized: the case of Freud', *Journal for the Theory of Social Behaviour,* vol. 1, no. 2

Davis, M., 1958, *Computability and Solvability,* New York, McGraw Hill

Dilthey, W., 1957, *Dilthey's Philosophy of Existence,* (translated with an introduction by W. Kluback & M. Weinbaum) London, Vision

Dilthey, W., 1961, *Meaning in History,* (edited with an introduction by H. P. Rickman), London, George Allen & Unwin

Duham, P., 1954, *The Aim & Structure of Physical Theory,* Princeton, Princeton University Press

Duham, P., 1969, *To Save the Phenomena,* Chicago, The University of Chicago Press

Durkheim, E., 1964, *The Rules of Sociological Method,* New York, The Free Press

Einstein, A., *et al.*, 1923, *The Principle of Relativity: a collection of original memoirs on the special and general theory of relativity*, London, Methuen

Fichant, M., & Pecheux, M., 1969, *Sur l'histoire des sciences*, Paris, Maspero

Foucault, M., 1972, *The Archeology of Knowledge*, London, Tavistock

Galtung, J., 1967, *Theory & Methods of Social Research*, London, George Allen & Unwin

Garfinkel, H., 1967, *Studies in Ethnomethodology*, Englewood Cliffs, N.J., Prentice-Hall

Gödel, K., 1962, *On Formally Undecidable Propositions of Principia Mathematica and Related Systems*, Edinburgh, Oliver & Boyd

Goodwin, B., 1972, 'Science and Alchemy' in Shanin (ed.), 1972

Gurwitsch, A., 1959, 'Alfred Schutz (1899–1959)', *Philosophy & Phenomenological Research*, vol. 20

Gurwitsch, A., 1966, 'The last work of Edmund Husserl' in *Studies in Phenomenology and Psychology*, Evanston, Northwestern University Press

Hegel, G. W. F., 1956, *The Philosophy of History*, New York, Dover Publications

Heisenberg, W., 1949, *The Physical Principles of the Quantum Theory*, New York, Dover Publications

Heisenberg, W., 1959, *Physics and Philosophy*, London, George Allen & Unwin

Hempel, K., 1963, 'Implications of Carnap's Work for the Philosophy of Science' in Schilpp, 1963

Hempel, K., 1965, *Aspects of Scientific Explanation*, New York, Prentice-Hall

Hindess, B., 1971a, *The Decline of Working Class Politics*, London, MacGibbon & Kee

Hindess, B., 1971b, 'Materialist Mathematics', *Theoretical Practice*, no. 3/4

Hindess, B., 1973a, 'Models and Masks: empiricist conceptions of the conditions of scientific knowledge', *Economy and Society*, vol. 2, no. 2

Hindess, B., 1973b, 'The empiricist conception of knowledge: A reply to Mr. Pickvance', *Economy and Society*, vol. 2, no. 4

Hindess, B., 1973c, *The Use of Official Statistics in Sociology: a critique of positivism and ethnomethodology*, London, Macmillan

Hindess, B., (forthcoming), 'Humanism and Teleology in Sociological Theory'

Hindess, B., & Hirst, P. Q., 1975, *Pre-Capitalist Modes of Production*, London, Routledge & Kegan Paul

Hindess, B., & Savage, S. P., (forthcoming), 'Talcott Parsons and the Three Systems of Action' in H. Martins (ed.) *Structural-Functionalism: a reappraisal*, London, Macmillan

Hirst, P. Q., 1975, *Durkheim, Bernard and Epistemology*, London, Routledge & Kegan Paul

Hodges, H. A., 1944, *Wilhelm Dilthey, an Introduction*, London, Routledge & Kegan Paul

Hodges, H. A., 1952, *The Philosophy of Wilhelm Dilthey*, London,

Routledge & Kegan Paul

Hollis, M., 1970, 'The Limits of Irrationality', in Wilson, 1970

Husserl, E., 1962, *Ideas: general introduction to pure phenomenology,* New York, Collier-Macmillan

Husserl, E., 1969, *Formal and Transcendental Logic,* The Hague, Nijhoff

Husserl, E., 1970a, *The Crisis of European Sciences and Transcendental Phenomenology,* Evanston, Northwestern University Press

Husserl, E., 1970b, *Logical Investigations,* London, Routledge & Kegan Paul

Husserl, E., 1970c, *Cartesian Meditations,* The Hague, Nijhoff

Husserl, E., 1973, *Experience and Judgment: Investigations in a Genealogy of Logic,* London, Routledge & Kegan Paul

Jones, B., 1975, 'Max Weber and the Concept of Social Class,' *Sociological Review,* vol. 23, no. 4

Kant, I., 1949, *Foundations of the Metaphysics of Morals,* Indianapolis, Bobbs-Merrill

Kant, I., 1950, *Critique of Pure Reason,* London, Macmillan

Kant, I., 1963, *On History,* Indianapolis, Bobbs-Merrill

Kant, I., 1974, *Logic,* Indianapolis, Bobbs-Merrill

Kaufmann, W., 1960, *The Owl and the Nightingale,* Garden City, N.Y., Anchor Books

Kleene, S. C., 1966, *Introduction to Metamathematics,* New York, van Nostrand

Kolakowski, L., 1972, *Positivist Philosophy,* Harmondsworth, Penguin

Koyré, A., 1965, *Newtonian Studies,* London, Chapman & Hall

Koyré, A., 1968, *Metaphysics & Measurement,* London, Chapman & Hall

Kuhn, M. H., & McPartland, T. S., 1954, 'An Empirical Investigation of Self-Attitudes', *A.S.R.,* vol. 29

Kuhn, T. S., 1962, *The Structure of Scientific Revolutions,* Chicago, The University of Chicago Press

Lakatos, I., 1974, 'Popper on Demarcation and Induction' in Schilpp, 1974

Lazarsfeld, P. F., 1954, 'A Conceptual Introduction to Latent Structure Analysis' in Lazarsfeld, P. F., (ed.), *Mathematical Thinking in the Social Sciences,* Glencoe, Ill., The Free Press

Lazarsfeld, P. F., & Oberschall, A., 1965, 'Max Weber & Empirical Social Research', *A.S.R.,* vol. 40

Lévi-Strauss, C., 1966, *The Savage Mind,* London, Weidenfeld & Nicolson

Lévi-Strauss, C., 1968, *Structural Anthropology,* London, Allen Lane, The Penguin Press

Liebniz, G. W. von, 1902, *Basic Writings,* La Salle, Open Court

Lucas, J. R., 1970, *The Freedom of the Will,* London, Oxford University Press

Lukacs, G., 1971, *History and Class Consciousness,* London, Merlin Press

Lukacs, G., 1972, 'Max Weber & German Sociology', *Economy and Society,* vol. 1, no. 4

Mach, E., 1959, *The Analysis of Sensations,* New York, Dover Publications

Mandelbaum, M., *The Problem of Historical Knowledge,* New York, Harper Torchbooks

Martin, R., 1964, *Logique contemporaine et formalisation,* Paris, P.U.F.
Marx, K., 1974, *Capital,* vol. 1, London, Lawrence & Wishart
Mendelson, E., 1966, *Introduction to Mathematical Logic,* New York, van Nostrand
Merleau-Ponty, M., 1962, *The Phenomenology of Perception,* London, Routledge & Kegan Paul
Merleau-Ponty, M., 1964a, *The Primacy of Perception,* Evanston, Northwestern University Press
Merleau-Ponty, M., 1964b, *Signs,* Evanston, Northwestern University Press
Mill, J. S., 1967, *A System of Logic,* London, Longmans
Nagel, E., & Newman, J. R., 1959, *Gödel's Proof,* London, Routledge & Kegan Paul
Neumann, J. von, & Morgenstern, O., 1954, *The Theory of Games and Economic Behaviour,* Princeton, Princeton University Press
Outhwaite, W., 1975, *Understanding Human Behaviour: the method called 'Verstehen',* London, George Allen & Unwin
Parsons, T., 1966, *Societies: evolutionary and comparative perspectives,* Englewood Cliffs, N.J., Prentice-Hall
Parsons, T., 1971, *The System of Modern Societies,* Englewood Cliffs, N.J., Prentice-Hall
Piaget, J., 1971a, *Structuralism,* London, Routledge & Kegan Paul
Piaget, J., 1971b, *Biology and Knowledge,* Edinburgh, Edinburgh University Press
Pickvance, C. G., 1973, 'Althusser's "empiricist" conception of knowledge: A comment on Mr. Hindess's review article', *Economy and Society,* vol. 2, no. 4
Pivcevic, E., 1971, 'E. Husserl: *The Logical Investigations', Mind,* vol. Lxxx, no. 319
Popper, K. R., 1959, *The Logic of Scientific Discovery,* London, Hutchinson
Popper, K. R. 1963a, *Conjectures & Refutations,* London, Routledge & Kegan Paul
Popper, K. R., 1963b, 'The Demarcation between Science and Metaphysics' in Schilpp, 1963
Popper, K. R., 1972, *Objective Knowledge,* Oxford, The Clarendon Press
Popper, K. R., 1974, 'Intellectual Autobiography' and 'Replies to my Critics' in Schilpp, 1974
Quine, W. V. O., 1963, *From a Logical Point of View,* New York, Harper Torchbooks
Ricardo, D., 1971, *The Principles of Political Economy and Taxation,* Harmondsworth, Penguin
Rickert, H., 1962, *Science and History: a critique of positivist epistemology,* London & New York, van Nostrand
Ricoeur, P., 1967, *Husserl: an analysis of his phenomenology,* Evanston, Northwestern University Press
Rosser, B., 1939, 'An Informal Exposition of Proofs of Gödel's theorems and Church's theorem' *Journal of Symbolic Logic,* iv
Rudner, R., 1966, *Philosophy of Social Sciences,* Englewood Cliffs, N.J., Prentice-Hall

Sartre, J-P., 1965, *The Problem of Method*, London, Methuen

Schilpp, P.A., (ed.), 1963, *The Philosophy of Rudolph Carnap*, La Salle, Open Court

Schilpp, P. A., (ed). 1974, *The Philosophy of Karl Popper*, La Salle, Open Court

Schutz, A., 1962, *Collected Papers I: The Problem of Social Reality*, The Hague, Nijhoff

Schutz, A., 1964, *Collected Papers II: Studies in Social Theory*, The Hague, Nijhoff

Schutz, A., 1966, *Collected Papers III: Studies in Phenomenological Philosophy*, The Hague, Nijhoff

Schutz, A., 1967, *The Phenomenology of the Social World*, Evanston, Northwestern University Press

Schutz, A., 1970, *Reflections on the Problem of Relevance*, New Haven & London, Yale University Press

Shanin, T., 1972, 'Models and Thought' in Shanin (ed.), 1972

Shanin, T., (ed.), 1972, *The Rules of the Game: cross-disciplinary essays on Models in Scholarly Thought*, London, Tavistock

Smullyan, R. M., 1961, *Theory of Formal Systems*, Princeton, Princeton University Press

Stinchcombe, A. L., 1968, *Constructing Social Theories*, New York, Harcourt, Brace and World

Strawson, P. F., 1959, *Individuals*, London, Methuen

Tarski, A., 1956, *Logic, Semantics, Metamathematics*, Oxford, The Clarendon Press

Torrance, J., 1974, 'Max Weber: Methods and the Man' *Archiv. europ. social.*, xv

Volosinov, V., 1973, *Marxism and the Philosophy of Language*, London and New York, The Seminar Press

Weber, M., 1930, *The Protestant Ethic and the Spirit of Capitalism*, London, George Allen & Unwin

Weber, M., 1959, *The Methodology of the Social Sciences*, New York, The Free Press

Weber, M., 1964a, *The Theory of Social and Economic Organisation*, New York, The Free Press

Weber, M., 1964b, *The Religion of China*, New York, The Free Press

Weber, M., 1968, *Economy and Society*, New York, The Bedminster Press

Weber, M., 1970, *From Max Weber*, (H. H. Gerth & C. W. Mills eds.) London, Routledge & Kegan Paul

Willer, J., 1971, *The Social Determination of Knowledge*, Englewood Cliffs, N.J., Prentice-Hall

Willer, D. & J., 1973, *Systematic Empiricism: critique of a pseudo-science*, Englewood Cliffs, N.J., Prentice-Hall

Williams, K. 1974, 'Unproblematic Archeology', *Economy and Society*, vol. 3, no. 1

Williams, K., 1975, 'Facing Reality: a critique of Karl Popper's Empiricism', *Economy and Society*, vol. 4, no. 3

Wilson, B. R., (ed.), 1970, *Rationality*, Oxford, Basil Blackwell

Winch, P., 1958, *The Idea of a Social Science,* London, Routledge & Kegan
 Paul
Winch, P., 1970, 'Understanding a Primitive Society' in Wilson, 1970
Wittgenstein, L., 1961, *Tractatus Logico-Philosophicus,* London, Routledge
 & Kegan Paul

Index

abstraction, 5, 6, 36, 44, 191-5, 196-7
action; and behaviour, 27-8, 30, 34; and
  contradictory ideas, 9; and meanings,
  24-6, 34-5, 41, 50, 216; systems of,
  225; Weber's definition of, 24-6; *see
  also* rationalist conception of action
action frame of reference, 225
adequacy, 52; causal, 40, 41, 46, 48; of
  meanings, 40-1
alienation of subject, 106, 109, 110-12
Althusser, L., 5, 20-2 *passim,* 111,
  188-9, 196-211, 212-14, 216, 217,
  223-4, 227
analogical models, 149
analogy, 171
anthropology, 59, 60, 207
anti-rationalism, 82
a priori forms, 103-4, 115-16, 162
Aquinas, Thomas, 133
axioms, 145, 146-8
Ayer, A. J., 180

Bachelard, G., 22, 198, 204
Bachelard, S., 62, 93
basic statements, 173-4, 175, 180-1,
  186-7
Baumann, Z., 157, 161
behaviour, 24-7; and action, 27-8, 30,
  34; institutional patterns of, 70-1; and
  meaning, 34-5
Bergson, Henri, 55
Berkeley, George, 82
Bertalanffy, L. von, 149, 159
biology, 59, 60

calculus, 145, 147, 173
Carnap, Rudolf, 4, 17-18, 167, 186,
  194-5; semantic analyses of, 127-8,
  130-4, 136-8 *passim,* 140, 144, 150-2,
  155-6, 165, 172
causal explanation, 24, 34, 40-3

causality, 10-13 *passim,* 33, 36, 97,
  111-12, 122; structural, 206, 208
causal laws, 41-4, 45, 47, 117-18
causal significance, 24, 39, 42, 43-6, 48
Cavaillès, J., 85, 108, 112
central characteristics, 53-4
collective consciousness, 8
common-sense interpretation, 52, 54-5,
  60, 61, 62-3, 77
concept formation, 32-4, 35-6
conceptual conditions of existence,
  215-16, 220, 223-4
consciousness, 73-6 *passim,* 106, 109-11,
  216; cross-sections of, 127, 130,
  135-6, 138; fictitious, 71-2; and
  ideology, 201-2; individual, 171-2;
  and meaning, 79-80
constitution, 60-1
contradictory ideas, 9, 218-19, 224
conventionalism, 129
correspondence, correlation, 4-6, 132,
  146-7, 149, 154, 162, 177-8, 184-5,
  194-5, 198
cultural phenomena, cultural system, 14,
  217, 222
cultural sciences, 23-4, 84, 115-16; and
  value-relevance, 31-2; Weber's conception of, 25, 29, 35
cybernetic hierarchy of control, 217,
  222, 227

deductive testing, methodology of, 16,
  18-19, 170, 172-3, 175-6, 179-80,
  183, 186-7, 215, 221
Descartes, René, 102, 105, 108, 110
determinism, 10-11, 13
Dilthey, W., 25, 84
distinction, 4-6, 198
Duhem, P., 70
Duns Scotus, 133